# *How I Made the Sale That Did That Did the Most for Me*

# How I Made the Sale That Did the Most for Me

**FIFTY GREAT SALES STORIES TOLD
BY FIFTY GREAT SALESPEOPLE**

*Edited by*

J. MEL HICKERSON

**JOHN WILEY & SONS**
New York • Chichester • Brisbane • Toronto

Library of Congress Catalogue Card Number: 81-50244

ISBN 0-471-07769-0

Printed in the United States of America

10 9 8 7 6 5 4 3 2 1

**TO ALL SALESPEOPLE
YOUNG AND OLD**

# *Foreword*

Techniques change, but fundamentals do not.

Vast technological advances have been introduced into our society in the last generation or two—jet travel, communications satellites, computers—all producing the opportunity for individuals to cover more area, to know more, and to do it in record time. These improvements are real and readily available. However, in and of themselves they have no capabilities. Only as individuals become motivated does society benefit from improved technology. That is why this collection of true and inspiring personal experiences is even more important than the learning of new techniques.

Here in simple story form and easy to comprehend is a factual record of achievement that is both informative and challenging. Any reader can learn "how" and be inspired to reach for the personal satisfaction these individuals so obviously enjoyed. Example is indeed the best teacher. Read and reap a harvest of stimulating ideas. What worked for these "experts" will work for you now as it did for them in the past.

ARTHUR H. MOTLEY

# *Preface*

Between these covers are fifty chapters of encouragement and help for everyone who sells or hopes to sell. And *everyone sells!* Directly and indirectly several million of us sell products or services, and all of us sell ourselves . . . to ourselves and to our associates.

Our "Great Sales Story" specifications were simple. One story would be selected from each of fifty industries. The tale had to be true and told in a "How I Did It" manner, in the belief that sales successes presented in a factual and specific way would be more interesting as well as more helpful to the reader. Now that I have read and reread these stories, I believe that this book will be invaluable to the groups that contribute most to the art of selling: sales managers, general managers, and salesmen themselves.

In studying these Fifty Great Sales Stories, I perceive the makings of a "pattern of greatness." It includes these common denominators: the value of little things, the role played by fate or circumstance, the fact that people are not "sold" but that they "buy" (when the salesman makes an effective presentation), the importance of quiet perseverance, the value of creative imagination, and the priceless value of actual selling experience.

And now, before concluding this preface, I want to thank formally a number of people who encouraged and aided me in compiling this book of Great Sales Stories.

I wish to thank my fellow members of the Sales Executives Club of New York and Edward B. Flanagan, Executive Director, for every cooperation requested. Their moral support sustained me from the inception of the book to the formal announcement of publication.

One member of the club merits special thanks—William W. Stein, consultant for Reed, Roberts Associates, Inc., the largest tax insurance company in the United States. For it was Bill Stein who came to me a year ago and suggested that I update the book of Great Sales Stories that I compiled and edited some years ago. Bill is a Director of the Sales

Executives Club and Chairman of its Sports Advisory Board. And his qualifications for that chair would seem to be sufficient. He is a 1947 graduate of the Georgia Institute of Technology, where he won more letters than any other Georgia Tech athlete. Four in football, four in basketball, four in baseball, and two in track. Fourteen letters in all!

Above all, I wish to thank my co-authors . . . busy and patient people, stubborn and persistent individuals, sturdy and cooperative souls. And one of these co-authors deserves special thanks. Not only did James A. Fox contribute an outstanding chapter, he recruited others and put the facilities of his Fox Public Relations, Inc., at their disposal.

It is the fifty co-authors who have made this book possible. With their contributions and the contributions of other great salespeople throughout the land, one need not fear for the safety of our American system of mass sales to promote mass welfare.

J. MEL HICKERSON

*New York, New York*
*February 1981*

# Contents

MUHAMMAD ALI        *Selling Oneself in Boxing*    3
The Champion

GENE AUTRY        *A Ticket to Ride*    13
The Original "Singing Cowboy"
Owner of California Angels

Dr. COURTNEY C. BROWN      *Selling an Idea to*    31
Dean Emeritus        *Academics*
Graduate School of Business
Columbia University

RALPH E. CARPENTER, Jr.      *My Most Thrilling Sale*    37
Consultant
Christie, Manson and Woods International Inc.

DONALD J. CHRISTIE     *Know What the Customer Wants*    43
Vice President
Banque de Paris et des Pays-Bas (Paribas)

ROBERT A. M. COPPENRATH      *A Little Bit of Luck*    49
President
Agfa-Gevaert, Inc.

WILLIAM J. DAVIS      *Fund Raising—Another Kind*    53
Director of Development        *of Selling*
Lawrence Hall of Science
University of California

LOUIS F. DeMARCO     *Success in a Competitive Market*    61
Vice President
*Advertising Age*

FREDERICK W. DeTURK                    *Salesmanship*      73
President
Phelps Dodge Industries, Inc.


C. R. DEVINE                    *Countdown to Nonsmoking*      79
Vice President
Reader's Digest Association, Inc.


ROLAND A. EARLY                    *Persuasion in Selling*      85
Vice President
S & H Promotional Services
Sperry and Hutchinson Company


JAMES P. ECONOMOS                    *A Model Traffic Court*      93
Former Executive Director
Dr. Scholl Foundation


JOHN C. EMERY, Jr.                    *A Few Things I've Learned*      99
Chairman and President                    *in Selling a Service*
Emery Air Freight Corporation


WILLARD R. ESPY                    *The Princes Serendip Had Nothing*      105
Author                                         *on Cordially Yours*


TINA SANTI FLAHERTY                    *How to Sell 36,000 Legs*      113
Corporate Vice President
Colgate-Palmolive Company


JAMES F. FOX                    *Public Relations: The Nonselling*      121
Chairman                                         *Way to Sell*
Fox Public Relations, Inc.


J. SCOTTIE GRIFFIN                    *When the Product Is Enough*      127
Pastor
Hitchcock Presbyterian Church


JEROME S. HARDY                    *A Complete Sale*      133
Former President of the Dreyfus Corporation
Former Publisher of *Life Magazine*


J. MEL HICKERSON                    *On Selling Books House to House*      139
Compiler and Editor
*How I Made the Sale That Did the Most for Me (1981)*
*Sixty Great Sales Stories (1950)*

PAUL B. HICKS, Jr.                    *Selling a New Point of View*    147
Vice President
Texaco Inc.

RICHARD M. HYMAN                              *Try, Try Again*    155
Vice President and Sales Manager
Owens Brush Company

FRANCES BARTLETT KINNE         *Not Only Hope, but Also*    161
President                                                  *Benny*
Jacksonville University

ROGER M. KIRK, Jr.                    *Lysol Disinfects Its Image*    169
Vice Chairman
Brown & Williamson Tobacco Corporation

AUBREY C. LEWIS                      *The Direct-Honest Approach*    179
Vice President
F. W. Woolworth-Woolco Division

SETH C. MACON                          *Planting Seeds That Grow*    185
Certified Life Underwriter
Senior Vice President—Agency
Jefferson Standard Life Insurance Company

EDWARD A. McCABE                      *A Massive Selling Effort*    195
Partner                                                  *That Failed*
Hamel, Park, McCabe & Saunders

WALTER R. McCURDY          *Walt Disney's Dream—and the*    203
Vice President—Sales             *First Great Sale I Ever Made*
Bristol-Myers Products

VIRGINIA MICKUNAS              *From the Cellar to the Sky!*    207
Portraitist

JOHN MILSTEAD                              *A Sales Process*    213
Certified Association Executive
Executive Vice President
Florida Bankers Association

J. WILMER MIRANDON                      *Use Extreme Caution*    221
President
United Student Aid Funds, Inc.

ARTHUR H. MOTLEY                    *The Best Sale I Ever Made*    227
Past President
United States Chamber of Commerce
Former President of *Parade*

COLONEL BARNEY OLDFIELD                      *The Saga of the*    233
United States Air Force (Retired)      *Value-Added Valentine*
Corporate Director
Litton Industries

DAVID OTHMER                    *You May Never Be Together,*    243
Director of Broadcasting              *But You're Never Alone*
WNET-Thirteen

HOWARD D. PUTNAM                          *The Winning Spirit*    253
President
Southwest Airlines Company

Hon. ROBERT D. RAY              *Selling Oneself to the Voters*    263
Governor
State of Iowa

WILLIAM B. REMINGTON                    *Selling British Style*    273
Senior Vice President
Hellmuth, Obata & Kassabaum

DAVID P. REYNOLDS                    *My Most Satisfying Sale*    279
Chairman of the Board
Reynolds Metals Company

MILTON R. SCHEIBER         *The Very Tangible Intangible*    287
Director of Corporate Management Development
Lone Star Industries, Inc.

DAVID L. SCOTT                          *The Starvation Factor*    293
General Manager
The Pinnacle Club

J. L. SCOTT                          *Remember the Little Things*    297
Associate Director for Finance
Board of Trustees—Institutions of Higher Learning
State of Mississippi

MURIEL SIEBERT            *The Day I Made the*    303
Superintendent of Banks        *Stock Exchange Coed*
State of New York

Hon. WILLIAM E. SIMON      *Protecting Our Liberty*    311
President, John M. Olin Foundation
Former Secretary of the Treasury of the United States

ROBERT C. SINNAEVE               *Promises*    317
Vice President—Program Development
   and Services
United Student Aid Funds, Inc.

ERNEST E. SMITH, Jr.     *Every Person a Sales Person*    325
Executive Director
Florida Student Financial Assistance Commission

MILTON R. STOHL        *The Most Significant Sale*    333
President                            *in My Career*
Milton R. Stohl Associates

JOSEPH SUGARMAN         *The Ultimate Salesman*    339
President and Creative Director
JS & A Group, Inc.

DON VAN DER WEIDE    *Finding Problems and Solutions*    345
Certified Life Underwriter
New York Life Insurance Company

JOHN M. VOLKHARDT      *Focus on the User Benefit*    351
President
CPC North America

WILLIAM E. WALKUP           *Selling Yourself*    357
Former Chairman
The Signal Companies, Inc.

HARRY R. WHITE     *A Novel Approach Pays Off*    365
Former Executive Director
Sales Executives Club of New York

INDEX                                          371

# Contributors'Affiliations

**ADVERTISING AGE**
Louis F. DeMarco
Vice President

**AGFA-GEVAERT, INC.**
Robert A. M. Coppenrath
President

**AUTHOR**
Willard R. Espy

**AUTHOR**
J. Mel Hickerson
Compiler and Editor
*How I Made the Sale That Did the Most for Me (1981)*
*Sixty Great Sales Stories (1950)*

**BANQUE DE PARIS ET DES PAYS-BAS**
Donald J. Christie
Vice President

**BOXING**
Muhammad Ali

**BRISTOL-MYERS PRODUCTS**
Walter R. McCurdy
Vice President—Sales

**BROWN & WILLIAMSON TOBACCO CORPORATION**
Roger M. Kirk, Jr.
Vice Chairman

**CALIFORNIA ANGELS OWNER**
Gene Autry

**CHRISTIE, MANSON AND WOODS INTERNATIONAL INC.**
Ralph E. Carpenter, Jr.
Consultant

**COLGATE-PALMOLIVE COMPANY**
Tina Santi Flaherty
Corporate Vice President

**COLUMBIA UNIVERSITY**
Dr. Courtney C. Brown
Dean Emeritus, Graduate School of Business

**CPC NORTH AMERICA**
John M. Volkhardt
President

**DREYFUS CORPORATION**
Jerome S. Hardy
Former President
Also Former Publisher of *Life Magazine*

**EMERY AIR FREIGHT CORPORATION**
John C. Emery, Jr.
Chairman and President

**FLORIDA BANKERS ASSOCIATION**
John Milstead, CAE
Executive Vice President

**FLORIDA STUDENT FINANCIAL ASSISTANCE COMMISSION**
Ernest E. Smith, Jr.
Executive Director

**FORMER SECRETARY OF THE TREASURY OF THE UNITED STATES**
Hon. William E. Simon
President, John M. Olin Foundation

**FOX PUBLIC RELATIONS, INC.**
James F. Fox
Chairman

**GOVERNOR**
Hon. Robert D. Ray
State of Iowa

**HAMEL, PARK, McCABE & SAUNDERS**
Edward A. McCabe
Partner

**HELLMUTH, OBATA & KASSABAUM**
William B. Remington
Vice President

**HITCHCOCK PRESBYTERIAN CHURCH**
J. Scottie Griffin
Pastor

**JACKSONVILLE UNIVERSITY**
Frances Bartlett Kinne
President

**JEFFERSON STANDARD LIFE INSURANCE COMPANY**
Seth C. Macon, CLU
Senior Vice President—Agency

**JS & A GROUP, INC.**
Joseph Sugarman
President and Creative Director

**LITTON INDUSTRIES**
Colonel Barney Oldfield
Corporate Director: Special Missions and Projects

**LONE STAR INDUSTRIES, INC.**
Milton R. Scheiber
Director of Corporate Management Development

**MILTON R. STOHL, ASSOCIATES**
Milton R. Stohl
President

**STATE OF MISSISSIPPI**
J. L. Scott
Associate Director for Finance
Board of Trustees—Institutions of Higher Learning

**NEW YORK LIFE INSURANCE COMPANY**
Don Van Der Weide
Certified Life Underwriter

**OWENS BRUSH COMPANY**
Richard M. Hyman
Vice President and Sales Manager

**PHELPS DODGE INDUSTRIES, INC.**
Frederick W. DeTurk
President

**THE PINNACLE CLUB**
David L. Scott
General Manager

**PORTRAITIST**
Virginia Mickunas

**READER'S DIGEST ASSOCIATION, INC.**
C. R. Devine
Vice President

**REYNOLDS METALS COMPANY**
David P. Reynolds
Chairman of the Board

**SALES EXECUTIVES CLUB OF NEW YORK**
Harry R. White
Former Executive Director

**Dr. SCHOLL FOUNDATION**
James P. Economos
Former Executive Director

## THE SIGNAL COMPANIES, INC.
**William E. Walkup**
**Former Chairman**

## SOUTHWEST AIRLINES COMPANY
**Howard D. Putnam**
**President**

## SPERRY AND HUTCHINSON COMPANY
**Roland A. Early**
**Vice President**
**S & H Promotional Services**

## SUPERINTENDENT OF BANKS OF THE STATE OF NEW YORK
**Muriel Siebert**

## TEXACO INC.
**Paul B. Hicks, Jr.**
**Vice President**

## UNITED STATES CHAMBER OF COMMERCE
**Arthur H. Motley**
**Past President**

## F. W. WOOLWORTH-WOOLCO DIVISION
**Aubrey C. Lewis**
**Vice President**

## UNITED STUDENT AID FUNDS, INC.
**J. Wilmer Mirandon**
**President**

**Robert C. Sinnaeve**
**Vice President—Program Development and Services**

## UNIVERSITY OF CALIFORNIA
**William J. Davis**
**Director of Development**
**Lawrence Hall of Science**

## WNET-THIRTEEN
**David Othmer**
**Director of Broadcasting**

# How I Made the Sale That Did the Most for Me

**Muhammad Ali**

**The Champion**

# *Selling Oneself in Boxing*

*It is very difficult* to say which sale was the best; it depends on what people think is best and the one that did the most for me. I think joining the Muslim religion was the best thing that ever happened to me, but that was not a sale on my part—it was just the best thing that happened to me. If I had to say what I did to sell myself in boxing, that is different.

I was surprised to learn how fighters have to sell themselves to get status and to become known just to get a good fight—not even a title fight. So I had to do some thinking for a while. I told myself that I am good, but nobody knows it but me and a few people at home, a few in the Olympics, and a few in the boxing world. Of course, these people don't buy tickets to the fights, so what can I do to get myself known to the public?

I was watching television and a wrestler was on the show talking a mile a minute. He was saying how pretty he is, how good he is, and how the arena was sold out that day. Most of the people showed up to see him get beat, even me. I had to stay tuned in to watch the match hoping that he would lose.

I got up in my room and I told the reflection in my mirror, "You are pretty good looking . . . tall, dark, and handsome . . . you move very fast . . . so why not start with some 'bragging.' "

I am a very quiet person, very bashful, don't like to talk in front of people, very shy when it comes to TV, so I began to practice how to be a bragger.

One week before a fight, the promoter told me that tickets were not going fast enough; things were slow. What could we do? I told him to let me do something to sell the tickets. I got dressed in my best suit, walked down the street telling people how pretty I am, how I'm going to beat everybody in boxing. That my pretty face will stay pretty, no one can hit me in the face. I'm too fast, too pretty to lose. And the next day there was a mad rush to buy tickets for the fight. I went out again the next day, still talking and bragging; I was almost tired of hearing the same thing. I decided to add something new. I began telling the people what round I was going to knock this chump out in. Now they were really coming out to buy tickets. The fight was a sellout—now I had four days to figure out how to beat the man in the round I had predicted.

This gave me a few days to add some poetry to my talk, such as "This man is so slow, he will be out cold in four."

The night of the fight, the place was full, nothing left but standing room. People were calling me names—"Big Mouth," "Talker"—and yelling at me, "You can't do nothing but talk, you can't fight." I was in the ring talking a mile a minute. The fight started . . . round one (even), round two (I won), round three (tie). Now when the bell rang for round four, the fans stood up yelling and screaming at me, "You can win chump!" I had watched him close in the first three rounds. I figured I could take him. So I really went to work on him . . . hard right to the head, fast left jabs, right and left combustions. He was hurt; I did my shuffle, stopped quick, and landed three straight combinations—and he was out cold. People began to say I was lucky, but I predicted two more fights, started bragging early, and won both. Then I had a chance to really pop off—about to fight Sonny Liston for the title, I added even more to my talking. I began to name the fighters: I called Liston The Bear, and he was upset. I predicted the round and I beat Liston and won the heavyweight title. I began to call myself the prettiest champion ever, the fastest heavyweight, and the greatest of all times.

Selling myself sold tickets to fights. People wanted to see me get beat, and it made me win.

It is very difficult to reach down into the grab bag of your sales experiences and pick out the one you can label "most interesting." Even the ordinary sale is bound to represent one or more interesting slants, so that it is quite difficult if not impossible to pick out the most interesting.

Selling to a large industrial or institutional customer is more difficult than selling to a merchant for resale to his transient or "store trade."

Salesmanship, it sometimes seems to me, is a good deal like playing golf. The salesman has many clubs in his bag, each designed for a particular purpose. The effective salesman, just like the par-shooting golfer, knows what each club is for.

Salesmen constitute a tremendous force for molding public opinion. They are in touch with a greater number of people and have more opportunity for influence than any other single group in the country.

# THE RING RECORD
## OF
## MUHAMMAD ALI
(Courtesy of *Ring Magazine*)

**1960**

| | | | |
|---|---|---|---|
| October 29 | Tunney Hunsaker, Louisville | W | 6 |
| December 27 | Herb Siler, Miami Beach | KO | 4 |

**1961**

| | | | |
|---|---|---|---|
| January 17 | Tony Esperti, Miami Beach | KO | 3 |
| February 7 | Jim Robinson, Miami Beach | KO | 1 |
| February 21 | Donnie Fleeman, Miami Beach | KO | 7 |
| April 19 | Lamar Clark, Louisville | KO | 2 |
| June 26 | Duke Sabedong, Las Vegas | W | 10 |
| July 22 | Alonzo Johnson, Louisville | W | 10 |
| October 7 | Alex Miteff, Louisville | KO | 6 |
| November 29 | Willi Besmanoff, Louisville | KO | 7 |

**1962**

| | | | |
|---|---|---|---|
| February 10 | Sonny Banks, New York | KO | 4 |
| February 28 | Don Warner, Miami Beach | KO | 4 |
| April 23 | George Logan, Los Angeles | KO | 4 |
| May 19 | Billy Daniels, New York | KO | 7 |
| July 20 | Alejandro Lavorante, Los Angeles | KO | 5 |
| November 15 | Archie Moore, Los Angeles | KO | 4 |

**1963**

| | | | |
|---|---|---|---|
| January 24 | Charlie Powell, Pittsburgh | KO | 3 |
| March 13 | Doug Jones, New York | W | 10 |
| June 18 | Henry Cooper, London | KO | 5 |

**1964**

| | | | |
|---|---|---|---|
| February 25 | Sonny Liston, Miami Beach | KO | 7 |
| | (Won World Heavyweight Championship) | | |

**1965**

| | | | |
|---|---|---|---|
| May 25 | Sonny Liston, Lewiston, Maine | KO | 1 |
| | (Retained World Heavyweight Title) | | |
| November 22 | Floyd Patterson, Las Vegas | KO | 12 |
| | (Retained World Heavyweight Title) | | |

**1966**

| | | | |
|---|---|---|---|
| March 29 | George Chuvalo, Toronto | W | 15 |
| | (Retained World Heavyweight Title) | | |
| May 21 | Henry Cooper, London | KO | 6 |
| | (Retained World Heavyweight Title) | | |

| August 6 | Brian London, London | KO | 3 |
| | (Retained World Heavyweight Title) | | |
| September 10 | Karl Mildenberger, Frankfurt | KO | 12 |
| | (Retained World Heavyweight Title) | | |
| November 14 | Cleveland Williams, Houston | KO | 3 |
| | (Retained World Heavyweight Title) | | |

**1967**

| February 6 | Ernie Terrell, Houston | W | 15 |
| | (Retained World Heavyweight Title) | | |
| March 22 | Zora Folley, New York | KO | 7 |
| | (Retained World Heavyweight Title) | | |

**1968–1969** Inactive

**1970**

| October 26 | Jerry Quarry, Atlanta | KO | 3 |
| December 7 | Oscar Bonavena, New York | KO | 15 |

**1971**

| March 8 | Joe Frazier, New York | L | 15 |
| | (For Undisputed World Heavyweight Title) | | |
| July 26 | Jimmy Ellis, Houston | KO | 12 |
| November 17 | Buster Mathis, Houston | W | 10 |
| December 26 | Jurgin Blin, Zurich, Switzerland | KO | 7 |

**1972**

| April 1 | Mac Foster, Tokyo, Japan | W | 15 |
| May 1 | George Chuvalo, Vancouver | W | 12 |
| June 27 | Jerry Quarry, Las Vegas | KO | 7 |
| July 19 | Al "Blue" Lewis, Dublin | KO | 11 |
| September 20 | Floyd Patterson, New York | KO | 7 |
| November 21 | Bob Foster, Stateline, Nevada | KO | 8 |

**1973**

| February 14 | Joe Bugner, Las Vegas | W | 12 |
| March 31 | Ken Norton, San Diego | L | 12 |
| September 10 | Ken Norton, Los Angeles | W | 12 |
| October 20 | Rudi Lubbers, Jakarta, Indonesia | W | 12 |

**1974**

| January 28 | Joe Frazier, New York | W | 12 |
| | (American Heavyweight Title) | | |
| October 30 | George Foreman, Kinshasa, Zaire | KO | 8 |
| | (Regained World Heavyweight Title) | | |

**1975**

| | | | |
|---|---|---|---|
| March 24 | Chuck Wepner, Cleveland | KO | 15 |
| | (Retained World Heavyweight Title) | | |
| May 16 | Ron Lyle, Las Vegas | KO | 11 |
| | (Retained World Heavyweight Title) | | |
| July 1 | Joe Bugner, Kuala Lumpur, Malaysia | W | 15 |
| | (Retained World Heavyweight Title) | | |
| September 30 | Joe Frazier, Manila, Philippines | KO | 14 |
| | (Retained World Heavyweight Title) | | |

**1976**

| | | | |
|---|---|---|---|
| February 20 | Jean-Pierre Coopman, San Juan | KO | 5 |
| | (Retained World Heavyweight Title) | | |
| April 30 | Jimmy Young, Landover, Maryland | W | 15 |
| | (Retained World Heavyweight Title) | | |
| May 24 | Richard Dunn, Munich | KO | 5 |
| | (Retained World Heavyweight Title) | | |
| September 28 | Ken Norton, New York | W | 15 |
| | (Retained World Heavyweight Title) | | |

**1977**

| | | | |
|---|---|---|---|
| May 16 | Alfredo Evangelista, Landover, Maryland | W | 15 |
| | (Retained World Heavyweight Title) | | |
| September 29 | Earnie Shavers, New York | W | 15 |
| | (Retained World Heavyweight Title) | | |

**1978**

| | | | |
|---|---|---|---|
| February 15 | Leon Spinks, Las Vegas | L | 15 |
| | (Lost World Heavyweight Title) | | |
| September 15 | Leon Spinks, New Orleans | W | 15 |
| | (Regained World Heavyweight Title) | | |

| **Record** | **Total Fights** | **Won (KO)** | **Lost** | **Drew** |
|---|---|---|---|---|
| | 59 | 56(37) | 3 | 0 |

□    □    □

"A king today must answer to the people," said Muhammad Ali simply. "A king belongs to the people."

The world heavyweight boxing champion was discussing the different reactions of people to different events. Today's Ali, strong, mature, pensive, considerate, admits that even at this stage in his long career he is still sensitive to the feelings of the crowd, particularly the younger element.

"You cannot ignore youth," he declared. "That's the trouble with sports today. The stars get so big they don't want to be bothered. I don't mean all of them, of course. The kids have lost their heroes and are almost forced to turn away from sports.

"The superstar can make lasting impressions on young people and if the athletes don't encourage them, you can lose them for good. I don't ever want to be accused of ignoring youngsters. I'll always remember the help I got as a kid. Nobody gets there by himself."

Muhammad concedes that the life of a super athlete has its pitfalls.

"With the achievement of greatness, people expect too much of an athlete. Each performance must outdo the other. I cannot put the blame on the opponent because the people came to see me."

The process of growing older and richer and wiser has only strengthened Muhammad's ties with his family. He will recall fondly how "my father walked up and down Boston Street (in Louisville) predicting 'My son is going to be another Joe Louis.' I was 12 years old then and I had just won my first fight on a TV show called 'Tomorrow's Champions.' I also weighed 112 pounds."

He will not talk about it but you will always find Muhammad's mother and father—Odessa Lee, whom Muhammad called "Bird," and Cassius Marcellus Clay I—on the fistic scene wherever it is. Aunt Coretta will be running the kitchen. Brother Rachman is ever present.

Boxing history's greatest, most exciting, and most controversial salesman was born Cassius Marcellus Clay II, in Louisville, Kentucky, on January 14, 1942. It is now 34 years later and the

"A Sketch of Muhammad Ali," press handout from Madison Square Garden and Top Rank, Inc., for Championship Fight, Muhammad Ali vs. Ken Norton, September 28, 1976.

tremendous demand for his services continues. Be it his vast ego—real or otherwise—or his fantastic showmanship that has made him a magnet whether you like him or not, or believe in his principles or not, he has played the key role in boxing almost from the time he turned professional in October of 1960.

Even before that, as an amateur and ultimately an Olympic Champion, he displayed evidence of a personality that attracted followers by the thousands. But for his refusal to accept induction, he might have become the greatest American hero of modern times. His action cost him three and a half years of ring work and millions of dollars in revenue, but fortunately, few of the skills that made him one of the most superb athletes in sports history.

This son of Cassius Marcellus Clay I, a Louisville sign painter, was a tot of destiny from the moment of his birth. It is said he started talking at ten months and there has been little stopping him since. He has mellowed considerably and matured physically and mentally. His statements, once quippy and more often humorously arrogant, are now expended with much thought. "I don't talk any more to hear myself," he says. "I have discovered that the youth of this country pay attention to me. On their account, I must say only what I feel is right and sincere."

Just as his father was a flashy, talkative man, young Cassius grew fast, talked faster, and had something to say about everything. He was a restless boy, with his share of fights in the street, and a good part of his amazing reflex action was developed ducking carefully aimed rocks. He was exceptionally fast.

In the public playgrounds, he played softball, basketball, and volleyball. He was a marbles champion. "I had the surest knuckles in Louisville," he claims. He was the pet of his mother, who affectionately called him "Gee Gee." Given a bike for being smart in school when he was twelve, he treasured it. One day the bike was stolen. Cassius reported the theft to policeman Joe Martin. Martin also happened to be the boxing instructor in the community gymnasium. He took young Cassius in hand, along with his brother, Rudolph Valentino Clay. The stolen bike was forgotten. The boys haunted the gym. Martin could see in Cassius a boxing natural. He not only showed the right moves, but also talked a great fight—even then!

Muhammad reveals in his book *The Greatest* that there was a time when he was afraid to walk the old streets of Louisville and his solution to this particular problem of the time contributed greatly to his road to the world championship.

"I was sixteen," he said. "In the gym, in boxing tournaments, in Central High, I was recognized as the King. I took on any fighter. I walked proud and confident, except when I heard Corky Baker was out on the streets. Whenever I walked through Sane Town or West End, with or without my gang, Corky was undisputed Lord of the Streets and wouldn't tolerate any rival.

"I had the Golden Gloves ahead of me, the AAU, the Olympics, all of which I was confident I'd win. But the crown that would make me feel most confident as a fighter was held by Corky. He terrorized everyone, including me. Already I'd made it known that my ambition was to become the world heavyweight champion, but this made Corky laugh."

Muhammad looks back at this chapter of his career as a turning point. He felt that unless he whipped Corky Baker all titles lacked credibility. He didn't want to fight him in the streets, where there were no rules. He wanted him in a gym, with gloves. It took several weeks of ingenious contrivance to lure Corky into a gym fight, but it finally happened and Muhammad still enjoys telling the story.

It was no contest. He was no match for the science of the ring and the speed of Ali.

"Before the second round was over," added Ali, "he suddenly stopped in the middle of the ring, screamed out 'Hell, no! This ain't fair!' and staggered out of the ring into the dressing room, got his clothes on, and left the gym. I was now the king of both the gym and the streets."

There was no stopping young Clay. In 1960 he won the National Golden Gloves heavyweight title in Madison Square Garden, although he was still a light heavyweight on the scales. He also won the National AAU and 1960 Olympic titles—both as a light heavy. He had 141 amateur fights, losing only seven. His personality captured the Olympic Village in Rome, where he talked to everyone who would listen. He became the hottest fistic prospect since Joe Louis. Everyone with money—and some without it—bid for the services of young Cassius. Ultimately, Clay signed with what became known as the "Louisville Group," which included eight millionaires among its eleven members.

Angelo Dundee, one of the ablest of trainers, was enlisted as top second, conditioner, and teacher. All of the young boxer's bouts were fought under the Louisville Group's aegis, including the title defense against Karl Mildenberger in Germany in September of 1966. His later fights, beginning with his defense against Cleveland Williams on November 14, 1966, in the Houston Astrodome, are independent of the original Louisville sponsors. Ali's poetic spoutings have become dimmed by his religious learnings but neither his religion nor his poetry had anything to do with his ability as a fighter.

He won the heavyweight championship in a controversial clash with Sonny Liston on a technical knockout in the seventh round at Miami Beach, February 25, 1964. His first defense was against Liston and he won that rematch on a knockout in a much-discussed first round at Lewiston, Maine, in March 1965. In November of that year, he stopped Floyd Patterson in the twelfth round of another highly speculative bout in Las Vegas. Ali successfully defended his crown nine times before his banishment from ring action. His last competitive effort as the recognized champion was against Zora Folley in Madison Square Garden with a seventh-round knockout on March 22, 1967. It was not until he fought and stopped Jerry Quarry in the third round in the City Auditorium of Atlanta, Georgia, on October 16, 1970, that he was permitted to return to any American ring.

The boy in him and the clowning seem to be gone with maturity. He remains an enigma, still the showman in training, but more settled and businesslike. He has four children—Maryum, seven; Reeshemah and Jamillah, who are six; and three-year-old Muhammad. More and more of his time is taken up with things other than boxing. He belongs to a world that sometimes makes family life difficult. There is his Muslim faith, and his people who need help. He has written his autobiography, *The Greatest*, and spends time plugging that. He finds it difficult to say no to causes but he realizes he is also a fighter—the Heavyweight Champion of the World.

Even now, he's talking about documentaries and films that have been built around him. He did his own TV special, which he will tell you himself was dynamic. He makes TV commercials. He doesn't allow himself to get bored. Most fighters at thirty-four have not only peaked out but want to get away from it all.

Not Ali. He has bought himself a new home and training camp, in Berrien Springs, Michigan—an eighty-acre affair that has become a new light in his eye. Boxing is his stage and his opponents and his followers the actors. He thrives on the unexpected. He plays a running game with the press. To understand Muhammad Ali you must take all this into consideration. He loves it and will fight hard to keep it.

And he will always tell you that none of this would have been possible without the friendship, guidance, and managership of Herbert Muhammad.

**Gene Autry**

# A Ticket to Ride

*I was picking when I should have been tapping*, but the customer didn't seem to mind. The opening of the door had startled me. I slid my feet off the counter top and moved to put away my guitar. But he motioned—with the hand that held the copy—for me to continue. Then he sat down at the scarred old writing desk in the waiting room.

I have long since forgotten what song, if any, he interrupted. I might have been just strumming, what they call *improvising* today. You did a lot of that to pass the long nights in the telegraph office; especially if you were in Chelsea, Oklahoma, as I was on that evening in the summer of 1927, working as a relief operator on the Frisco Line.

Near the end of the four-to-midnight shift all interruptions were welcome. When I finished whatever tune I had been playing, the visitor asked me to sing another. I did, with great energy. From time to time he nodded at me, looking up from the pages he was fussing over.

When he dropped his copy on the counter, he said, "You know, with some hard work, young man, you might have something. You ought to think about going to New York and get yourself a job on radio."

I knew who the customer was, even before I read the bottom of the last page and saw where he had signed it, *Will Rogers*. You couldn't spend any time in Oklahoma, after all, and not recognize that face or that voice, which had the sound of a man chewing on cactus.

His words encouraged me, but not quite to the point of quitting my job and barging off to bring Broadway to its knees. I saw Rogers several times that summer. He was visiting a sister in Chelsea, and he'd drop into the telegraph office to wire his columns back to the newspapers in the East.

A full year passed before I was prepared to take his advice. For one thing, I wasn't certain I wanted to throw away my "career" with the railroad. It paid well, for the times. It made you an important man in town. And for a lot of years I had never thought about being anything other than a telegraph operator.

For those under thirty it must be difficult to understand what the railroad once meant to this country. Not just in the movement of people, or the territories it opened, but as a romantic symbol of an age that once was and will never be again. Oh, sure, we still have trains today. But AMTRAK doesn't wave as well or toot as loudly when it goes by.

Many of my early memories are of the railroad, of people milling around the platform and dozing on the benches. It was like that in Tioga, Texas, where I was born, and where the tracks ran right through the heart of town. Folks would flock to the station when they heard the whistle of an arriving train, just to see who got off and who was leaving.

That was a more romantic time, a lilac time, just after the First World War and before the Great Depression. It was a time of gaslights and high starched collars and no Social Security. Along the line between Texas and Oklahoma, the twenties didn't roar much. There were few cars and no paved roads and not everyone could afford a radio. News traveled slowly, when it traveled.

And that was what made the telegraph office the center of our universe. Part of the joy of hanging around the railroad depot was watching, and hearing, the operator tap out his messages in Morse Code. We were the first to know about floods and election results and bank robberies. During the World Series we'd post the score by innings on a blackboard. By late afternoon maybe two hundred people would be standing there, watching the numbers go up, *seeing* the game.

I was in my senior year in high school, at Tioga, when I talked my way into a job at the depot. I'd get up every morning at five-thirty and work for an hour before school, sweeping out the station and unloading the baggage and mail. I'd return at noon to practice the Morse Code, and again after school. I'd even hang around the station at night, listening to the train orders, learning to figure the express and freight and ticket rates.

That was what I wanted and what I expected my life to be: a train dispatcher, maybe work my way up someday to superintendent. I earned a little money on the side entertaining at the Rotary Club and the Chamber of Commerce luncheons, but I saw no real future in that. It struck me as good experience, getting up in front of people, but I wasn't sure why. My other part-time job was more practical. It got me into the movies free.

After we moved to Achille, Oklahoma, I ran the projector at the Dark Feather Theater, where the daily fare usually consisted of Tom Mix and William S. Hart and Harry Carey, and all the serials. I got saddle sore just from watching. I taught myself how to thread the machine, an old Vidagraph, and how to run an arc light.

No, I didn't identify with those fantasy figures on the screen, flickering in the light of my own projector. But I could identify with the fellow under the green eyeshade at the railroad depot. And the railroad offered something real. It offered a hundred and fifty dollars a month and a better life. Those tracks led to other places and I planned to ride them out of the small towns that had been the only world I knew.

Let me say right off that there is no point in trying to glorify one's childhood. Growing up is simply one of the debts we must pay to society. It is hard for me, at best, to imagine anyone caring whether I slopped hogs as a kid. But if you are going to tell your story and wrap it between covers, what you came from ought to be included. As they say, a bar of music that made the man.

The essential facts are these:

I was born Orvon Gene Autry on September 29, 1907, at Tioga, Texas, the son of Delbert and Elnora Ozmont Autry. My grandfather was a Baptist preacher, William T. Autry, a practical man who taught me to sing when I was five in order to use me in his church choir. He was short a soprano. Grandpa's family had crossed the plains in covered wagons, coming to Texas with the early settlers (and adventurers) from Tennessee, the Houstons and the Crocketts. An Autry died at the Alamo.

I was twelve when I ordered my first guitar out of the worn and discolored pages of a Sears, Roebuck catalogue. The story that I bought it on the installment plan is untrue, the invention of a Hollywood press agent. Local color. I paid cash, eight dollars, money I had saved as a hired hand on my Uncle Calvin's farm, baling and stacking hay. Prairie hay, used as feed for the cattle in winter. It was mean work for a wiry boy but ambition made me strong.

I was ambitious mainly to get out of baling hay. The guitar would in time make that possible, but I had no sense of it then. By my fifteenth birthday I knew my way around whatever stages the town had. I was in all of the school plays, and when I sang my cousin Louise, Uncle Cal's daughter, would accompany me on the piano. I began to earn money in a Tioga café where the nightly collections amounted to about fifty cents.

My mother, who had been a beauty in her day, a gentle and dainty and thoughtful lady, always hoped I would be a professional man. But that dream went against the trend of my time and place. No one I knew as a child attended college. Where I grew up, in the line between Texas and Oklahoma, X was not a rating for dirty movies. It was the legal signature for about a third of the adult population.

But the pace was serene, the life pastoral. We were the sons of ranch hands and farmers and drifters. I knew how to ride a horse and milk a cow and drive a buckboard. I guess we were poor. Nearly everyone was. But the Autrys were never Tobacco Road poor. My father earned good money, when he felt like it, which was some of the time.

Father was a livestock dealer, a horse trader, a foot-loose, aimless man who loved people and animals and the smell of the good earth. He was uneducated and a casual provider, but he had a western sense of values. I remember him talking once about his younger brother, Homer, and saying proudly, "You know, son, that Homer is a fine man. He just won't hardly lie to you in a hoss trade."

Most of my early years were spent moving from one small town to another, all less than a thousand people, scratching a living out of the hardscrabble ground. From Tioga we moved across the Red River into southern Oklahoma, where we lived on a farm at a place called Achille. We pronounced it a-SHEEL, and it was so small you could start a crime wave by stealing three chickens.

That America doesn't exist any more, except in our imaginations, which may be the best place. The three most popular spots in town were the country store, the church, and the barbershop. In Tioga the barber was Old Man Anderson. He cut my hair until I was grown. I think of him half a century later and I can still smell the Lilac Rose talcum on my neck. Long after I was established in the movies I went back to see him. He trimmed my hair and I posed in his chair for pictures. The barbershop was as close to a public library as we had. Featured *Whiz Bang* comics and the *Police Gazette.*

The farmers and ranchers looked forward to receiving their copies of *Capper's Weekly,* which contained all the latest livestock news. It was owned by a man who later became a senator from Kansas. The big-city dailies from Tulsa and St. Louis arrived two or three times a week and it did not take a great deal of news to cause a stir.

The year I was seventeen, in 1924, the headlines told of the brutal murder of a little boy in Chicago named Bobby Franks. Two young men from wealthy families, Nathan Leopold and Richard Loeb, were accused and later convicted of what the press labeled "a thrill killing."

It was in the accounts of the murder trial that my school friends and I puzzled over a reference that was strange to us. None of us had ever before heard of the word "homosexual."

(Ten years later, as a star of the "National Barn Dance" on radio, I did a benefit show at the prison in Joliet, Illinois. One of the inmates was in charge of the entertainment and he went out of his way to put me at ease. He was a quiet, cultured fellow, assigned to the chaplain's office. "Mr. Autry," he said, "I'm Nathan Leopold. I want you to know that while you're here you have nothing to fear. You are probably safer inside these walls than on the streets of Chicago. If anyone made a move at you, the rest of the inmates would gang him on the spot. They know if anything happened, it would be the end of these privileges.")

We lived in a small corner, and we did not always learn in it quickly, but we learned. When radio began to sweep the country, finally reaching Tioga, I taught myself out of a magazine article how to rig my own crystal set. You began by wrapping a copper wire around a salt box. You needed a tuner and a little crystal about the size of a thumbnail. You ran an antenna from the top of your house to the nearest pole, back into the bedroom window and tied it to the "set." Then you'd take a cat whisker, turn it until you found a frequency, put on your headphones and listen to the radio.

When the Fields Brothers Marvelous Medicine Show came to town one summer, looking for a local boy to sing with them, I was recommended to Professor Fields. I traveled with them for three months, softening up audiences with mournful ballads before the professor began pitching his wares: liniment and pills and his own product, a patent medicine called "Fields' Pain Annihilator." This experience so hardened my instincts that, even today, I am not offended by television commercials that sell remedies for stomach gas and underarm odors. Besides, I earned fifteen dollars a week. For a teen-aged boy, in the 1920s, this was more than money. It was the riches of Arabia.

No one in Tioga ever accused the Autry boy of being lazy. I was up milking the cows before the first light and had done a fair day's work by the time I left for school. Later, when we lived in Achille, I rode a horse five or six miles to class. Along the way I did the addition tables in my head. I was good at math, enjoyed it, and knew it might lead to a job with the railroad.

They had in those days, in small towns, a custom called First Monday. Trade day. The ranchers and farmers would pour into town and trade anything under the sun. It was a big day, a festive day.

Father stayed close to the stockyards, the cattle pens. He was a whittler. I can see him yet, working on a stub of wood, one boot raised on a rail, standing there for hours at a time, talking and whittling and bartering. He dealt mostly with the ranchers but, sometimes, with the drummers. These were the merchants who carried their goods in a trunk. They would come into town on the early train and rent a horse and buggy, then make the rounds, stopping at all the country stores and ranches and farms, drumming up business. Father would trade for chickens, eggs, cloth, leather, or whatever they had.

When I was younger he invited me to come along on some of his trips. We would ride twenty-five or thirty miles across the border into Texas, sleeping at night in our wagon. Other times he and Uncle Homer would buy mules, by the hundreds, and sell them at auction to the plantation owners along the Mississippi Delta. When it came to judging stock no one outsmarted my father. But as a businessman he was not very astute. Some days he would bring home five hundred dollars. Other days he would bring home only the lint in his pockets.

Delbert Autry was a handsome man whose sandy hair, same color as mine, showed no traces of gray up to the day he died at eighty-five. He was well liked, but rigid in his ways. Every son, at some point, may wish he had known his father better. As I grew older, I found myself drawing closer to my Uncle Calvin, on whose farm I had done the chores that paid for my first guitar.

Mother encouraged my interest in music, though she never imagined I could make a living at it. She wanted her first-born son to be a professional man, anything other than a farmhand or a cattle trader. At night she sang to us, hymns and folk ballads mostly, and read psalms. I was practically raised on the Twenty-third Psalm. She played the piano, and a guitar in the Latin style, and on Sunday she was the church organist.

We lost her in 1930 from a disease the family never discussed, but which I suspect was cancer. She had been ill quite a long time and suffered terribly with stomach pains. No one ever heard her complain, but her health was never very robust. She didn't weigh much over one hundred pounds.

My father drifted off soon after Mother died and I became the head of the family. I looked after, and supported, my two sisters, Veda and Wilma, and my brother Dudley, who was ten. Years later, under the name of Doug Autry, he tried mightily to break into show business. He traveled with a circus, sang with small bands, worked country club dates and one-nighters wherever he could find them. Doug chased rainbows but I was a poor one, after all, to discourage him, to tell him the effort would not be worth while. I had caught mine.

I always regarded the death of our mother as a tragedy, because I was then on the verge of making the kind of money that might have prolonged her life or made her last days more bearable. The money came too late. She died old at forty-five.

She had gone years without proper medical care. We didn't know about clinics and specialists in Tioga and couldn't afford them if we had. The family had no savings. At fifteen I had gone to work at the railroad as an apprentice for thirty-five dollars a month. Even in those days that salary would barely keep you alive. As a telegraph operator, moving from town to town, I was able to work my way up to one-fifty, a "steady income," as we referred to it proudly in those Depression times. I was able to send part of my pay home, but not enough to help Mother.

The last time I saw her my first records had been released and were attracting notice. I was on my way to Chicago to start a career in radio. If Mother knew she was dying she didn't let on. I talked about postponing my trip. She insisted I leave. "You go to Chicago, Gene," she said. "There might not be a next time."

The telephone call came a few days after I stepped off the train. She had gone into a coma. Within a week Elnora Ozmont Autry was dead. She never saw me in pictures. She didn't live to see me own a ranch, instead of working on one. She had every mother's nervousness about the future of her son.

The last question she asked me, was I *sure* I ought to give up my job with the railroad?

*The railroads were still a link* to the Old West. Not that I was especially looking for one. The old outlaws had died off or gone to prison, but tradition dies hard in the Southwest and you still read of an occasional train holdup.

One occurred in the little town of Waleeka, Oklahoma, shortly after I had become a full-fledged telegraph operator on the Frisco Line. The Matt Kimes gang hit my station. They were among the last of a special kind of desperado, bred in Oklahoma, whose imagination was limited to banks and train depots. This was just after midnight and the ticket window was down, as a safety precaution. Worked fine, except that when I heard a knock I raised it. Pointed at my nose was the barrel of a gun.

The man holding it said, "This is a stick-up. Let's have the money." If that sounds no more inspired than the average movie dialogue, I can assure you there is no clearer way of getting across the message. One of the gang held the gun on me and another came around and cleaned out the cash box. It contained only change, at most a hundred dollars.

When they left they locked me inside a meat car standing on the platform, what we called a "reefer," used to refrigerate meat between transfers. I was trapped in there for nearly two hours, until the next train came through and stopped. Luckily for me, the signal was down and no train ever runs a red signal. When the train came in, the crew tried to rouse the operator, meaning me, and I kept kicking against the door, hard as I knew how.

You couldn't yell loud enough to be heard outside those cars. They kept looking around and finally one of the crewmen heard me thumping away and let me out. It was so cold in there I thought my ears would fall off.

Of couse, this was one scene you would never find in a Gene Autry movie, unless Smiley Burnette or Pat Buttram played it.

I never carried a gun, even though we were in the middle of the Oklahoma oil fields, mean country, and robberies were a part of the job. The railroad instructed us to turn over the money without resistance if we were held up.

Later, when I was working in Bristow, the Kimes gang struck the bank. A crowd gathered outside while they were emptying the safe, and about that time I sauntered out of my office to see what was going on. It was just a few blocks from the station and the word spread fast. I joined the crowd just as one of the robbers, holding a shotgun, backed through the door. I heard him yell inside, "Matt, they're ganging up pretty heavy out here. You better get that loot and get the hell out."

They all started pouring out then and one of them shouted, "Stand back, or some son-of-a-bitch is going to get hurt." Then he fired the shotgun straight up and blew out a window upstairs, over the bank. Four of them piled into a car and drove off.

I had seen Matt Kimes only twice, but I was getting mighty tired of running into him like that. I was reminded of him years later, in 1934, when I arrived in Hollywood to make motion pictures. I met a fellow who was then playing character parts in Westerns, who had actually held up a train in Oklahoma, back in the days when it was still Indian Territory.

His name was Al Jennings. He had gone to prison, served five years of a life sentence, and settled in California, a fine place for a man with stories to spin. He claimed, among other things, that he had run for governor of Oklahoma. There is no record that he did, but it is possible Jennings ran without letting Oklahoma know.

He was an entertaining cuss whose career as an outlaw was brief and somewhat comic. Along with his three brothers, Al failed in his first two attempts to rob a train. The first time he stood on the tracks and tried to flag down the engineer, who ignored him. Al was nearly run over. The next time they rode alongside a roaring locomotive and fired their pistols in the air as a warning. The engineer waved and kept going. They finally robbed a small passenger train of sixty dollars, and Al and one brother were captured a day later. The other two rode into a nearby town and tried to pick a fight with Temple Houston, the son of Sam Houston and a famous lawman of his day. Houston shot them both, killing one.

Al Jennings was a little bitty fellow, dried up like a prune. Kimes was short and stocky and homely. I don't know if there is a conclusion to be drawn from that about bandits as a type, except that the ones I met were not very pretty. Off the screen, either.

When I was a young boy in Achille, listening to the stories of the old-timers, I understood that there was a kind of glory attached to that life. Oklahoma was not what you would call well policed in those days. Three of the popular pastimes of the young rogues of that day were drilling for oil, drinking moonshine whiskey, and cheating Indians.

They were mostly Choctaw and Cherokee. In Oklahoma, each of the Indians was given a portion of land, maybe a hundred acres or so. But they were never trained or prepared for the business dealings that would be coming at them. When the automobile came in, many sold off their land at a fraction of its worth, just to buy a big car they didn't know how to drive.

I had seen the Indians exploited and considered it then, as now, a tragedy. It was no protest on my part, but later when I made my own pictures, I had no taste for the stock cowboy-and-Indian scripts and we avoided them.

From my desk in the telegraph office, I could see the changes taking place all around me. As I say, sooner or later everyone in town dropped by to send a message, or receive one, or watch the trains pull out.

Will Rogers had dropped by and, after a year had rolled on, I had reason to think seriously about what he had said to me. The Depression had given me a reason. It had grown more severe, business had fallen off, and the Frisco Line was cutting back. I didn't know if my singing talent had improved, but I was quite sure that my prospects with the railroad had not. I knew it wouldn't be much longer before I'd be unemployed.

So one morning when the eastbound train pulled out I was on it. I was nineteen, riding free on my railroad pass, and with a hundred and fifty dollars tucked in a sock in my one suitcase. I slept in a chair car for the three days and nights it took us to reach New York. They didn't serve meals on the train out of Chelsea. There was a chain of Fred Harvey

restaurants along the route of the Frisco Line, and when the train stopped you'd dash in for a quick meal.

Actually, I didn't take the train directly into New York. I stopped off in Chicago, and saw the second Dempsey-Tunney fight on September 22, 1927, under the lights of Soldier Field. While I was in Chicago I looked up Jack Capp, later the president of Brunswick Records, then in charge of the division that made their "race" records—what we call soul music today. I told Capp I had a railroad pass and was going on to New York. He gave me the name of a friend of his at Okeh Records, Tommy Rockwell.

I had no appointments and no clear idea of what I would find when I got there. But I had a few names to call and a pure heart. I didn't know enough to be discouraged.

The train went into Newark and you rode the ferry across the Hudson River. That was when I had my first look at the New York skyline. It was purely a shock for someone from the flatlands of Texas and Oklahoma. I thought to myself, "My God, if I ever get in there I wonder if I can find my way back?"

When the ferry docked, they herded you onto a bus and dropped you at a station across the street from Grand Central. For a dime I checked my suitcase and guitar in a locker and walked outside. I looked around, found a policeman, and asked him, "Where's Times Square?"

He pointed west and said, "Over there about five blocks."

So I walked over to Times Square. It was early on a Sunday morning and the streets were absolutely deserted. The buildings, the empty shops, the whole scene, had the look of a woman the morning after a party, when she wakes up in her flannel nightgown, her hair a mess and no make-up. I had seen Times Square and Broadway in newsreels, always at night with the lights on and the people thick as syrup. This wasn't the way I had pictured it.

But I went back later that evening and the place had sprung to life. It was just an explosion of neon lights and milling crowds. I had on boots and a cowboy hat and western clothes, and a few people shot me a curious look, but most of them were dressed funnier than I was.

I had checked into a hotel on Forty-fifth Street, near Broadway, called the Riley Hall. It wasn't exactly a New York landmark, but the price was right. I planned to stay three weeks to a month. I figured that was how long my bankroll would last me, and that's how much leave the railroad had granted me. See, I hadn't yet quit my job. I had confidence in myself, but no one had ever accused ol' Autry of being *reckless*.

Will Rogers had told me to try radio, but I had another idea. I planned to call on the record companies. It seemed to me that the quickest way to get on radio was to cut a record.

I had met the mother of Johnny Marvin, then a recording artist of some popularity at Victor. I stopped off one day in Butler, Oklahoma, where the family owned a café. Mrs. Marvin told me to look up Johnny if I ever got to New York, and I took the precaution of getting his address and phone number.

When I reached Johnny, he told me his younger brother, Frankie, had just gotten into town and we had a lot in common. Like me, Frankie was broke and trying to get started. I moved into his room at the Manger Hotel, which later became the Taft. We'd both make our separate rounds during the day, and play pool at night. It wasn't much of a social life, but neither one of us had any money to blow on women.

As the weather grew colder, we took turns wearing Frankie's topcoat. It was the only coat we had between us.

The days turned into weeks and I lugged my guitar up and down Broadway, to the rhythm of the record company doors slamming in my face. At the time, there was only a handful of companies—Victor, Columbia, Brunswick, Edison—and I tried them all, day after day, hoping for an audition. My first problem was to get past the reception desk.

I had been waiting for hours in the anteroom at Victor one day, guitar across my lap, when the thought must have struck the receptionist that I might not ever leave. She glanced up, smiled nervously, and asked what kind of songs I did.

"Cowboy stuff, mostly," I said, "And some hillbilly. When I can get anyone to listen."

"I'll listen," she said. "Go ahead, play something."

That was all the encouragement I needed. An audience of one. I was halfway through "Jeannie, I Dream of Lilac Time," when Nat Shilkret, the man who wrote it, by then working for Victor, strolled into the room. He stopped for a moment, then ducked into another office and reappeared with a fellow named Leonard Joy. I now had an audience of three. Joy turned out to be the Number Two man at the company, in charge of promoting new artists and their records.

Joy asked me to come back the next morning. "We're recording a band," he said, "And if you'll be here then we'll cut a test and see what you sound like." There were no tapes then, of course. It was all on wax.

To me the whole process was magic. I didn't sleep much that night. Stayed up for hours, practicing.

When they opened the offices the next morning I was waiting on the doorstep like a bottle of milk. I sang "The Prisoner's Song," a weepy tune, and a Jolson hit, "Climb Upon My Knee, Sonny Boy," probably not the smartest choice on my part, and we cut the test record. After everyone listened to the playback, Nat Shilkret asked me to step into his office.

"You got a nice voice for records," he said, "but you need experience. My advice is go home. Take six months, a year. Get a job on a radio station. Learn to work in front of a microphone."

I didn't feel like a failure. But time had run out on me. I had been in New York a month and had stretched my money as far as it would go, living on five- or ten-cent hamburgers and all the coffee I could hold for a nickel.

When I said good-by to the Marvin boys, Frankie offered a piece of advice. "Forget that Jolson stuff," he said. "Learn to sing some yodel songs. That's more to your style."

With that I rode my railroad pass back home to Oklahoma. Shilkret had given me a to-whom-it-may-concern letter, saying I had potential, and I used it to wangle a radio show over KVOO in Tulsa. I was billed as the Oklahoma Yodeling Cowboy, backed up by Jimmy Wilson's Catfish String Band. Meanwhile, I had gone back to my job as a relief operator working up and down the Frisco Line. The idea of paying for radio talent had not yet caught on in the Southwest.

For the next six months I traveled more back roads than a bootlegger, singing at Kiwanis clubs and high schools and private parties all over the state. And it was during those last days on the railroad that I began to write my own songs, with Jimmy Long, who worked with me as a dispatcher. Jimmy was older, settled, a good influence. Together we came up with one called, "That Silver-haired Daddy of Mine." I sang it on the air in Tulsa and the response delighted us.

Now, for the first time, I read about myself in a daily newspaer. As a favor to a friend, George Goodale, a reporter for the Tulsa *World*, interviewed me. The story made light reading, about a struggling young telegrapher who wanted to be a big-time singer, and we had to buy the managing editor a half gallon of corn whiskey to get it published. Cost three bucks, as I recall. Years later, George became my press agent.

I was ready to try New York again. I had gained experience and exposure and the next step, I thought, was a record contract.

On October 9, 1929, backed up by the guitars of Frankie and Johnny Marvin, I cut my first record for Victor. Johnny had written one of the sides, "My Dreaming of You." Jimmy Long had composed the other, "My Alabama Home."

The rules of the record business were a little loose then. It was not uncommon for an artist to do the same song for more than one company under various labels. So two weeks later I made a test record for Columbia, which released it on the Velvatone label. One of the songs was "Left My Gal in the Mountains," written by a friend of mine named Carson Robinson.

Two other young singers were in the studio that day cutting records. One was Rudy Vallee and, yes, he had his megaphone with him. I consider Vallee one of the great performers of all time, still going strong, still popular, in his seventies. One of my first guest appearances on network radio would come on Rudy's show, "The Fleischmann Yeast Hour."

The other singer was an ample, sweet-faced girl named Kate Smith. The general sales manager at Velvatone was then Ted Collins, who resigned later to manage Kate's career. It proved to be a shrewd move. By the 1940s, Collins was wealthy enough, and foolhardy enough, to buy a pro football team, the Boston Yanks. Eventually, the team went broke, but whenever Ted needed to raise money to meet his payroll all he had to do was book Kate somewhere to sing "When the Moon Comes Over the Mountain."

But I remember that recording session best for the way we did it. I walked into the studio with nothing but my guitar and my own courage. Our equipment consisted of two old-fashioned horns. I sang into one and the engineer, an old-timer named Clyde Emerson, placed the other on the chair in front of my guitar. They did it that way to avoid having to pay a royalty to RCA, which owned the rights to the microphone and other electronic recording gear.

We had no arrangements. I just kept singing until Clyde Emerson was satisfied, and that was it.

I was under some pressure by then to sign an exclusive contract with Victor, but I wanted a few days to think about it. I had been given the name of Arthur Sattherly, the new head man at American Record Corporation, a division of Columbia. American had put together a series of chain store deals that meant big numbers. Under separate labels, it would produce records for such companies as Sears and W. T. Grant and Kresge's. Tin Pan Alley was impressed.

Sattherly had just taken over and he was looking for a new artist to launch his own drive. "Victor is big," he said, "but they have lots of stars. You can get lost over there. With us, you can be Number One." That sold me.

The next day I called and gave my regrets to Loren Watson, the boss at Victor. Then I walked over to the American offices at 1776 Broadway—a nice, patriotic address—and signed a contract with Art

Sattherly. I was to be paid an advance of fifty dollars a side for each record I cut, against royalties.

My first recording date under that contract was set for early December. Six sides. That came to three hundred dollars. It meant I could coast for a while. But more than that, signing with American meant a turning point in my career. On the Conqueror label, I would soon crank out several for Sears, and it was through this connection that I was invited to appear on the "National Barn Dance," on station WLS (World's Largest Store).

Sometimes you can yank on one stitch and an entire sweater will unravel. Well, this was my stitch. Hit records, a movie career, a happy marriage, goodies and groceries all came to pass. I was en route to Chicago in 1932 when I stopped off in Springfield, Missouri, to visit my friend, Jimmy Long.

And there I met the girl I was to marry, a coed with blue eyes and skin like rose petals. She was Jimmy's niece, Ina Mae Spivey— eighteen, an Oklahoma girl, living with the Longs while she attended music college in Springfield. We had only a few dates in the next month or so, but I was a frequent guest in Jimmy Long's parlor.

I was now a regular on the "National Barn Dance," and making thirty-five dollars a week singing on radio for Sears. By night I played the tank towns of southern Illinois. Three months after I met Ina Mae Spivey, I was booked into St. Louis, and Jimmy joined me for the show. The next day, his wife and niece came over on the train to go shopping.

I went off with Ina and we agreed to meet the Longs for dinner in a little café on the city's south side. We arrived early. As we sat there, I suddenly blurted out, "Honey, let's get married."

She said, "Gene Autry, are you out of your mind? We hardly know each other. This is only our fourth date. Besides"—fine feminine logic—"I just brought enough clothes for the weekend."

I convinced her we would overcome that problem. The next thing I knew, we had rushed off to get a license and find a wedding chapel or a justice of the peace. A Lutheran minister married us and his wife witnessed the ceremony. When we rejoined the Longs—by now a couple of hours had passed—Jimmy was not very happy with us. "Where have you two been?" he demanded. "Jessie and I were starting to worry."

Ina said, "Uncle Jim, Gene and I got married."

Jimmy said, "I don't believe it. Gene would have told me. I know he would." He looked at me sharply. I sort of ducked my head.

Then Jessie said, "Jimmy Long, today is April Fool's Day. Don't you know a joke when you hear one?"

And for the first time I realized the date *was* April 1, 1932. I turned to Ina and said, "I hope you weren't fooling, honey. I wasn't." She reassured me, with a kiss, and the snug little booth in the corner of a short order restaurant became the scene of our wedding reception. She was only eighteen. I was twenty-two.

I now had steady work, a wife, and a hit record. "That Silver-haired Daddy of Mine," the song Jimmy Long and I had spun off one night in a railroad depot, was off and running. A month after its release, thirty thousand copies had been sold.

A year later, Art Sattherly met with Bev Barnett, my first press agent, and an idea was born: a gold-plated copy of "Silver-haired Daddy" to celebrate the half-millionth record sold. When the sales hit a million, they gave me another one. And that was the start of the gold record tradition.

There was a touch of irony in all this. The early thirties marked the heyday of Al Jolson, the era of Mammy songs. I thought back to that first, fumbling audition in New York, when I had sung a Jolson hit. Now I had one of my own, and it went against the trend. Equal time for daddies.

☐    ☐    ☐

Gene Autry has had two incredibly successful careers. Born Orvon Gene Autry on September 29, 1907, he went on to become one of the most famous movie stars of his generation. He began his movie career in 1934, and during the next twenty years appeared in ninety-five feature films. Autry became a fixed image in American minds as the good cowboy with the white hat, on his horse Champion.

Along the way he has sold over 40 million records. After his phenomenal career, he went on to have another equally successful business career, which included the ownership of hotels, ranches, radio and television stations. Currently, he is frequently in the news as owner of the California Angels baseball team.

*Dr. Courtney C. Brown*

# Selling an Idea to Academics

*It has often been said* that selling an idea may be as hard—or harder—than selling merchandise. Ask any politician. Or better still, ask an academic administrator who has tried to sell an idea to his faculty. If it's an idea related to the curriculum, look out!

The campus of a great university is unique: someone once called it organized anarchy. It was into this chaotic environment that I—a businessman—plunged fresh from eight years work in the beautifully structured administration of Standard Oil Co. of New Jersey. I had been invited to be the Dean of the Graduate Faculty of Business at Columbia University. Over the years I had acquired some ideas of how a program of graduate business study should be organized. Unfortunately, those thoughts had not been developed in collaboration with my newfound faculty—or with any other faculty for that matter.

Faculty control of the curriculum is a sacred cow in the academic world. There are very good reasons why this is, and should be, deriving from the long evolution of the university. These institutions originated in Europe in the thirteenth century as collegiums, clusters of scholars gathering in population centers to offer their own courses and admit their own students, from whom they would collect their own fees. It was a very personal system. What was taught was the result of each scholar's study, inquiry, and reflection. The same holds true today in so-called higher education. Nothing is more highly prized on the academic campus than intellectual integrity, together with the preservation of the opportunity to follow one's broadly informed and carefully reasoned convictions with unimpaired objectivity. A professor builds his intellectual capital in very much the same sense a businessman builds his production capital.

The Columbia business faculty had been accumulating an inventory of intellectual capital for more than a quarter century when the new

**31**

Dean arrived. Only naiveté could explain his intention to sell the idea of revising the curriculum. Had it not been for frequent expressions of discontent from individual members of the faculty, it would have been pure bravado. But each expression of discontent always referred to the content of another's courses or to the lack of balance and integration in the whole instructional program.

Business education got its start in the United States at the Wharton School of the University of Pennsylvania. The organizational pattern of the curriculum used there was followed in the mid-1950s by most other business schools, including Columbia. The spectrum of business was organized into vertical segments for specialized study: insurance, real estate, banking, transportation, and so on. Several fields of study—accounting, statistics, personnel, administration, for example—cut horizontally across these specializations. Apart from these studies that were required, the student elected a field of specialization. Harvard was the first to modify this basic pattern with its heavy use of the case method of instruction, appropriated from the law schools of the nation. The Columbia school had looked at the case method and rejected its use as the principal method of instruction—wisely in my judgment.

Four or five attempts at curriculum revision had been made prior to my arrival. Two professors would compare their courses for overlaps. Many were found, but they were always in the other fellow's courses. Little was done to explore significant areas of business not adequately represented. Such areas did not happen to coincide with any faculty member's major interest. Needless to say, the successive efforts had not been successful, and the students' discontent with the curriculum was then shared to a degree by the faculty.

It was clear that another round would be futile if we used the same approaches. Something new must be tried. It must be subtle, avoiding at all costs the implication of imposing ideas by the Dean. It must avoid emulation of others; that had been tried without success. Indeed, whatever was done must derive from fresh thinking, analytical consideration, and from discussion by the faculty, individually and collectively. With only a modest bit of nudging from the Dean, we decided to adopt a new and novel procedure that, so far as we were aware, had not been used before in efforts at curriculum revision.

Initially, we rejected the comparison of our course offerings with those of other business schools, regardless of their quality. We were not even interested in analyzing what we were doing and had been doing. But being a business school operating at advanced levels of instruction, we were keenly interested in what business was doing, what the business community was thinking, and in the nature of the major concerns and problems of business.

Only after a thorough and comprehensive examination had been made of the entire business spectrum would we be ready to assign its several parts to specific courses of study for further development. The idea that was sold to the faculty was not the adoption or modification of specific course materials. Rather it was the acceptance of a novel procedure for a study of the whole curriculum that started with business, then moved to phases of business, and finally to the design of specific course materials that would be developed by members of the faculty themselves.

It was an ambitious enterprise. Everybody felt a bit threatened. But the adopted procedure had the merit of focusing initially on business; only as a last step would course materials be used to express the major characteristics of business. Moreover, it was a group exercise that created its own requirements as it progressed.

The faculty was constituted as a committee of the whole to review each successive progress report. Three major areas of interest were identified at the outset: the environment in which business operates, the oranizational and administrative arrangements characteristic of business, and the communication and analytical tools used by business. A third of the faculty was assigned to each of these areas with a senior member identified as chairman. The Dean obtained a foundation grant to arrange faculty visitations, thus relieving the chairmen from teaching duties. Each group took its assignment seriously, making frequent and comprehensive reports for review and discussion by the full faculty.

The nature of important matters of interest that should be included in each of the assigned areas gradually emerged from these reports and discussions. It was concluded that business operates in an environment that is conditioned by three main variables: the state of the economy, concepts and attitudes inherited from the past, and the interplay of physical, technological, and human resources. That meant three basic courses of study that all graduate business students should take. Macroeconomics and microeconomics were established subjects, but the other two required new materials and new design. One new course that resulted was a novel study of the modern corporation that we called Conceptual Foundation of Business. It was our way of presenting the societal and ethical issues that increasingly confront business decision making. It was reasonably successful. We gave to our geographers the task of studying the several interrelated resources. The results were disappointing, for their training was related to physical resources and their location rather than to demography or technology and the interplay of all resources.

We also found it necessary to develop new courses in the second major segment of business interest. Behavioral science was a subject then much discussed in academe. We felt the need to develop our research more extensively to relate this body of emerging knowledge to behavior and decision making in the corporation. Another course, administration and structure of the firm, had long been given and fitted nicely with the study of behavioral patterns. The legal framework within which the corporation is managed, including regulation, provided the material for a course to round out the second major segment of identified business interest. Again it was felt that all graduate students should be exposed to these three courses of study.

The tools of business had long been a part of the curriculum. An attempt was made to blend accounting and statistics, as is frequently done in business, but without success. The teaching staff had lived too long in their separate compartments. The mathematics of operations research was a fascination, however. Several members of the faculty developed a course that made extensive use of the computer to test business assumptions and decisions mathematically through fast computation. Again it was felt comprehensive exposure to all the tools of business was essential to graduate business study.

In each of the three major segments of business, the faculty had identified essential materials that required three courses of study, making a total of nine courses. Several of these meant newly designed syllabi, a very large task if adequately done. But the faculty was not through. It was felt that as a capstone in the last term of study the student should be exposed to the process of group decision making, using the knowledge acquired in earlier terms of study. This was accomplished by presenting a course conducted entirely with the case method of discussion. That made ten courses required of the total twenty stipulated for the MBA degree. Another five courses, it was decided, could be taken in a field of concentration such as finance, marketing, international business, or transportation. The remaining five courses could be selected at random by the student from offerings in the faculty of business or even in other graduate faculties of the university.

The adoption of this program of study did several things. It achieved the integration and balance long sought by the faculty. It approached the study of business as a comprehensive activity with an emphasis on the reciprocal influences between business and society at large. It shifted the primary purpose of graduate business education from preparation for the first job to preparation for a business career. And as a significant by-product, it made redundant much of the specialized course materials that had been accumulated under a different program of course offerings designed to serve a different purpose. The total number of courses offered was reduced from 130 to 80.

An attempt to revise the curriculum through comparisons with other institutions could not have had such favorable results. Nor could the comparison of the content of different courses offered by the Columbia faculty of business have been fruitful. That had been tried before, several times. Had the Dean disclosed his ideas of curriculum revision to the faculty, he would have been resented. But the selling of an idea for a procedure leading to curriculum revision proved to be feasible and successful. Indeed, it resulted in a revision that had the integrity to attract widespread faculty and student attention throughout the nation and abroad.

Dr. Courtney C. Brown is Dean Emeritus and Paul Garrett Emeritus Professor of Public Policy and Business Responsibility of the Graduate School of Business of Columbia University. He is a recent Chairman of the Board of Directors of the American Assembly.

Born in 1904, in St. Louis, Missouri, he was educated at Dartmouth College and did graduate work in economics at Columbia University. During World War II he served with the Department of State and the War Food Administration in negotiations with other countries to procure their exportable surpluses of supplies needed by the Allies. Following the war, he was associated with the Standard Oil Company (New Jersey) as Chief Petroleum Economist and Assistant to the Chairman of the Board.

Dr. Brown has had long personal experience with the boards of both business and charitable corporations. He has served on the boards of directors of Esso Standard Oil Company, American Standard, American Electric Power, the Borden Company, Uris Buildings, and the New York Stock Exchange. At present he serves on the boards of Associated Dry Goods, the Columbia Broadcasting System, Union Pacific Corporation, and the West Side Advisory Board of the Chemical Bank. He serves on the Executive Committee of two of these companies, and as Chairman of the Audit Committee of another, the Conflict of Interests Committee of a second, and the Executive Compensation Committee of a third.

His experience on the boards of not-for-profit corporations is equally wide; he has served on the boards of the Interracial Council for Business Opportunity and the New York Advisory Board of the Salvation Army. Currently, he is a member of the boards of the American Assembly and the Academy of Political Science. He is an honorary director of the Council for Financial Aid to Education (which he assisted Alfred P. Sloan, Irving Olds, and Frank W. Abrams to found in 1952).

Dr. Brown is a member of the Board of Trustees of Columbia University.

*Ralph E. Carpenter, Jr.*

# My Most Thrilling Sale

*Upon graduation from college* I entered the insurance business, specializing in selling corporate retirement plans. Over the years I learned many lessons in selling. The most important: never let an opportunity slip by, no matter how obscure. Example—a phone call from a stranger who wanted to see me the next day, when I was leaving town at 9 A.M. So I suggested a breakfast meeting. This meeting set in motion a sale that produced for me over $800,000 in commissions during the next ten years, a sale I could easily have missed.

After twenty-six years of selling insurance retirement plans I became a partner in a Wall Street firm and spent twenty years there. During this time there were many exciting sales experiences—closing a tough investment banking deal, after three months of trying to close, by getting on the phone at 8 A.M. and refusing to give up until all parties agreed at 7:15 that evening. Another time I found myself in a hotel in London faced with selling $3,000,000 in bonds in three hours. For three weeks a series of transatlantic phone calls had set the stage so that when the time for action arrived the bonds could be sold.

After retirement from Wall Street I became a consultant to Christie's, the art auctioneers, and my avocation, the collecting of art and antiques, became my vocation. As on Wall Street, where the essence of business is to find buyers and sellers of securities, at Christie's we find buyers and sellers of works of art. After so many years in finance it never occurred to me that I would experience at Christie's my most thrilling sale.

It began one morning on a plane headed for Detroit. I had heard of the existence of a rare and important piece of furniture made in Newport, Rhode Island, circa 1760, that might be for sale. During the plane trip the big question that kept going through my mind concerned the authenticity and condition of the piece I was about to see. It reminded me of moments in the insurance business when the insurability of the prospect was always a worry. In the world of art and antiques the value of objects depends so much on condition and whether they are of the right period. New feet or a replaced drawer can have a devastating effect on the price at auction. The patina and condition of the finish is important. A piece that has been "skinned" and refinished is less desirable. If this piece was "right" it would be one of the most important pieces of American furniture known and one of the most valuable.

The owner met me at the airport. Driving to his home we learned that we were both graduate engineers and began to speak the same language. Our discussion at first was largely about the auto industry, in which he played an active and important role. We immediately developed common interests as my family also had a long history within the industry. He then spoke of how he had acquired the piece we were to see and now I learned for the first time that two competitors had seen this piece a year or so earlier. This added to my worries. By the time we arrived at his home I had the impression that our conversation had developed a common respect for each other, a good base to build on.

As we entered the front door I felt a surge of emotion. Would I see what I hoped for or what I feared? There it was in a sunny corner of the room. My first quick glance brought reassurance. Proportions and patina were all that one would want. But was the reassurance about to disappear after an inspection of the feet and the inside? The drawers were all removed and passed careful inspection. Right! Right! Right! But let's make sure. Look carefully again. Every detail of construction and condition met the test with flying colors.

But now, with apprehension of condition and quality disappearing, a new concern took its place. Would this great piece of furniture be consigned to Christie's or the competition? After all, they did know about it. General conversation gave way to specifics. If consigned, what would be the date of the sale? How would it be advertised? Was there sufficient time to advertise it effectively? How would it be transported safely to New York? What tax considerations are there? What would be the amount of the "reserve"? (If the bidding did not reach the reserve, the piece would be "bought-in" and returned to the consignor.)

As I left my new friend at the airport many decisions were still to be made. I had attempted to answer his questions, reassure him, and explain our procedures, but he still needed time to sort it all out in his mind.

So as I flew back to New York my concern centered on what needed to be done to successfully consign and sell this wonderful piece of furniture. To do so was particularly important to me because I have been identified with Newport cabinetmakers through a study I wrote and published in 1953. Because of this association with Newport furniture it would have hurt my pride to fail to obtain a price equal to its worth.

The days that followed were filled with frequent phone calls. Slowly all was resolved and several weeks later the piece arrived at 502 Park Avenue. It had been carefully packed and driven to New York by the owner.

It was now necessary to bring buyers into the picture. The auction sale was still several months away but the marketing effort that precedes a sale includes many time-consuming activities. First photographs, black and white for the press and advertising. Color transparencies to be sent to collectors and institutions. Letters to be written. Private viewing arranged. Each interested buyer examined the piece inside out, top to bottom. When a knowledgeable curator or collector is considering the purchase of an important and costly item there are always many questions to be answered. Is it as good as others of its kind? Is it worth more or less than the last one sold? Any restorations?

Finally the day of the auction is here. It is 10:00 o'clock. The auction is at 2:00 o'clock. At 11:00 a prospective buyer arrives by plane. He has not seen the piece, only a photograph. Can I meet with him, and can we look at the piece together? We are sitting on the floor, people are milling around us. We are looking at the piece, a four-shell kneehole bureau by the Townsend Goddard family of cabinetmakers. As we finish and go off to lunch I offer one last thought. "If you want to own one of the very few four-shell kneeholes and do not buy this one, you must be prepared to wait for five to ten years, maybe fifteen, before another one becomes available."

It is now 2:30. The auction has been going for thirty minutes. The four-shell bureau will soon come up. There in the first four rows are the serious bidders, but how interested? The bidding starts at $50,000 and soon advances to $100,000 but I am still worried as to whether it will continue. If it does not reach the reserve all the effort and time spent to get the consignment will go for naught. Failure to meet the reserve would put a blight on a fine piece of furniture. But the bidding advances the price to $130,000. A short pause, two quick bids, and the hammer hits hard! Sold for $140,000 plus 10 percent! A world auction record for a single piece of American furniture.

Today this Newport piece occupies a prominent space in the reception rooms of our State Department in Washington, D.C.

□  □  □

☐  ☐  ☐

Ralph E. Carpenter is a consultant to Christie, Manson & Woods International, Inc., Fine Art Auctioneers since 1766. In this capacity, he is involved primarily in finding sellers and buyers of a great variety of arts and crafts, applying an expertise gained as a collector of art since 1932.

Following graduation from Sibley College of Mechanical Engineering, Cornell University, in 1931, he entered the life insurance business and soon specialized in the sale, design, and administration of corporate retirement plans. He was retained as a consultant by nationally known corporations, advising them in all phases of their retirement and employee benefit plans. In 1958 he became a partner of Reynolds & Co., which later became Reynolds Securities, Inc. During his career with Reynolds, he instituted a formal sales training program, then became head of Institutional Sales and later head of the International Division and served as President and Director of Reynolds Securities S.A.

Upon retirement from Wall Street several years ago, Mr. Carpenter was invited to join the Christie's organization where he is active today.

*Donald J. Christie*

# Know What the Customer Wants

*In the last semester of business school*, most prospective graduates are faced with one of the toughest sales jobs of their lives: convincing those responsible for hiring the executives of the future that the graduate fits the bill. I was no different from my classmates. Although I had spent three years in the Army and a short period of time working for an airline, before going to business school my experience with banks was limited to waiting in lines at my local branch to get checks cashed. Still I had set my sights on becoming a banker.

Through my readings and discussions with acquaintances, I had decided before entering business school that while in the MBA program, I would focus my studies on banking. The major New York banks had excellent training programs that could take the uninitiated student and turn out a professional banker. The jobs available were very appealing; as a "Calling Officer" a young person would rapidly be exposed to the major corporations in the United States and have the opportunity to meet the senior executives who ran them. Although my knowledge of the industry was limited, I liked what I knew.

As a means of attracting students, most major New York banks conduct on-campus discussion panels staffed by experienced officers who outline the structure of their bank, the types of jobs to be filled, and the kinds of people being sought to fill the jobs. In addition, many banks conduct full-day tours of their headquarters. The programs are beneficial, in that they help students make informed decisions about their careers. Much of the coordination of these activities between the personnel departments of the banks and the students at Columbia was handled by the student-run American Finance Association (AFA), and I had the good fortune to be elected the officer of the group dealing with the commercial banks. I was able to meet the people running the recruiting programs, and I was assured of seeing all the banks (because many of the tours were limited to a modest number of students, not every student got to see every bank). This exposure gave me a chance to analyze the personality of each bank and get a feel for what each wanted. I was put in a favored position above my classmates, and I unconsciously began to get a little cocky.

May graduates typically do most of their interviewing in February and March. The process is nerve wracking. It starts with the preparation of a résumé planned to attract the attention of the interviewer who, during the course of one day on campus, will see up to ten students for a mere half-hour each. The popular assumption was that each interviewer could pick two, at most three, interviewees for a "callback" and more detailed discussions at bank headquarters. We all hoped that the "best" students would not be on our schedule with the same interviewer.

Because of my contacts, I was able to short-cut this process with several banks. During the Christmas vacation, I arranged full-day interviews with three of the biggest banks. I did my homework; I knew what they wanted and I felt that I was it. After receiving three rejections in quick succession, I realized that I had miscalculated; but what went wrong? Was I not cut out to be in this business? Had all this work been for nothing? I was rapidly learning humility, as my ego plunged.

My depression was interrupted by a call from the head of recruiting for one of the banks. He wanted me to come down to the bank for a little chat. "Don, you were liked by everyone. They all felt you have good skills, but you came on too strong, and you just about blew one fellow out of his chair. Tone it down and you'll do just fine." I thanked him for the advice and checked with the other two banks. Same story; too aggressive.

Although all banks claim they want aggressive individuals, I had obviously missed a part of the story and had focused on the wrong meaning of the word. What they wanted were people with drive, the ability to keep pushing, and *tact*. I altered my style and things started going better; callbacks came from Chicago and the South. Each time I flew back to LaGuardia, however, I realized that I wanted to stay in New York.

Although Bank of America was a California bank, it had an office in New York, and it was looking to bring some people on board. At that time, BofA conducted its recruiting program differently from other banks. A hall was rented on campus, and a catered affair was arranged.

Just about everyone whose résumé indicated an interest in banking was invited. The informal atmosphere during cocktails, as well as the seating arrangement at dinner, created an environment much more personal than that presented by many banks, which crowded a lot of people into an auditorium with speakers on stage at the podium. While I had not met anyone at this bank through my position at school, the introduction I received that evening made me very excited about the bank and the people working for it.

I was determined to get an interview, but this time I used the normal procedure at school and signed up for the half-hour interview on campus. I woke up on the designated morning with a fever; but decided not to postpone the interview lest I miss my chance. My previous failures had taught me a few lessons, and I felt that my style had improved, but I came out of the interview frustrated. I could not tell how it went. Things didn't seem to click, and I did not feel that I had established the kind of rapport I wanted. I went home and crawled into bed. Three days later, the rejection letter arrived.

I was convinced that BofA was the place for me and decided to try again. I had met the assistant to the head of recruiting at the dinner and decided to start with her. When she picked up the phone, I told her my story and explained about the fever. She was sympathetic and promised to check into it. Two days later, she called to say that the decision could not be changed.

Needing more advice, I started talking to some of my professors, one of whom was on the Board of Directors of a major corporation. He had seen my work in class and felt that I had a good grasp of what I wanted and where I was heading. He encouraged me to speak with the Dean of Placement at school and, unknown to me at the time, he called the Dean and put in a good word on my behalf. "You're talking too much," the Dean told me. "People can read your résumé and that goes a long way in selling you. Keep your mouth closed and listen more. Slow down!" he told me, "but don't worry. It's a lot easier to get someone with energy to slow down than it is to build a fire under someone who doesn't have any. You'll do fine." He got me another interview at BofA.

The time for graduation was getting near when I walked into the office of the head of recruiting. I expressed my appreciation for the chance to get together and chat. We were interrupted several times during the conversation. The telephone rang and some people went in and out of his office. I sat back, relaxed, and took it in stride. We talked about banking, the kind of people working at BofA, and the largest bank in the United States, which was founded by an Italian immigrant.

He asked me if I would like to come back and spend a day talking to some more people. "Sure, I'd love to." I could hardly restrain myself. It was difficult to walk out of the bank like a normal human being. I wanted to shake the hand of everyone I saw there. I had passed the big hurdle.

Offers had come to me from other banks, but I wanted to work for BofA. On the way to the bank, for the big day, I kept telling myself to relax, to remember everything that my professors and the Dean had told me. The two officers I met in the morning had been at BofA for many years. I could feel that our conversations were going well and that these fellows liked me. I had lunch with a younger officer who, like me, had an interest in Asia. Finishing my coffee, I felt confident the day was going well. As we walked back to his office, he told me that he thought that I had a lot to offer the bank. He then took me to what was to be the final interview of the day.

When he introduced me to one of the senior BofA officers in New York, I was a little nervous. I realized that this was one of the fellows I had talked to extensively the night of the dinner at school in those days when I was pushing too hard. He remembered me as well, but I hoped not too well. I saw a humidor on his desk, so I offered him one of my cigars. As we both lit up, I kept telling myself to relax and to let him do the talking. Our conversation seemed to be going smoothly, and he told me to expect a call from the bank. When it came from the head of recruiting, "Don, I'd like to offer you a job at BofA. Can you start in July?" "Of course" was about all I could get out.

A week later, I saw the Dean at school. He congratulated me and added, "By the way, I heard that the person they just hired had changed 180 degrees from the person they met at dinner."

While I'm not sure I had changed that dramatically, I did learn a lesson about sales; know what the customer wants and what you have to offer. The fit between the two does not have to be exact, but it should be close. If it is, "No" is seldom a *final* answer.

**Donald Christie is New York-based Vice President of Banque de Paris et des Pays-Bas (Paribas). He is responsible for corporate calling in the northeastern United States. Before joining Paribas, he spent three years with Bank of America's New York office calling on companies in the chemical, rubber, and forest products industries.**

After serving three years in the U.S. Army where he was trained as a Chinese interpreter, Mr. Christie received his BA in Chinese Language from the University of Massachusetts, Amherst, where he was a Commonwealth Scholar. He then went on for an MBA degree from Columbia University. While at Columbia he was Vice President of the school's chapter of the American Finance Association and was also a member of the International Fellows Program. He is currently attending the evening JD program at the School of Law of Fordham University.

*Robert A. M. Coppenrath*

# A Little Bit of Luck

*This is a true story*. It happened in 1960, the spring of 1960 to be exact, and it is so unusual that it is hard to believe.

The country is Canada. The city Ottawa. I was the president and chief executive officer of a medium-size Canadian company that specialized in the warehousing, servicing, and distribution of a Belgian imported product. There was a big bureaucratic problem in Ottawa for which I had set up an appointment with Mr. R. D. of the Customs and Excise Department. But let me not run ahead of my story.

It all started in January 1959 when my pregnant wife, our two-year-old daughter—just out of a cast for a dislocated hip—and I came to Canada as landed immigrants. After six stormy days in the middle of January, we landed in Halifax, Nova Scotia. From there we took the train to Toronto, a trip of exactly three days and two nights. My poor young wife could not believe her eyes when on the third day we had still seen nothing but snow! She was convinced I had taken her to Siberia. As I mentioned, this was the middle of January and this is the way things are in Canada in the middle of winter. All this under bright sunny skies during the day and bright shining stars during the night. This is when we remembered the snide remark made by Voltaire when he referred to the fact that Napoleon had bought Louisiana *pour quelques arpents de neige*!

We settled in Toronto and all went well. I started the business after first liquidating another one that had gone broke for a number of reasons too long to explain here (and totally irrelevant to the subject at hand). Soon a substantial problem developed on the customs and excise side, necessitating a visit with the officials to try to sort out the problem. It was a matter of life or death, and we very much wanted our corporate venture to thrive.

I was somewhat leery of flying, so I took the 11 P.M. train from Toronto to Montreal. It was scheduled to stop at around 7 A.M. in

Ottawa. After a good double Canadian Club failed to put me to sleep, I settled in my sleeper, taking one sleeping pill and then a second. When I awakened, I noticed that the train was at a standstill and it was quarter to eight, which gave me all kinds of tremors. The attendant told me how he had tried to waken me, then continued to tell me that the locomotive had developed engine trouble and would not proceed to Montreal, but rather to a service station forty miles outside of Ottawa.

I was still in pajamas, but I was happy that I was not on my way to Montreal. I started to wash and shave when the train started to roll; when I was completely dressed, the train was still rolling, which annoyed me to some extent because I felt it would bring me farther and farther from my target, the center of Ottawa, right next to the Grand Hotel Chateau Lauier.

At the end of my patience, I pulled the alarm. The train stopped. I was the only passenger, of course. I jumped out of the last car, ran over some tracks, climbed an embankment and discovered to my great satisfaction a vast amount of traffic going one way—the morning traffic into the city. This gave me a good feeling, for I had no idea where I was. By this time it was quarter to nine.

As I crossed the street through this traffic, it started to rain. A car stopped in the middle of this slow-moving traffic jam. The driver, instinctively sensing that I was lost in the rain, gave me a sign to jump in. I thanked him profusely, even more grateful when I learned we were on our way to Ottawa Center. I told him what had happened to me, whereupon he inquired about my accent. I told him I was from the Lowlands of the Old Country, that I was an importer, and that I was here on business with the Customs Department for a most difficult problem. Hearing this, the driver looked at me and said, "My dear sir, you must have the luck of the Irish. My name is R. D. and you are Mr. Coppenrath, and you are supposed to have an appointment with me at 9:00 in my office."

The surprise was great—and we nearly had an accident, for we burst into laughter. Incredible. I might have flown to Ottawa. I might have driven. I might have gone a day earlier. I might not have taken sleeping pills. The train might not have developed engine troubles. I might have ended up in Montreal. I might not have pulled the alarm. There are a lot of things I might or might not have done but no, I had to do all I did and meet my contact in a traffic jam among thousands of cars somewhere on a road of which I cannot even recall the name. All I know is that it paralleled the Canadian Pacific Railroad track!

Well, believe it or not, we settled our business in the car in a most satisfactory way. He promised all the help he could offer with the remark that he was not going to break the lucky spell of a young immigrant with a problem. The same day I took the train back.

It gave me the time to put my house in order and build a successful business. This was the most effective and successful selling job that I ever was involved in. For a number of years we exchanged Christmas greetings, and then one day I was informed that my benefactor had passed away. As the saying goes, all you need is a little bit of luck.

Robert A. M. Coppenrath joined Agfa-Gevaert, Inc., in August 1969 and became its President in March 1970. Prior to this he had spent eleven years in Canada as President and General Manager of Photo Importing Agencies, Ltd., a company he founded. In 1964 this firm became the exclusive agent for the distribution of Agfa-Gevaert products throughout the Dominion.

Born in 1928, in Antwerp, Mr. Coppenrath earned his BBA and MBA degrees at the University of Antwerp. After moving to Canada, he continued his education with postgraduate studies in marketing at the University of Waterloo, Ontario, and completed a seminar in finance sponsored by Columbia University.

Mr. Coppenrath is a director and chairman of the Belgian-American Chamber of Commerce in the United States, a member and vice president of the Sales Executives Club of New York, and a trustee of the Aviation Hall of Fame of New Jersey. He has been awarded several Belgian decorations including Knight of the Order of the Crown and Officer in the Order of Leopold II.

**William J. Davis**

# Fund Raising—
# Another Kind of
# Selling

*This sales story* is of course my story, but in reality it is a tale of a sales campaign involving volunteers who received nothing but personal satisfaction for giving their time and energies and money on behalf of an institution of higher education.

Some, often those with the most confidence and zeal for the activity, were professional salespeople. But there were many men and women who had little or no sales experience to begin with and less desire to "make the call." But once excited with the task and properly motivated they would rise to the occasion to equal and sometimes excel the "pros."

After spending a year cutting his fund-raising teeth on a $1,200,000 capital campaign to provide money for construction of the Owen D. Young Library at St. Lawrence University in Canton, New York, this thirty-year-old, newly appointed alumni secretary was assigned, as one of his many duties, direction of the college's annual alumni fund campaign.

The St. Lawrence alumni fund had attained less than average success through the years with about 17 percent of its 8700 alumni donating a total of $50,000 annually, chiefly as a result of an appeal letter from a volunteer chairman and a series of mimeographed personalized letters from class representatives to their classmates.

Shortly thereafter, this neophyte fundraiser attended a national conference of educational fundraisers held in Bretton Woods, New Hampshire, at which the institutions with outstanding records of alumni support (Dartmouth, Princeton, Yale, and Harvard) were praised, cited, and almost worshiped by those present. This meeting provided the incentive to try to raise St. Lawrence to the lofty heights of alumni giving.

How could a small college located in northern New York hope to compete with institutions known for great traditions of alumni giving? Consider the story about a Dartmouth alumnus and an alumnus of a lesser-known institution. They were chatting one day, and the Dartmouth man was asked: "Do you give to your alumni fund?" "You mean you don't have to?" was the incredulous response.

The successful institutions boasted large staffs devoted to the annual fund, as well as volunteer class agents or fund managers who would not take no for an answer, and high-powered publicity campaigns directed to the alumni in support of their annual giving programs. St. Lawrence possessed an alumni secretary who also edited the quarterly alumni magazine, coordinated alumni meetings throughout the east, and served the college's Alumni Council as well. An assistant alumni secretary, a secretary, an alumni records keeper, and a bookkeeper/clerk provided the staff for the alumni office.

Obviously, the competition with the "big boys" was not going to be a simple task. First, an analysis of our strengths and weaknesses was in order. The great strength (though really untested) seemed to be a strong sense of loyalty on the part of St. Lawrence alumni, but doesn't every college president feel he has unusually loyal and dedicated alumni?

The weaknesses were a long-time failure by the institution to communicate more effectively with alumni, lack of techniques for doing so, and the absence of any tradition of alumni financial support. Recent graduates, who at that time equaled nearly half of the alumni body as a result of the post-World War II boom in college enrollments, were especially reluctant to contribute.

With this in mind, a plan for improvement was formulated, even though on the surface it would appear that only a minor miracle would enable St. Lawrence to make major strides in this direction.

Since all the "pros" in the fund-raising field stressed personal solicitation (face to face, person to person) as the single key to successful fund raising (selling), it was decided to operate our annual fund in much the same manner as a capital campaign with, of course, a reduced budget and considerably less costly fanfare.

We needed something to dramatize this fundraising effort and thereby cause someone who had never given to at least think about it, or perhaps remember, so that a call or visit might convince the alumnus to become a contributor. A challenge offer seemed to be the most likely way to dramatize the appeal. Several major donors, mostly trustees of the university, were sold on the concept of becoming "Angels," or challengers, and they collectively offered to match all new gifts to the fund as well as all gifts from persons who increased their contributions over the previous year's. We had the offer and now we had to tell the prospects again, and again, and, yes, one more time, if necessary. The campaign was launched in December and was to finish in September. It developed as follows: every class agent was encouraged to write no less than three and in some cases as many as five letters to classmates. Letters were prepared from samples we felt would *elicit a favorable response* (money!); if an agent wanted to originate or modify the samples this was perfectly fine. A sales dinner for the metropolitan New York area agents was planned to spark enthusiasm, outline goals, and thank them in advance for their vital assistance.

The fund chairman, selected from the Board of Trustees, with the encouragement of the university's President and the Chairman of the Board, sent a special appeal letter to the major donor prospects in December saying "give now, or pledge, and pay later," thereby enabling them to take advantage of contributing in either of two years. In January, a letter from the fund chairman was sent to all prospects officially announcing the opening of the campaign and asking for a response in the enclosed postage-paid return envelope.

As this was going on, we began seeking area chairmen for the personal solicitation phase of the campaign. The President of the university would usually telephone candidates for area chairmen and sell them on the need for their voluntary services. These area chairmen, all alumni, a few nongraduates, were the most prestigious available and often the busiest, but they seldom declined. (The Prexy was himself a supersalesman.)

Once they were selected, the Alumni Secretary would go to their areas, meet with them, and help with the selection of their leadership committees. The leadership committees would in turn select workers for their teams and a subsequent kickoff meeting would be scheduled several weeks later. These kickoff meetings, usually held over coffee and dessert at a local hotel or restaurant, were of vital importance: here inspiration, encouragement, and training in getting the gift (making the sale) were dispensed with enthusiasm. When possible the President or one of the Deans of the university would attend these kickoff meetings to thank the workers for their willingness to give their time and their energies for alma mater. Each succeeding week a new area would begin its task of selection and solicitation. Rivalries sprang up between areas and area chairmen. The northern New Jersey chairman vowed to gain a higher percentage of participation than the Westchester County chairman, and a friendly wager ensued. We stressed participation rather than dollars in these early days, feeling that once an alumnus had made the first gift, followed by a second, a habit pattern would have begun (he or she might even enjoy participating!) and in the future, as our alumni prospered and the institution did its job of attempting to upgrade contributions, the dollar amounts would grow accordingly.

Bimonthly bulletins were sent to all chairmen, leaders, workers, and class agents detailing progress to date. These bulletins showered the leading classes and geographic areas with praise and called for greater efforts on the part of all involved. A page in the university alumni magazine was also devoted to highlighting our progress.

As response to the class agent mailings was being received so were the gifts from the area campaigns, requiring an up-to-the-minute records system. There were times when a prospect might receive a letter from the class agent on Monday and on Tuesday or Wednesday be visited by an area worker, thereby enhancing the importance of the gift. Credit was given both the area and class in determining performance in each category.

By May we could see that the campaign was beginning to bear fuit. Hundreds of gifts from persons who had never given to the university were being received. There was still more work to be done. A small but loyal group of alumni met in a New York City real estate company office provided by the president of the alumni association and began the first "phonethon"—telephoning alumni all across the country and especially in locations without a heavy concentration of alumni, where no formal area campaigns existed. Armed with a sales pitch for those who needed it, they proceeded with excellent results. The "natural salesmen" required no prepared sales pitch. They just spoke with enthusiasm, interest, and persistence and the pledges followed accordingly.

In all instances follow-ups were made, including pledge reminders, personalized thank yous from the chairman, and meeting reminders.

A special letter from alumnus Kirk Douglas, personally signed and mailed from Hollywood, was sent late in the campaign to those who had not contributed. This was followed by a "last call" appeal from the General Chairman, Allen D. Marshall, Vice-President and Secretary of General Dynamics Corporation. The alumni were beginning to feel the excitement of the challenge and the success of the campaign as the student body, through its leaders, offered to participate, responding to a special minichallenge from the Angels' committee.

When the campaign ended in September 1961, 4663 alumni of the 8772 had contributed $123,580 for a 53.3 percent participation figure, and the university had been cited for a national award by the U.S. Steel Foundation for outstanding improvement in alumni support among private coeducational colleges.

This could be the happy ending of this story, but 1962 was just ahead and what would we do for an encore? Only more of the same. So we began 1962 by enlarging the Angels group, which then offered to give $5,000 for each percentage point of alumni participation over the 55 percent level. Eighty-nine alumni represented one percentage point, therefore once the 55 percent level was attained, each person's gift, when combined with eighty-eight others, was worth about $55. This was an exciting fact to exploit. When 55 percent was eventually reached late in the fund year, the Chairman of the Board of Trustees, who was the "head Angel," sent a personal check for $55.05, made payable to St. Lawrence University, to each alumnus who had not yet contributed, urging him or her to place a personal check with the Chairman's and return both to the university in the enclosed postage-paid envelope. A gimmick, yes, but it worked. A total of 595 alumni responded with their own checks. We also increased the area solicitation program, enlarged the phonethon, and informed the alumni with great emphasis on how their tremendous response the previous year had resulted in the U.S. Steel award. For the second consecutive year our effort at "educational" fund raising involving the student body was brought into the Annual Fund campaign. The previous year 90 percent of the undergraduates had responded to a challenge from the Angels. This year the Angels offered to give $1000 for each percentage point of participation the students could increase above 95 percent. Again, the students accepted the challenge with enthusiasm. A student chairman and his committee directed a personal solicitation program complete with pledge cards, captains, and workers, achieving 99.1 percent participation. Once again, as in 1961, the highest gift permitted was 10¢. A total of 1310 students each gave a dime. These results were not included in the overall totals, but this effort to establish a high-level giving pattern with these classes succeeded, with obvious results to the present day. The 1962 campaign was carried on with great gusto; participation increased to 65.1 percent, and the dollars to $146,734. The National Grand Prize for Improvement in Alumni Support among all private educational institutions in the nation was awarded by the U.S. Steel Foundation to St. Lawrence University.

And now, one more time: in 1963 we did it all over again with a few new wrinkles and St. Lawrence recorded the highest percentage of alumni participation in annual giving ever attained by a coeducational institution—70.7 percent—a record that still stands some seventeen years later. I left St. Lawrence to become Vice-President of Kalamazoo College shortly thereafter, but the college has continued its excellence in alumni support ever since. This then is a story of the beginning of a program that has continued to thrive and to prosper. A story of dedicated individuals, a great product (higher education), persistence in all efforts, and the employment of sound sales techniques that proved to be the catalyst to ensure success for all involved.

□   □   □

William J. Davis is Director of Development for the University of California's Lawrence Hall of Science, a world-renowned science and technology center located in Berkeley, California.

A native of Utica, New York, and graduate of St. Lawrence University with a major in history, he began his business career as a reporter for the *Watertown* (New York) *Daily Times*.

Mr. Davis next served in the Public Relations Department of Bucknell University with responsibility for sports information, until returning to his alma mater as Assistant Director of Admissions in 1954. He subsequently was appointed Alumini Secretary and Director of Annual Giving, serving in this capacity until 1963 when he joined Kalamazoo College (Michigan) as Vice President for Development. At Kalamazoo, Mr. Davis directed a capital campaign that resulted in $9 million being contributed in response to a challenge offer from the Ford Foundation.

In 1967, he was named Assistant to the President of United Student Aid Funds, Inc., a nation-wide not-for-profit corporation based in New York City, which guarantees bank loans to college students. He later became Vice-President and Treasurer with responsibilities for lender and college relations, fund raising, and several state agency loan programs.

Mr. Davis moved west in 1974 to become Special Consultant and Campaign Director for the University of California's Natural Land and Water Reserve System, an effort by the university to acquire and preserve for all time, for study and research, samples of the various habitats indigenous to the State of California. In 1977, after directing a successful $2 million fund raising effort for the NLWRS, Mr. Davis was named Director of Development for the Lawrence Hall of Science, where he is currently implementing a complete development program for this organized research unit of the University of California.

**Louis F. DeMarco**

# Success in a Competitive Market

*Getting a job on the* Advertising Age *sales staff* was one of the most important sales of my career.

When *AA* ran a salesman wanted ad, the competition was intense for many reasons. *AA* was a very prestigious publication and clearly on its way to becoming the leader in its field. It was the only newspaper in a fast-paced, quick-changing business. Other long-established "how to" or feature magazines in the field were unable or unwilling to keep pace with the changing reader needs of the market and were being swept aside by *AA*'s momentum.

Another reason the position was eagerly sought was the fact that salesmen were to be paid on a straight commission basis. There were still many publications offering salary plus quota commission or bonus systems, but a straight commission setup that paid you in direct proportion for every inch of advertising space you sold was rare. It was unbelievable that the one offering straight commissions also happened to be red hot and obviously gaining strength. *Ad Age* did not need to offer such a generous plan but they wanted only the best, and . . . it worked.

I found myself among a crowd of applicants most of whom had much more experience than I. To stand out I would have to make an extraordinary impression. No simple recitation of my experience or even a superlative résumé would be sufficient in this field. So I approached it as I would any sales situation. I tried to put myself in the chair of the man doing the hiring. What were his needs and what problems would he face trying to satisfy them?

As always, I began by analyzing the depth of my product knowledge. In fact, there were at least three products involved in this case.

**61**

I, of course, was the product being sold. My product knowledge in that area was thorough and I would decide how to use it after my study of the other two products involved. Another product involved was *Advertising Age*.

The third product was Jack Gafford, the man doing the hiring.

I did my research in reverse order because I had already learned that whoever got the job would be reporting directly to Mr. Gafford. It would be a close relationship, and he had better approve of my attitudes and style as well as my qualifications or I would lose out.

So I set about finding out as much as I could about Jack Gafford.

It wasn't a very difficult assignment because Jack was a well-known, almost legendary figure in the business. He was a unique, enormously effective, often flamboyant salesman. I learned much about his style from people who knew him. He was intense and obviously impatient with dull or inconclusive calls.

He often behaved as though sales calls were exciting battles that must be won on the spot and he willingly took risks to make something happen. For instance, there were many stories of vicious attacks on the competition. It seemed reasonable then to assume that his enthusiasms were quickly spent. I would have to make it easy for Jack to make a fast decision about me or risk having any good impressions I made fade as other good candidates commanded his attention.

Jack's self-confidence was another characteristic frequently mentioned. Evidently, he often made sales simply because his confidence so overwhelmed prospects they bought on the assumption he must be right.

I gathered most of this information from friends in the media who were Jack's customers—buyers of space in *AA*. One friend arranged a meeting with an *AA* salesman, who gave me valuable information about Jack's personal and professional history. For example, despite his rough, irreverent public image, Jack admired strong family men and was capable of an almost courtly grace when he met employees' wives. He was especially respectful of his elders. I also learned that Jack felt his salesmen should cultivate the classic Brooks Brothers Madison Avenue look (Brooks was where he bought all his clothes), and he was absolutely disdainful of the salesman who did not wear a hat.

It became clear that to break out of the pack, I would have to demonstrate traits with which he could identify. A plan was beginning to take shape in my mind.

As in any sales situation, all this "homework" was beginning to build my confidence. I was certain I already had an edge on the competition.

Therein lies the greatest value of thoroughly preparing for a sale. Rarely will you use all the bits and pieces of gathered information, but the sure knowledge that you are prepared to draw on it provides an aura of confidence that pervades the call from beginning to end. Confidence is the most important characteristic of good selling. The confident salesman radiates authority and genuine enthusiasm. Those are the elements that create the ideal sales environment—one in which the respect of the buyer becomes automatic. It cannot be faked if you are unprepared and thus necessarily unsure of yourself.

Using the same *AA* contact I then moved on the second phase of my research—learning all I could about *AA*. I studied the history of the publication and its competition. I pored over every piece of sales material available, paying particular attention to its own ads. As an avid reader since my college days I had come to understand its purpose very well, but I nonetheless talked to one of the editors, who provided more insights.

It was all extremely impressive.

*AA* was a powerful publication getting stronger all the time and destined to become one of the great publications of all time. I felt certain I was already qualified to sell *AA*—and I knew precisely how I would put it all together. When I originally asked for an interview I took my first risk by saying a road trip prohibited my coming in for at least two weeks. I needed time to do my research and I wanted to get in late when the need to fill the job was more urgent and impressions of earlier candidates were beginning to fade. There was a possibility he would hire one of the first people interviewed, but it was not likely because he probably would feel compelled to see several candidates before making a decision.

My research used up one week and the remaining week was spent preparing and refining my presentation. I also made a point of buying a Brooks Brothers hat (fortunately I already had some of their suits).

I arrived for my interview and made a point of carrying my hat and coat with me when called into Jack's office. After the usual firm handshake, damned if he didn't compliment me on my choice of hat, which was exactly the same as his own. I was off to a fine start.

I led him through my résumé embellishing each point with clear, precise examples of achievement: bonus receipts, sales records, complimentary letters from customers and employers, and so on. Watching for interest on his part, I would slip in bits of information about my attitudes and work habits. He was enjoying it and drawing me out. At one point he admitted that he liked what he saw but asked why he should choose me over several more experienced candidates. If you listen hard enough the prospect will always tell where he needs help in making the decision to buy. Listen closely and he will always tell you when to make your big play—when he is ready to close. It is the moment when all the preparation pays off. I still have the notes from that day. Remembering his own reputation for feistiness, my response went like this:

"Mr. Gafford, I would be doing a disservice to both of us if I were to allow false modesty to get in the way of the truth at this point. A silly polite answer now would just be a waste of all the valuable time you have given me and I might lose this job. *AA* will survive very well without me if that happens, but you will have lost the opportunity to add to your staff an absolutely dedicated, truly outstanding salesman . . . one who is determined to do everything necessary to become the best in the business. And I will have lost a career opportunity that I want more than anything I can imagine. *AA* is not a good or outstanding publication—it's a great publication and with great salesmen it will get the business it deserves and become a gold mine. I, of course, don't know who you have seen, but I am willing to bet I am a better salesman than any of them . . . by far. I say that because of all I have worked with none—not one—is even close to being as hard working, determined, hungry, successful, or smart as I am."

He was smiling at this point so I started to move to the clincher.

"Of course, you only have my word and this pile of documents to go by so why not check some references? But I can't believe you would be impressed by some carefully selected list of cronies. Here is a copy of my entire account list, big and small. You select the names or pick them at random. I am not the least bit worried about the answers you'll get. But really, there is no reason in the world why you should take my word, or any candidate's word, for how well he can sell for you. What you have heard so far is conversation—history and promises. But in answer to the question, 'why should you choose me?' . . . You should choose me because I am willing to stick my neck out now and demonstrate my ability—I am going to *prove* I can sell *AA*."

It was obvious he had no idea what I was going to do but he was having a great time and his attention was riveted.

At that point I asked permission to set up a table-top presentation board with an adhesive face. After asking him to pretend he was the publisher of a mass circulation magazine, I used a combination of his own sales materials and some I had created to launch into a ten-minute sales pitch for *Advertising Age*, slapping points on the board as I went. I concluded with the entire story facing him and quickly hit the highlights again before closing by asking for the order.

He roared his approval, repeating "You've got the job, boy—you've got the job." In fact, he called the salesmen who were not on calls into his office and had me go through the presentation again, saying it was better than any they had ever produced, which didn't exactly endear me to the staff.

The point is that the importance of preparation can never be overstated. That kind of audacious approach might not have worked with anyone but Jack Gafford.

That sale was personally very important to me because it was the start of a joyful and rewarding career at *AA*.

There were many others along the way but the most important came fifteen years later. It was a sale that had an effect on the whole industry—maybe even the entire economy.

It reaffirmed my belief that a strong sales story, well prepared and clearly stated, could successfully move thousands of minds as easily as one.

A brief sketch of the ways in which American business was drifting toward mismanagement will be helpful in setting up this sales story. At the outset it should be understood that American advertisers have led our economy forward. They are largely responsible for the enviable standard of living we have enjoyed for decades. The consumer's freedom of choice among an ever-widening circle of goods and services could not have been possible without advertisers. So in the late 1960s, when advertisers began to lose faith in their ability to keep the economy moving, it was not unlike a salesman doubting his ability to make something happen. And the prophecy is always self-fulfilling. Many advertisers began to accept predicted economic conditions rather than shape new conditions.

Clarity of purpose is an essential prerequisite of good management. *Consequences must never be confused with causes.* Because ours is a sales-based economy, the mission of all companies is to sell something. No company will succeed by deliberately minimizing its sales effort. Those who cut sales budgets in tough competitive situations invariably lose market shares. They are companies who forget their mission is to maximize sales. When that kind of management finds itself confronting diminished profits, it chooses to increase short-term profits by cutting sales costs. Advertising, which is overwhelmingly the most effective mass selling tool, suffers the deepest cuts of all. The MBA theory is that ad plans represent unspent dollars and cutting ad budgets simply transfers dollars to the profit side of the ledger. The long-term result is inevitably no profits. Such managements confuse the profits and sales functions of their enterprise. Profits are always the consequence of sales—never the cause of sales.

It is absolutely impossible to run a profitable operation over an extended period with an ongoing policy of cutting the sales effort. *No company can economize its way to success in a competitive market.* Now, back to the sales story.

In the late 1960s the drift toward "bottom-line" managements accelerated with the popularization of the MBA. Despite a lack of academic or practical experience in the most important function of all business—sales—MBAs were moved into decision-making positions. Danger signs were flashing, but MBAs were ill-prepared to deal with them. Sales experience would have taught them that when profits decline, the need is to sell more—not less. They, however, chose to react to symptoms rather than causes. They increased short-term profits by cutting the sales effort. The relief could only be temporary. In the long run it would produce a disastrous result.

During all this I had successfully persuaded many of our customers to increase their advertising in this environment. However, the enchantment with bottom-line management was so widespread, the idea that advertising no longer had the power to lead the economy was so pervasive, that it was impossible to keep pace with the defections on the basis of personal calls.

A company-by-company approach was too slow to prevent the damaging recession that would surely result if managements continued to decrease their commitment to advertising growth. The problem was massive and had to be dealt with on that scale.

It was at that point that I decided to use the most effective mass-selling technique—advertising. I decided to use the direct mail method of advertising for several reasons:

**1** It provided an opportunity to reach a large yet selective audience.

**2** The list's community of interests would allow me to employ uniquely appropriate examples to illustrate my points.

**3** The message was complex and needed to be studied, in an environment I hoped would be free from the competition of other ads or editorial matter.

**4** Finally, direct mail, when well executed, is a very personal medium. I had to persuade the reader that the message was of critical importance.

I accomplished all this by creating a piece that had the appearance of a personal letter. It was sent to our customer list of publishers and broadcasters who were advertisers in *Advertising Age*.

The response exceeded our expectations—by far.

Indeed, we even received commitments for additional space by return mail when the most we hoped for were indications of interest that would provide an opportunity for follow-up.

However, we still had not achieved the massive turnaround necessary, and the responses told us why. They told us that although many agreed with our premise about the importance of increasing advertising, their own customers did not. The major advertisers who ran advertising in our customers' magazines and newspapers and on their TV and radio stations were cutting back.

At this point we decided to reach beyond our own prospect universe. We would do for our customers what they should have done for themselves. We would take the message directly to *their* customers. Since *Advertising Age* reaches more advertising and marketing managements than any other medium, we decided to run the direct mail piece as an "open letter" in *Advertising Age*. We did so with very few changes for, although we detailed the ill effects of cutting advertising as it affected magazines, the broader implications for all business were clear.

The reaction to the ad overwhelmed the earlier response. Requests to reprint the message poured in. Thousands of copies of the message were circulated by individual companies and industry groups. Many, such as the Canadian Railroad Association, made small alterations in the copy for their particular audiences.

The consciousness level across a broad span of industries was raised. The threat was given shape and made visible. An insidious trend that had begun to erode the importance of the sales function in the minds of great numbers of businessmen had been exposed and reversed. Most important, a predicted recession had been averted because ad budgets began to grow at an accelerated rate. From less than 1 percent growth in 1970 to 6.1 percent in 1971, ad budgets doubled to 12.3 percent in 1972, greater even than the growth of the GNP, which was 10.1 percent in 1972.

I cannot avoid selecting this as my most important sale and it is therefore reproduced here.

# An Open Letter to Advertising Executives

*A selected group of publishing executives received this letter last month. Their response has been surprising—and rewarding. Because of this heavy response—and because the principles discussed are relevant to all business, we believe this letter merits much broader readership among concerned advertising executives.*

Dear Publisher:

Some of what I am about to discuss in this letter will not specifically apply to your situation. However, the general subject is one that I believe deserves the attention of all major publishing executives.

In recent years many magazines have undergone a subtle but significant change. They have moved away from publishing management toward financial management. Often the same people remain in charge, but their operating philosophies have changed.

The "bottom line" is king.

It can now be said that major magazines live and are successful for one of two reasons. Either they are making money or there is visible evidence that they soon will be making money. Financial managements have displayed very little patience with diminishing profits. Budget cutting, particularly promotion budget cutting, has reached epidemic proportions. The trouble with eliminating a magazine's own advertising in response to one bad quarter is that it almost certainly will result in worsening the profit picture for the next quarter, thereby setting the stage for further cuts.

It is a suicidal cycle.

The fine editorial product that reaches and penetrates an audience must be sustained by a steady influx of advertising revenues. More than ever, editorial content and advertising content are interdependent. No magazine will succeed by sacrificing one to the *imagined* benefit of the other.

Correctly, almost no publisher would think of allowing economy moves to jeopardize the editorial product. To do so is to risk losing readers. But what growing numbers of publishers seem to have forgotten is that it is just as bad to economize at the expense of promotion which stimulates the cash flow that makes good editorial possible.

It must be remembered that magazines are a unique kind of business. We do not sell toothpastes or tractors, we sell markets . . . specific numbers of people delivered on a regularly scheduled basis. Unlike most product manufacturers it is not possible for us to make swift, substantial economies by simply stopping the production line and living off our inventories. There are no inventories. There are, instead, fulfillment commitments. Whether the circulation is 7,000,000 or 70,000 those magazines must be produced every issue date . . . those guarantees met. Advertising makes it possible. It provides the cash flow that buys the paper, people, postage and almost all else that is needed to meet your fulfillment commitments. Cut the cash flow, which is what happens when publishers cut their own advertising, and eventually fulfillments and even editorial will have to be cut.

The Saturday Evening Post has shown us the consequences of that kind of cycle.

In today's market the publisher who produces excellent magazines must acknowledge that he is equally in the business of selling advertising. If he does not believe his advertising can work for him, he has nothing to sell his customers and is, frankly, in the wrong business.

No one in publishing is going to economize his way out of a tough competitive situation. It is, instead, the one sure way to lose ground. Would you tell your prospects to wait until things get better? Of course not. You tell them to fight back . . . sell their way to success. So, what should you do to increase profits? Very simply, you should do what you've been telling your customers to do. You should advertise. You must *make* things get better. You must seize opportunities. And the opportunities have never been better for publishers with courage and vision.

While overly cautious competitors are pulling in their horns, you sell your way into a bigger share of the market.

While advertisers are taking harder looks at media, you give them more reasons to buy your magazine.

Find the courage to establish a stronger than ever franchise while others are running scared.

No less than an absolute faith in advertising will carry magazines through this difficult time into an era of unprecedented growth. Magazines must fight their way clear, and their own advertising can be the most effective weapon. Promotion is modern publishing's plasma. Common sense dictates that in difficult times you increase the flow.

If you've already ordered your promotion budget cut—rescind the order.

If you're thinking of cutting your promotion budget—forget it.

And if you really want to take a giant step forward building bigger profits than ever . . . right now is the time to substantially *increase* your magazine's promotion budget. Call in your people today and say, "We've waited long enough, pour on the advertising and let's bust our way out of the doldrums."

May I hear from you?

Very sincerely,

Louis F. De Marco
Advertising Director

Unfortunately, the lessons learned in averting one recession were quickly forgotten when economists unleashed a torrent of dire predictions in the second half of 1972. The growth of advertising expenditures dropped from 12.3 percent in 1972 to 7.8 percent in 1973 while the GNP rose to 11.6 percent and we plunged into the worst recession since the great depression.

Shortly after recovering from that debacle the economists went to work predicting the next imminent downturn. They were relentless and unified in forecasting another recession every quarter since 1977. We were equally relentless in predicting continued growth. They were wrong—we were right. Why? There had been no recession through 1979 because American businessmen remembered the lessons learned in 1973. Advertising expenditures grew at a faster rate than the GNP every year since 1975. Instead of decreasing ad expenditures in the face of bad forecasts, advertisers increased them. Today, however, they are not keeping pace with growing inflation and the "real dollar" impact of advertising budgets is being eroded. Consequently a 1980 recession is likely to continue into the first quarter of 1981 if advertisers forget the necessity of selling their way clear with increased budgets. However, on the chance there are faint hearts out there, we have run an updated version of that successful earlier ad, and it too is reproduced here.

The only limits to a good salesman's influence are in the prospect's mind. A well-planned, carefully executed sales story can successfully influence thousands as easily as one.

Louis F. DeMarco has been publisher of *Advertising Age* since May 1977. In three years the income of the publication increased almost 100 percent. Mr. DeMarco is proud of this statistic, because he believes that "a successful sales performance is the universal imperative of all enterprises. The sale of something is the common purpose of all companies. That 'something' may be a product, a service, or even a charitable cause. If the sponsoring organization does not do a good job of selling, it will simply cease to exist." Mr. DeMarco learned the techniques of good salesmanship very early. He had to because "the competition among shoeshine boys working Brooklyn barrooms back in the 1930s was fierce."

As a teenager he had a variety of after-school and summer jobs. One, selling bad furniture polish door to door in a poor neighborhood

# An open letter to All Advertisers

Dear Advertiser:

Congratulations!

You are largely responsible for defeating the predicted recession of 1979. In fact, you have done it four years in a row confounding the "economists" who are now confused enough to suggest that maybe we are in a recession and don't know it.

Congratulations to you for recognizing that advertising provides the energy that keeps the American economy growing. It is our great energy resource. We have plenty and...it is renewable.

Most importantly, congratulations for having the courage to back your insights with increased advertising expenditures in 1979, 1978, 1977, and 1976.

It's time someone thanked you because it certainly did work. Business was just fine all those years when, according to the wizards, it wasn't supposed to be good at all. It was supposed to turn down. At least that is what economists and various other "experts" were insisting as far back as the winter of 1976. They were particularly emphatic about a recession arriving in 1978. When no recession developed in 1978 the "experts" insisted it would surely arrive in the first quarter of 1979. When that didn't happen, they predicted a recession would start in the second quarter. By June they were obviously wrong again so, they tried a new tactic.

They simply "declared" a recession. For those of us unable to recognize it, they announced that the recession had already started way back in April. They were, of course, wrong again.

Not only are many economic forecasters pretty bad at predicting the future, it now seems evident they can't even predict the past.

Why are they so wrong so often? What is going on?

What lessons did you, the advertiser, learn in 1975 that seem still to elude many forecasters?

Possibly the most painful lesson learned was that cutting advertising budgets in response to a predicted drop in sales assured only one thing—a drop in sales, probably swifter and deeper than predicted. Those who cut budgets to "wait and see" what the economy did, usually saw the competition running off with larger shares of market.

This sequence is documented in a serious study done by the American Business Press. It is called "How Advertising in a Recession Period Affects Sales." Its conclusion: "Companies which do not cut advertising budgets in periods of recession post greater increases in sales and net income than companies which cut back their advertising in times of economic turndown." Copies are available from the American Business Press.

You cannot economize your way out of a tough sales situation.

However, you certainly can sell your way to success and, in good times or bad, THE MORE YOU SELL, THE MORE YOU WILL SELL.

That is exactly what you, the advertiser, did in 1976, 1977, 1978 and 1979.

Despite the bleak forecasts of that period, ad expenditures grew at a faster rate than the G.N.P.

Result: There was no recession in those years.

In 1973, 1974 and 1975 the reverse was true. The G.N.P. grew at a faster rate than ad expenditures and we suffered a very damaging recession.

So we learned a lesson that cannot be overstated. When forecasts are bad, we need to advertise more—not less.

Ours is an aspiring, upwardly mobile society. Advertising responds to these impulses and, when successful, creates the sales that provide payrolls, profits, taxes and all else needed to keep the economy moving. Movement is the key to understanding the critical relationship between Americans and advertising. When advertised products satisfy consumer aspirations, movement takes place. The movement of goods in massive amounts requires massive amounts of advertising. And

that is how you beat off the impending recessions. You authorized enormous ad budget increases (largest ever) in the face of dire forecasts, and you created sales and profits way beyond anything thought possible at the time. Still, economists seem unable to understand the power of advertising. Perhaps they don't know how to fit it into their models. Models constructed of past performances that have no relevance today...models that make no allowance for potential sales responses to increased advertising.

Maybe many economists discount the power of advertising because it refutes their contention that we are the helpless victims of uncontrollable circumstances. They seem to view the economy as something beyond our influence. Some kind of inexorable force moving us toward an inevitable destiny about which we can do nothing.

That is nonsense. We are the economy. You and I and the millions who both produce and buy the nation's output. We are the economy and we do have the power to give it direction.

Therein lies the key to continued prosperity.

We must have faith in one powerful truth—WE CAN MAKE A DIFFERENCE.

We must reject the hopeless despair of the helpless victim mentality.

We must have confidence in our ability to excel at what we have done in the past to create the most envied standard of living the world has ever known.

Most importantly, we must have COURAGE. Courage enough to give action to that faith and confidence. For advertisers, the way is clear.

In the face of all the bleak forecasts, you must not cut advertising expenditures. For if you do, you will forfeit your ability to make something happen. You will become one of the victims.

The courageous will, instead, increase advertising expenditures and, while other overly-cautious competitors are pulling back, the courageous will pull ahead. The evidence supporting that simple notion is overwhelming. Act on it and you will help your company and the economy which, always remember, is you.

In summary, I urge you to:

1. Keep faith in the belief that you need not be a victim—that what you do is very important and will help shape the economy.

2. Have confidence in your ability to recognize and respond to consumer aspirations.

3. Find the courage to back that faith and confidence with increased advertising budgets.

Faith, confidence and courage are the hallmarks of American business that do not fit into the forecasting models used by economists.

Remain firm in those convictions. Act upon them now and 1980 will be another good year for your company and... we will again share this same kind of happy review in January, 1981.

Happy New Year,

Louis F. DeMarco
Publisher.
Advertising Age

P.S. You might be interested in just how good 1979 was for Advertising Age.

Our fully-paid circulation reached an all-time high of more than 76,000, generating circulation revenues of $1,750,000. Our renewal percentage is an impressive 76%. We carried 3,730 pages of advertising which represents a 471 page gain over 1978. And, yes, we have increased our advertising budget for 1980.

70

during the Depression, was spectacularly unproductive, but a valuable lesson was learned. Clearly, selling the wrong product to the wrong people at the wrong time was difficult, unprofitable, and (despite the canard about Eskimoes and refrigerators) not very satisfying. He became interested in the prospects of selling the right product to the right people at the right time and embarked on an intensive study of good salesmanship that continues even now.

Although the personal call, one-on-one selling, is always fun, his first love is that great American invention—mass selling. His fascination with selling thousands or millions of products—the movement of goods in tonnage lots through the use of effective advertising—started while attending Fort Hamilton High School in his hometown, Brooklyn, New York. He began to prepare himself for a career in advertising by taking writing and layout courses, and he sharpened those skills by writing and selling advertising space for the school newspaper.

World War II came along and in 1943 Mr. DeMarco enlisted in the Army Air Force. While in the Air Force, he took a correspondence course in advertising through the U.S. Armed Forces Institute. By September 1946 he was once again a civilian and enrolled as a Marketing/Advertising major at Pace College. He supported himself with a part-time job at Erwin Wasey Advertising until he and three other students formed their own advertising agency. When he graduated the agency dissolved and Mr. DeMarco went to work as a copywriter for Gunn-Mears advertising agency. Pursuing a plan designed to provide a well-rounded background of experience in a variety of media he worked for a display house, sold advertising space for the New York *Daily News* and, in 1953, joined the sales staff of *Advertising Age*. It was the end of his job-hopping strategy. Like a kid in a candy store, Mr. DeMarco found himself at the very heart of the business he loved. *Ad Age* was both the repository and the source of the industry—the reporter of news, the recorder of trends, the marketplace of ideas. It *was* the advertising and marketing business.

Mr. DeMarco moved through the ranks of the *Advertising Age* sales staff, finally heading it as Advertising Director in 1970, at which time he was also made a Vice President of the parent company, Crain Communications. He became Publisher in 1977.

Mr. DeMarco is a Vice President of the New York Sales Executives Club and a member of many industry organizations.

*Frederick W. DeTurk*

# Salesmanship

*Although the art of salesmanship* and the profession of salesman are commonly characterized by the tragic image of Willy Loman, it seems apparent to me that almost all interpersonal business and professional relationships encompass a large measure of selling. It is, in fact, the element of salesmanship—substitute persuasion if you will—that represents the heart of such relationships. It would be hard to rate as a success the priest who cannot persuade his congregation to believe in God, the teacher who fails to create enthusiasm for his subject, the doctor who prescribes a treatment a patient is not inspired to follow, as well as the merchant whose wares lie unsold on the shelves.

If I am right that salesmanship is a key element in the success of almost any business or profession, it follows that a successful sale is an experience to be savored. In reviewing a lifetime of sales, those that stand out in my mind are not necessarily those with the largest dollar value or product volume. In fact, the one that represents my personal high and did the most for me did not involve a product or a monetary value at all. It was the sale of an idea. To fully understand my sense of achievement, it is essential to have a feeling for the environment in which the sale occurred.

□

After graduation from the University of Michigan, I spent about a year and a half fulfilling undistinguished assignments in industry before joining forces with Uncle Sam in support of the Korean police action. Fresh from that experience, I accepted the position of Advertising Manager with Phelps Dodge Copper Products Corporation, at that time the major manufacturing subsidiary of Phelps Dodge Corporation. Phelps Dodge Corporation was at that time, and is today, one of the largest miners of copper in the world. The position of Advertising

Manager with its manufacturing subsidiary should not be confused with those carrying the same title at the better-known consumer products firms. I doubt that our total advertising budget in 1953 would have been sufficient to pay the taxi fares of one product management department of Procter and Gamble. When, in 1955, our agency put together a daring request for $1,000,000 to be spent in corporate advertising and presented it to the parent company management, we waited fearfully for the Chairman's reaction. I'll never forget his disinterested shrug and statement, "They're only asking for $1,000,000; I spend that much on a shovel." So much for the value of advertising!

□

Lest anyone conclude from this I look upon Phelps Dodge with disdain, let me quickly correct that impression. The corporation's roots go back to the eighteenth century, and its growth parallels closely that of the United States. The original leaders of the company were deeply religious, and an article appearing in an early edition of *Fortune* called Phelps Dodge "Presbyterian Copper." This attachment has, indeed, had a strong impact on the company's *modus operandi*, and it remains today one of the most ethical secular organizations I am acquainted with. In fact, the Presbyterian view that only charity which is anonymous is truly charity probably contributed to the historical reluctance of Phelps Dodge to trumpet its successes to the press. In any event, the close-lipped character of the corporation led to the memorable sale that is the subject of this story.

□

Through the early 1950s, Cornelius Kelly of Anaconda was acknowledged to be the spokesman of the copper industry and as a result Anaconda was the best-known of the copper companies. Phelps Dodge, meanwhile, let its deeds speak for themselves and what little publicity and public relations activity took place at headquarters was handled by a young and obscure Advertising Manager named Fred DeTurk. The Chairman of the Board of Phelps Dodge was gruff, powerful, hard-driving Louis S. Cates, nearing the end of a highly successful career. The President was a short, brilliant, chain-smoking lawyer named Robert G. Page. One of Bob Page's teachers at Harvard Law described him as a man "with the finest legal mind and the best-developed taste for bourbon whiskey I've ever known." Also on the senior staff of Phelps Dodge, serving as a Vice President, was Cleveland E. Dodge, a descendant of one of the founding families and a great lay leader of the Presbyterian Church. The business press would have been delighted with the opportunity to interview any of these gentlemen.

One member of the fourth estate, Byron Mack, Managing Editor of *Forbes* had suggested to me that a cover picture would be the reward for an interview with any major officer of Phelps Dodge. However, given the existing attitudes and methods of the company, such an interview seemed highly unlikely. But then occurred one of those unexpected circumstances that make life an adventure to be lived and not a battle to be won. Cornelius Kelly, the industry spokesman, died. With the brashness of youth, I decided to go for broke and suggest that Bob Page make himself available for the *Forbes* interview and try to assume the spokesman position formerly held by Kelly.

□

When I suggested to Page that the opportunity existed for him to become spokesman for the copper industry, his reaction was a mixture of amusement and puzzlement. Amusement at the audacity of his young Advertising Manager and puzzlement as to why he would want the position in the first place. In any event, he decided to give me an audience with the company's big three—Page, Cates, and Dodge—to discuss the matter.

Adrenalin was flowing on the day of the meeting. Page seemed willing to let me try. Cates was essentially negative but not to the point of blocking the program if the others felt it was worthwhile. The swing vote belonged to Dodge. After thoughtful consideration, he suggested that my arguments regarding the potential benefits to Phelps Dodge seemed to him to have some merit. I believe to this day that Page felt that giving me the go-ahead represented very low risk on his part, primarily because he considered it improbable that I could really arrange the exposure I was proposing. He didn't know about my commitment from Byron Mack of *Forbes*, which was, incidentally, a magazine highly regarded by the Phelps Dodge management. When he asked me how I would go about this business of making him a spokesman, I suggested that a good start would be to get a feature story in a prestigious financial magazine, perhaps *Forbes*.

The game was won when Bob Page said the words I remember as though they were uttered yesterday. "If you can arrange an interview with *Forbes*, I'm available." The interview went very well, and with his appearance on the cover of *Forbes*, "Puckish" Bob Page began his tour as industry spokesman.

I don't know the extent to which this position helped Phelps Dodge, but I do know that the company has never gone back to its position of reticence with the press and security analysts. Certainly the experience was exhilarating to me and surely didn't hurt my career.

◻   ◻   ◻

Frederick W. DeTurk is president of Phelps Dodge Industries, Inc., the manufacturing subsidiary of Phelps Dodge Corporation. Born in West Reading, Pennsylvania, he spent most of his teen years in Garden City, Long Island, New York. He left his parents' home to attend The University of Michigan, graduating with a bachelor of arts degree.

Shortly after graduation, he returned to Long Island where he held two junior-level jobs ("undistinguished assignments in industry," as he describes them) for a year and a half until he joined the U.S. Army in 1951. After two years of service in the Counterintelligence Corps, his career started with Phelps Dodge.

After fifteen years in various marketing and sales positions, Mr. DeTurk was awarded executive posts of progressively more responsibility, first as Assistant Vice President of Phelps Dodge Industries in 1968, next as President of Phelps Dodge Communications Company (a division of Phelps Dodge Industries) from 1969 to 1978, then as Vice President–Personnel of Phelps Dodge Corporation (the parent company) from 1978 until December 1979, when he was elected to his present position.

In 1978 Mr. DeTurk completed Harvard University's Advanced Management Program.

*C. R. Devine*

# Countdown
# to
# Nonsmoking

*Just as the Heimlich Maneuver* has become the world's accepted emergency measure for saving people choking on food particles, the Devine Countdown may one day achieve similar eminence as the *only* effective way to stop smoking once and forever.

Until the Countdown becomes more widely known, the world's innumerable—and appropriately miserable—cigarette smokers will have to make do with the plethora of methods said to be helpful in ridding them of this foul and obnoxious habit.

☐

These various and traditionally ineffective systems have included such nostrums as a chewing gum that makes you ill if combined with the noxious weed, psychotherapeutic sessions similar to Alcoholics Anonymous meetings, fake cigarettes, acupuncture, pierced ears, hypnotism, and more. The Danish Cancer Society has just started to market "No Smoke"—a package of imitation cigarettes invented by Hans V. Aaberg of Copenhagen. They look like the real thing but are made of mentholated fiber that won't burn. Presumably you can suck on these things all day and eventually kick the habit.

Then there's the "cut down" (*not* to be confused with our soon-to-be-famous Countdown) system, a decision to cut from twenty cigarettes a day, for example, to ten. This *never* works, although it has been tried millions of times by beleaguered smokers.

Least effective of all known methods for most people is the one that requires character and will power beyond the average mortal's innate capacities—"cold turkey"—eschewing the lethal weed at a given instant and swearing by all that's holy *never* to light up another. I have countless friends and acquaintances who've stopped cold turkey dozens of times but who've all succumbed again to the deadly habit. Those who do succeed for a while with this method frequently go into traumatic suspense and lose all contact with the real world. Some fidget uncontrollably when they feel the urge to smoke. Some can't sleep, or be civil to friends or strangers, or eat, or think, or walk, or talk. An appreciable number of these cold turkey aficionados go into catatonic behavioral patterns from which they can be saved only by grabbing a cigarette, lighting up, inhaling deeply, and forgetting the whole abortive attempt at prolonging their lives.

Among the "substitute" methods have been chewing tobacco, puffing it through cigars and pipes, and even walking around holding and constantly handling unlit cigarettes. This method is almost as worthless as the tapering off or cut down method.

□

Here is where the Devine Countdown comes in. It requires only two basic steps, one mental, the other physical.

□

*First*, the cigarette-smoking victim, like the alcoholic, must come to a clear self-determination that smoking *is* bad. This involves an intelligent awareness that the evidence against cigarette smoking is overwhelming. Not only does it trigger such grisly diseases as cancer of the lips, tongue, gums, throat, larynx, and bladder, it indisputably is a principal cause of a wide assortment of cardiovascular disorders, many usually fatal.

The smoker has only to think of all those helpless, countless, microscopic cilia that line the lungs to appreciate how a blast of hot tar and nicotine can make them curl up and wither away. Those still hooked on cigarettes know perfectly well the hacking cough most of them enjoy, the breathlessness when climbing stairs, and the general feeling of malaise they frequently suffer—all are inevitable and chronic concomitants of cigarette smoking. Heart specialists all over the world have quickly achieved an impressive consensus—cigarette smokers suffer cardiac and circulatory problems in far greater numbers than nonsmokers.

☐

Ok, realizing all this, you've successfully completed Step 1 in the Devine Countdown. Then comes Step 2, which requires only minimal will power—and even that is applied gradually and in small doses. It involves giving up cigarettes *for limited times* in each day until *nonsmoking* takes over as the habit syndrome. For example, stop smoking until 8 A.M. each day. (I used to have a college roommate so severely hooked he'd light up his first cigarette each day *before* he got out of bed.) Lots of cigarette smokers start off their daily diet of tar and nicotine with their cup of morning coffee. The Devine Countdown, at the outset, merely requires that you give up this first and frequently most compelling urge to smoke. Then, smoke as frequently as your habit requires the rest of the day.

A week later—or even a month later—hold off that first cigarette until 10 A.M. Then, at the interval most suitable to you, abstain until noon—or after lunch. Then, finally, until cocktail hour or after dinner.

By that time, you've gotten *used* to doing without but all the while you're smugly aware that, at a certain later hour, you can smoke all you want. The secret of this extraordinarily simple but effective system is that it requires practically no character or will power at all. It just gets you slowly but inexorably into the habit of *not* smoking—a habit that gradually but inevitably takes over from the previously uncontrollable smoking habit.

☐

The final coup de grâce can be struck on any easily remembered day. (I chose New Year's Eve 1952.) You will know that day when it arrives. After weeks and even months of applying will power *gradually*, you're ready for final foreswearing and can throw away what's left of that last pack because you've smoked too many during the last hours of that last day. *Most* of that day, the Devine Countdown has prepared you for this final release from cigarettes.

☐

For a few months, you will feel the urge to smoke at times, but all those weeks of gradual disentanglement will reap their reward. You've already learned to sweat out a few hours of temptation. No longer is it traumatic self-deprivation. At last you are free!

□  □  □

C. R. (Bob) Devine is Vice President of the Reader's Digest Association, Inc. Previously Deputy General Manager of Reader's Digest International Editions, he has served as chairman of the International Committee of the Magazine Publishers Association. He was 1962–1964 President of the International Advertising Association, and its Chairman and Chief Executive Officer in 1976–1980. He is President of the International Federation of the Periodical Press. He has served as Vice President of the International Executives Association and is now a Director of that organization.

Mr. Devine joined the Digest in 1955; prior to that he was Assistant Advertising Director of *U.S. News & World Report*. A graduate of Princeton University (where he was business manager of the *Daily Princetonian*), he worked with the Salisbury, Maryland, *Times* and Compton Advertising, Inc. During World War II he served almost five years in the Army, having enlisted as a private and subsequently been commissioned in the horse cavalry before that branch of the Army became mechanized. His assignment then shifted to the airborne infantry. He later rose to the rank of Major while serving in the campaigns of Central Europe and the Rhineland.

He is a member of the Council on Foreign Relations, the Squadron A Club, the Military Order of Foreign Wars, the Association of the United States Army, the Sales Executives Club, the Public Affairs and International Economics Affairs Committees of the National Association of Manufacturers, the Public Relations Society of America, the English-Speaking Union, and the Foreign Policy Association. Mr. Devine is a trustee of the American University in Cairo, a trustee of the Vail-Deane School in New Jersey, a director of the American Hospital of Istanbul, a director of the America-Italy Society, a member of the Board of Managers of the Harlem YMCA, a director of the Society for the Rehabilitation of the Facially Disfigured, and a director of the Metropolitan Opera Association. In June 1976 he received an honorary degree as Doctor of Humane Letters from Fairleigh Dickinson University.

*Roland A. Early*

# *Persuasion in Selling*

*Making an important sale* is like a victory, but sometimes the anticipation can be as exciting as the achievement. Early in 1977, I felt I was closing in on a sale that meant a great deal to me. It wouldn't be my biggest sale by a long shot, nor would it be a breakthrough into a new market or even add money to my income. But it meant a lot to me. I had been working on it for more than twenty years. At last I was getting close.

My job is to manage the sales of the S&H Green Stamp service to retailers in seven Southeastern states and my target this time was a sixteen-store grocery chain in North Carolina. I had been trying since the late 1950s to persuade the owner to use stamps. In those days his chain had only three or four stores. He was a Carolina country boy, hard-working, proud, skeptical, and very careful with his money. I certainly understood the type. I had grown up in that part of the country, too. When I first met the store manager, I had been traveling my sales territory for S&H for about two years, more or less learning how to sell the service as I went along.

When I called on this manager, as I did sporadically, he showed no interest in stamps at all. No matter what approach I took, his response was quick, definite, and completely negative. But those were days of rapid growth for S&H Green Stamps, and so I sought business elsewhere; there were plenty of challenges to occupy my day. Rather than attack his fortress, I respected his wishes, kept his good will, and continued to visit him. We could always talk about the weather or how the fishing was.

Now, in 1977, the time was ripe. For one thing, he had volunteered more than a passing interest in our service. He was actually warming up to the idea of stamps. I wasn't to find out why until later. Meanwhile, the conditions in his market were almost ideal for his taking on stamps. None of his competitors used stamps of any kind. He had a reputation for quality and fair dealing. The local economy was strong.

I knew that if he began giving S&H Green Stamps to his customers, his sales would increase by 15 to 20 percent within months. I needed no computer or market research study to tell me this. I had seen it happen too many times over the past twenty years to have any doubt about it. This is not to say that I do not believe in computer reports and market research surveys. I most certainly do. But this was a classic situation.

Even as I explained this to him over several visits, I could see that he wanted to believe me but remained reluctant, doubtful.

This attitude did not surprise me. It's one I had seen many times in my career. You see, those of us who sell promotional plans are selling a promise. We have nothing tangible to sell—only the promise of what will occur if our prospect buys our service.

In this case I was asking my prospect to commit two percent of his sales—and his reputation—to giving away S&H Green Stamps to his customers. This was a $500,000 annual commitment on his part.

Although *I* knew he could realize between $3.5 and $5 million in additional sales from the traffic this promotion would generate, first *he* had to promise me half a million dollars to pay for it. He was not the marketing vice president of a multibillion-dollar corporation. He was the owner of a small supermarket chain that he had built through serious labor over thirty years. It was *his* money. In his industry, a profit margin of 2 percent of sales is well above average. And investing half a million dollars in something that couldn't be seen, touched, or resold—a mere promise—was a frightening prospect.

It was going to be a tough sale. But then, twenty years ago it had been an impossible one.

Years of experience had taught me to have faith in the service I sold. Somehow, I had to transmit my faith—my absolute certainty—to my prospective client.

It was something, of course, that I had done hundreds, maybe thousands, of times over the years.


*Back in the early 1950s*, when stamps were beginning to catch on, and I was beginning to learn how to sell them, one of our basic sales missions was to explain how stamps work. They work the same way today they did then and it may help the reader to understand the system.

The merchant licenses the stamp service from S&H, paying us according to the number of stamps given away. Usually, one stamp is given for each 10¢ a consumer spends. The consumer saves the stamps until she or he has filled enough books to get some desired item. It takes

1200 stamps (from purchases of $120) to fill one book, which is worth about $3 in merchandise at retail value.

It is then S&H's responsibility to provide the consumer with valuable and memorable merchandise in exchange for this stamp collection so that the customer will return again and again to stores that offer stamps.

S&H has been operating its system in essentially this manner since 1896, the year Thomas A. Sperry and Shelley B. Hutchinson formed their partnership.

The fact about stamps is that, other things such as price, service, and value being roughly equal, the consumer will make a special effort to shop at stores that offer stamps and the extra value they deliver.

That was the basic pitch then; it's the basic pitch now. It's the truth.

The idea, while hardly new, was often met in the 1950s by outrage from the very merchants it was designed to help. Sometimes all the merchants in a town would "agree" not to give stamps.

Our job was to change their minds. One of my earliest successful attempts at that was instrumental in creating the faith I had in what I sold.

A service station association in a key town in my territory had convinced all operators to stay away from stamps, circulating petitions and lists of their evils.

The association had done its job well. The environment for stamps and stamp salesmen was hostile. My company sent six salesmen into town with the assignment to break the boycott. Not a single one of them succeeded. In a week's time they were all sent back home and there I was, alone in my territory, frozen out.

I went to the largest, most modern, most progressive service station in town and somehow got to see the manager. He wanted to throw me out immediately.

"You haven't heard one good thing about stamps, have you?" I managed to blurt out. "But don't you think that if they can cause this much commotion, there must be something to them?" I had hit a nerve. He grumbled that he had seen some stations giving stamps in a larger city to the north—outside my territory.

"Well," I said, "the next time you drive up that way, you just stop in and ask the managers what they think about stamps. You'll hear lots of good things."

To tell the truth I did not have any idea which service stations gave our stamps or what their managers might say. I only knew that this manager would never listen to me.

"All right," he said, "but you better not be lying to me. I'm fed up with you stamp salesmen. If you're lying to me, so help me if you come into my station again, I'll shoot you, I mean it."

I didn't know whether I had made a sale or signed my death warrant. I truly had second thoughts about going back.

But after a week or so, I couldn't resist. The manager saw me coming and started yelling: "Come in here. I want to talk to you. Give me that contract." He signed up on the spot and eventually became the cornerstone to my business in that town.

You might say S&H Green Stamps saved my life.

One of the themes of this chapter is the importance of believing in what you sell; the other is the power of the third-party endorsement. One such endorsement helped me set a sales record that probably stands to this day.

I was trying to persuade an oil company distributor to offer his licensees—local service stations—the option of using our stamps in their stations. In effect, he would pick up some of the cost as a service to his licensees and as a way of selling more gasoline (there seemed to be plenty of it around in those days).

He would not listen. He was angrily opposed. I handed him my card, which he threw into his desk drawer. I didn't think I had a chance.

A few days later he summoned me to his office.

"I saw that Dinah Shore show you people put on TV. If you can sponsor a show like that you must know something. Tell me about those stamps of yours."

I told him. Within a few days, he asked me to visit his service stations. He even sent his son along to show me the way. The father had called ahead and all we did was walk in, get the contract signed, and walk out. I "sold" twenty-eight new accounts that day, breaking the one-day record of a legendary salesman who was then a top officer in our headquarters. I believe the record still stands.

Another third-party endorsement got me involved with an account I didn't want. A call came into our office for a salesman to visit a store in a tiny town in rural North Carolina. It was hardly on the map. It was at least ninety miles from the nearest redemption center or other store giving stamps. I didn't want to make the call, but one day I felt obligated.

To reach this town I had to drive miles on dirt and sand roads. I came to a river. There was no bridge. Instead there was a small, two-car ferryboat that putted across the river attached to a cable. The ferryboat was on the opposite side of the river.

I called out to the operator.

"Can't come now," he hollered back, "having a sandwich." After I finally got across, it was still miles from that river to the store that wanted to give S&H Green Stamps.

It was a crossroads store selling farm supplies, feed, horse collars, canned goods. The owners were wonderful people. I told them they didn't want stamps. They had no competition. It was too far from the redemption center. I couldn't come by very often to help or deliver stamps. There was really no point in it. None at all.

No, they said, they had heard from friends that stamps were good, that S&H was best, and that's what they wanted.

I relented and signed them up. As the months passed, their business increased by more than enough to pay for the stamps. And I found myself making that long trip far more frequently than I intended. The owners used to fix lunch for me, marvelous country lunches of homemade foods. Sometimes we would eat outside.

*These were among* the twenty years of experiences that helped me know for a certainty that, in 1977, this sixteen-store supermarket chain would prosper with S&H Green Stamps—prosper beyond the owner's fondest hope.

But I could not determine how to convince him.

An associate and I made several calls. We explained all the circumstances that pointed toward success. We described the redemption centers we would open to serve his customers. We talked about the advertising and promotion plans we would use to launch the stamps. We told him the sales and traffic increases he could reasonably expect.

He wanted to sign up, but he just couldn't bring himself to do it. His whole life had taught him to be cautious about things he couldn't touch.

During this time I discovered why he had become receptive after all these years. He served on a business committee with another supermarket owner from another part of the state. This owner had built up his business over the years just as my client had done. But the other merchant's business had grown somewhat faster. My prospect was impressed and perhaps felt competitive. The other merchant used trading stamps.

Our sales calls continued. Each time we came back with more information, different proposals, answers to his questions.

After the end of the fourth such meeting he still had not agreed.

I had reached the end of my rope. There was nothing more I could think to say or propose. I was exasperated.

Suddenly, I became angry. Without thinking, I stood up. I pulled the contract out of my pocket and signed it as fast as I could. I tossed it in front of him and slapped the pen down on top of it.

"Now listen," I said, "sign this thing. Sign it right now."

He looked at me, startled. Then very gingerly, carefully, he picked up the pen and signed the contract. As I stood there glowering at him, he quickly shoved the contract back across the desk, almost as if it was hot, and dropped his hands into his lap. For a while he just stared down at his desk. He looked as if he felt guilty.

My anger broke immediately, of course, and we made certain arrangements to move toward our launch date and my associate and I left.

I never used such an intimidating close before or since, nor have I ever discussed that particular outburst with the supermarket operator. Nor have I ever felt the need to remind him that after he took on stamps his sales increased by nearly 40 percent, almost twice as much as our most flamboyant promise.

◻ ◻ ◻

Roland A. Early, a native of Raleigh, North Carolina, has been employed by The Sperry and Hutchinson Company for more than twenty-five years. He joined S&H in Goldsboro, North Carolina, and worked as a fieldman (salesman) for five years before being named a supervisor. He held that position for a year before being promoted to State Manager, Then, a year later, he was made a District Manager in Jacksonville, Florida, where he had under his direction half of the southern sales force. After serving three years in that job, he was promoted to Regional Manager in Atlanta and subsequently was made an officer and a vice president of the company. He is currently one of five persons holding the title of Regional Manager and Vice President in the S&H Promotional Services division.

When he was being considered for the S&H job, he was on the verge of joining the North Carolina Highway Patrol. Fortunately for S&H, he chose "selling" as his career.

**James P. Economos**

# A Model Traffic Court

*The greatest sale I ever made* was on March 17, 1959, when the county commissioners were convinced that they should engage my services as Director of the Traffic Court Program of the American Bar Association to install a model Traffic Court for Dade County, Florida.

In 1957 the State of Florida had adopted an amendment to its Constitution establishing a home rule Metropolitan Government for Dade County, which includes Miami and Miami Beach among its twenty-six municipalities. This Home Rule Charter authorized the county to provide for certain uniform laws, rules, and regulations on a county-wide basis. This authority included a county traffic ordinance superseding all municipal traffic ordinances. It also included the creation of a Metropolitan Court with exclusive jurisdiction over all traffic offenses committed within the county, thereby excluding such jurisdiction for the twenty-six municipal courts and their judges.

After the concept of Metropolitan Government had been adopted, some groups still strongly opposed the constitutional amendment. A sequence of litigation was instituted immediately after the new county commissioners implemented the new charter with the uniform traffic code for the county and appointed the three judges and clerk of the new Metropolitan Court. All appeals to the Florida Supreme Court resulted in support of the Home Rule Charter and steps taken to make government effective.

Finally in early 1959 the Metropolitan Government was able to consider long-range plans. It was deemed advisable to begin enforcement of the uniform county traffic ordinance and to provide for a court with adequate judicial, administrative, and clerical personnel to administer justice in an impartial manner. Plans were under way to build a new court facility and the adherents of Metropolitan Government were determined to offer the citizens of Dade County a model Traffic Court. It was at this period that the Metropolitan Government approached the American Bar Association Traffic Court

Program for assistance. The committee supervising this program agreed that I should undertake the task of selling the County Commissioners on my ability to install a model Traffic Court for Dade County.

This necessitated a preliminary survey of the twenty-six municipal courts, the combined traffic case load, the traffic law enforcement activity of the several police departments, as well as a review of traffic accidents, fatalities, injuries, and property damage. This survey included interviews with local judges, chiefs of police, safety officials, and local bar association members.

After completing the survey I was ready to present the proposal to the ten county commissioners of Dade County. The date set for this effort was St. Patrick's Day.

At the appointed time, I was introduced to the commissioners, who were all present. I outlined the results of the preliminary study, explained the need for additional judges, prosecutors, administrative and clerical personnel, the additional court requirements to be a part of a new court facility, the adoption of a no-fix uniform traffic complaint and ticket, the need for a training program for all personnel required to process the no-fix traffic complaint and ticket, and the proposed budget. It was also recommended that the Dade County Bar Association appoint a committee to review the qualifications of all attorneys seeking appointment to the new court. Finally I submitted the amount that we requested for our professional services. It doesn't take much imagination to determine the number of questions all these recommendations generated. Although answering them took considerable time, it was evident that the proposal was going to be accepted when one of the commissioners asked how soon all of this could be accomplished. A July 1, 1959 starting date was finally negotiated. The county commissioners unanimously approved the proposal to install a model No-Fix Traffic Court for Metropolitan Dade County.

The next three and a half months were most hectic. Suggestions to cancel the agreement were heard more than once. Not only was it necessary to continuously protect the agreement but the County Manager scheduled several meetings with municipal officials and I was required to outline the relationship between the municipalities and the new program. These meetings eventually developed into new sales efforts to secure cooperation as well as support for the total program.

As my staff, assembled for this effort, progressed with their assignments, I was required to overcome opposition even without the administrative departments of the Metropolitan Government. For example, the plans for a court facility had to be revised to accommodate the needs of the new court, yet justification for the recommendation had to be repeated before final approval was achieved.

The setting up of the training program for the introduction and processing of the no-fix uniform traffic complaint and ticket had to be carefully reviewed. Finally a six-week training program was scheduled for 1527 police officers as well as prosecutors to be assigned: all clerical personnel classes had to be scheduled to suit the convenience of all chiefs of police and the hours of attendance had to be staggered so all could be accommodated with a minimum of absence from duty assignments. This training program was a success until the very last week.

It suddenly dawned on twenty-six mayors and twenty-six chiefs of police that they no longer had the ability to recall traffic tickets issued by their own enforcement personnel. Likewise, no longer would any of them be able to call on another mayor or chief of police to perform a similar "courtesy" for their constituents who had run afoul of traffic regulations in another municipality or participate in granting like "courtesies" to their fellow mayors or police chiefs. This no-fix aspect of the program was an essential element for its success.

Another phase of the program required additional reselling. This was the effort to secure the appointment of qualified judges. The county commissioners possessed the power of appointment. However, its exercise required some political finesse as well as jockeying to secure support for the favorite candidate of each commissioner. The commissioners were cautioned to nominate only those lawyers who were likely to receive a favorable recommendation from the bar association screening committee. The program called for ten additional judges, but it was a coincidence that there were also ten commissioners. The result, of course, was to have each commissioner nominate one candidate. The bar screening assisted materially in determining the caliber of the nominees who were finally selected. Accomplishing this result assured the success of this sale.

Now this number of judges permitted the scheduling of court sessions in such a manner as to assure every traffic defendant of a trial on the first appearance in court. Prior to this it was customary for courts to require a defendant who wished to plead not guilty to make a second appearance in court to contest the charges. To eliminate judicial coercion to plead guilty, court sessions had to be scheduled in a manner that would have the judge, the prosecutor, and the defendant (with or without an attorney) all present at the same time. This was done first by staggering the court sessions into four each day—for example, 9 A.M. to 10:30 A.M., 10:30 to 12 noon, 2:00 P.M to 3:30 P.M., and 3:30 to 5:00 P.M. This plan then required the police chiefs to assign three to five officers for one of the court sessions every two weeks. This plan then depended on each assigned officer writing all traffic tickets issued by him for his assigned court day and session. This scheduling went into effect on July 1, 1959 and was followed for a number of years until other court developments and increasing case loads interfered with the continuance of the trial on first court appearance. It had, however, demonstrated the efficacy of the plan through the reduction of court appearances by a defendant to secure his day in court.

The lack of court facilities at the beginning of the program necessitated the use of a central court location and outlying court locations; this was the only way to ensure enough courtrooms for the scheduling required by this plan. Since each municipality wanted to have the honor of retaining its own courtroom for the convenience of its officers, there was considerable jockeying among the mayors and police chiefs. Selling the assignment of courtroom locations was another major facet of the total program. It emphasized the need to secure support for each part of the program by selling each component separately and continuously.

Further opposition to the Metropolitan Government efforts to make its Home Rule Charter work resulted in an investigation instigated by the Grand Jury. I was required to make two appearances before this august body. Others, both for and against the program, also were required to express their views as to the progress being achieved by the staff working on the installation. Finally the Grand Jury rendered a favorable report.

An interesting by-product of the opposition was the antagonism of a television commentator. To overcome his diatribes I finally accepted an offer to appear on his program. In his initial introduction he called me "Mr. Expensimos." Of course he used this way to complain about the cost of operating a model Traffic Court. Fortunately this appearance allowed me to show that the court's revenue exceeded the expenses as well as providing a greater opportunity for a "Day in Court" for Dade County citizens and visitors.

Finally the communities realized a traffic safety dividend. It was noted that during the first three months of the new court, the traffic accidents were reduced substantially. A reasonable conclusion is that the media exposure throughout this period constantly emphasized the no-fix uniform traffic ticket as well as other parts of the program right up to the starting date of July 1, 1959 and for several weeks thereafter. When the effect of the media exposure was exhausted, the effort to retain high traffic safety required more effective enforcement.

This was a hard sale that required constant reselling during the entire installation as well as during the shakedown period to make the administrative machinery function effectively. It demonstrated that a model Traffic Court had been established in Dade County.

□   □   □

James P. Economos received a BS (Accountancy) and LLB from the University of Illinois. He retired as Executive Director of the Dr. Scholl Foundation on December 31, 1980; he served as Director of the Traffic Court Program of the American Bar Association from December 1, 1942 to January 1972. He is now practicing law in Chicago.

He is a member of the American Bar Association, serving as National Chairman of the Junior Bar Conference in 1943-1944, member House of Delegates, 1942-1944, Secretary of Special Committee to Improve Administration of Justice, 1943-1946, and Assistant Secretary, 1948-1951. He is a member of the Fellows of American Bar Foundation and the Illinois State Bar and Chicago Bar Associations. He has directed and participated in traffic court conferences at many leading law schools throughout the country since 1947. He has directed surveys of traffic courts of ten states and thirty cities. In 1959-1960, he assisted the government of Metropolitan Dade County, Florida, in establishing a Metropolitan Court, superseding twenty-six municipal courts for the purpose of hearing traffic charges.

Mr. Economos has contributed articles on traffic courts to various publications, most recently to the *National Civic Review* and *Reader's Digest*. He is the author of a book entitled *Traffic Court Procedure and Administration*.

He is a member of the National Committee on Uniform Traffic Laws and Ordinances, National Committee for Traffic Safety, is Past Chairman of the Committee on Alcohol and Drugs of the National Safety Council, and was Secretary of the Committee on Enforcement-Courts of the President's Committee for Traffic Safety, Chairman of the Traffic Conference-NSC, 1968-1969, and Vice President for Traffic-NSC Board of Directors, 1969-1972.

Mr. Economos was the recipient of the Paul Gray Hoffman Award for distinguished professional service in highway safety in 1970.

*John C. Emery, Jr.*

# *A Few Things I've Learned in Selling a Service*

*Here beginneth the story* of an idea that was born during World War II, became a commercial venture at the end of the war, and grew from a $30,000 business in 1946 to a $560 million business in 1980. The principle behind the business was to put together a world-wide, door-to-door, air freight forwarding service utilizing the belly and freighter capacity of the scheduled airlines for our airlift. Since the business wasn't capital intensive, because we neither owned nor operated aircraft, the financing of the new venture was accomplished with only $250,000 garnered through the sale of Emery Air Freight common stock to the public. And that original quarter of a million dollar seed money was the last nickel we've ever had to borrow from anybody!

Our first year of business, in 1946, we did a fantastic job! We sold $30,000 worth of our new air freight service and lost $90,000 for the effort. In 1947, our sales soared to $300,000 but our losses zoomed to $120,000. By the middle of 1948, we had just enough cash left in the bank for two more pay periods. But then something happened that proved that luck is just as important as skill in business. Our largest competitor, the Air Express Division of the Railway Express Agency, chose that moment in time to go on a nationwide strike. As a result, many Air Express shipments were diverted to the good guys from Wilton, Connecticut, and helped put us into the black for the first time. I still light candles in church every Friday in honor of those wonderful guys from Air Express whose timely strike saved us from what later happened to them. In 1975, they went bankrupt.

One long-range corporate objective we've had over the years is to double our sales and profits every five years. So far we seem to be pretty much on target. We reached our first million dollars in sales in 1949.

**99**

Five years later we reached $5 million. By 1959 we had more than doubled again to become a $14 million business. Five years later in 1964, we reached $35 million, and in 1969 our revenue exceeded $97 million. In 1974, we more than doubled it again to $213 million. In 1979 domestic and international air freight sales easily exceeded $500 million.

The five principal management concepts we follow are equally adaptable to any growing, profit-oriented organization. In the gospel according to Emery, we believe:

**1** You must have a product or service with a measurable difference. And you must be able to describe, prove, and promote differences rather than emphasize similarities between what you and your competition offers.

**2** You must take *nothing* for granted, and *never* be satisfied with things as they are! Today, you and I are living in a business world of dramatic change and uncertainties. Whereas Emery had one basic air freight service for the first twenty-five years of our existence, we now offer four different service levels or concepts. And a fifth new service dimension, a personal air courier service, was added recently. We believe the buying public wants choices and variety in what they buy, not simply a single choice. What we offer is what I call our multifaceted approach to our cafeteria style of service offering. In short, an à la carte approach toward constantly creating new services to meet the needs of the ever more sophisticated and discerning buyer whose tastes, values, and needs are constantly changing.

**3** Our third foundation stone is that you must have a basic understanding of what creates profits—the *real name of the business game*. Having an outstanding product or service isn't the whole answer. More sales by themselves won't necessarily produce profits to the degree you may want. Hard-hitting sales, marketing, and finely tuned pricing programs won't either. Nor will effective cost control programs by themselves, even though you may have the greatest computerized management information system in the world. But if you blend each of these separate ingredients together (an outstanding, measurably different product or service; sales growth; effective marketing and pricing programs; and good cost controls combined with fast feedback systems), you'll get what the stockholders want—orderly and predictable profits and growth according to plan that minimizes big surprises.

**4** You must have a sales and management team whose personal capacity stays ahead of your corporate growth. But even a good team of today really isn't good enough for tomorrow. Key people are forever being promoted or transferred out of their present jobs. Or they're pirated away by your competitors. Or they can get hit by a truck. Not an Emery Air Freight truck, of course! Therefore, for every key job you have, whether you're President or a Sales Manager, you must know who replaces whom—if, as, and when! It's what I call the "bench strength" factor, without which your great momentum of today could come to a screeching halt if you lost one or more of your key people.

**5**   Finally, you must have a long-range plan of how you want your company to evolve and the basic business you intend to be in over the years ahead. I call ours our plan for 1990 because that's the year I'll retire. I figure if we haven't met our long-range goals by that time, it will be too late for me to worry about it anyway. A good long-range plan that sees your corporate role in the marketplace in the years ahead better permits more orderly short-range plans and the development of priorities. They simply serve as a securer foundation or sequential stepping stones for your future corporate path. In our case, by 1990 I see our company evolving into becoming not just an air freight company but a multimodal high-speed logistics systems company. By then we'll be in the air, as we are today, on the oceans, on the roads, and on high-speed rail links like AMTRAK. And if a pneumatic tube becomes a more efficient method of high-speed transportation than the iron bird, then we'll be aboard that, too! Railway Express died because it continued depending on the dying national rail system when it should have switched to a primary trucking operation, as UPS now does.

In terms of the selling principles we preach and practice with our people, I'd like to share with you the six main points we emphasize in training our salesmen:

**1**   Few sales are ever "closed" by the number of words the salesman uses. Therefore, ask questions, listen carefully, sell specifically. Never make the mistake of presenting your product or service before you know exactly how it can best be tailored to your prospect's needs. And remember the purpose of every sales call is to get the prospect to take "observable action" while you are there. It's not enough that your prospect promises to "keep you in mind" or that he promises to call with an order at an early opportunity. "Observable action" means this prospect does something concrete *now*, while you're there, to thereby convert vague future promises into real commitments to you and your company.

**2**   Selling by words is not enough. Particularly if you are selling a service or an intangible, make your sales points more powerful by using visual aids on every one of your sales calls.

**3** Your prospect must feel *you* are enthusiastic about your product or service if you ever expect to make him an enthusiastic buyer. That's the best kind! Enthusiastic buyers!

**4** Particularly in selling a service or an intangible, over 50 percent of the sale is you, the salesman—*not* the company you represent. No matter how good your service is, it's a rare day when it will ever sell itself.

**5** If you have ever been called on by a salesman, think back on how many ever sent you a "thank you" note, reemphasized the main points of your discussion, and closed with another request for your business. Or how many took the time to cover these same points in a follow-up phone call to you a few days later? Only one salesman out of 100 takes advantage of the power of a timely phone call or follow-up letter *after* a personal visit. To help your prospect think of, and remember, you rather than your competitor, use the simple technique of follow-up letters or phone calls—*at least* after your more promising sales calls.

**6** Your present customer needs as much selling emphasis as your newest prospect. The easiest time for a competitor to move in on your old account is when you start *servicing* and *stop selling* him. Remember that people like to be kept sold on your service so that they continue to feel their initial decision to use you remains a sound one.

Finally, last year I was given an honorary Doctor of Laws degree by Manhattan College. And at their graduation ceremonies where this highlight in my academic life took place, I suggested to the graduates four rules to "live and work by." I'd also like to share them with you:

**1** The most important thing about the business world is not the companies that comprise it but the people who represent it. A man is known by the company he keeps and a company is known by the quality and integrity of its people. Never forget or underestimate your importance as an individual. If you're ever engaged in selling a product or a service, remember that people buy people first, companies second. No matter how good the company or institution you represent, remember that people must believe in you before they can believe in who or what you represent. Also, remember that corporate integrity is the sum total of the personal integrity of employees in their relationship with others.

**2** In whatever you do in your life, take nothing for granted and never be satisfied with things as they are. Complacency, or satisfaction with things as they are, is the same as quicksand in this world of an ever-increasing rate of change. Taking nothing for granted applies equally to a marriage relationship or to operating a business.

**3** In dealing with a business associate, the most prevalent way of trying to correct or change others is through a time-honored device known as "constructive criticism." In my opinion, constructive criticism destroys; it doesn't cause change. It's the worst possible method of trying to change human behavior. Positive reinforcement of what a person does well is the best way to assure improved human performance. In business today, most of us live in an environment in which 90 percent of the time we're told what we've done wrong, but only 10 percent of the time do we hear what we've done right. I advocate a reversal of the percentages. If you will positively reinforce good performance 90 percent of the time and be constructively critical only 10 percent of the time, you will help establish the kind of business environment that will truly prosper and grow.

Finally, remember you have three basic priorities in life. Do your best to never get them out of order. Your first priority is to take care of your health. Without it, you're of less and less value to yourself, to your family, or to your job. Your second priority is to your family, for most of us the reason we were put on earth. Your third priority is to your job. If you can prioritize your life, remembering your health first, your family second, your job third, you'll most likely be a most successful and happy person, and that's a worthy objective in life, I'm sure you'll agree.

John C. Emery, Jr., is Chairman, President, and Chief Executive Officer of Emery Air Freight Corporation. He joined Emery in the early stages of the company's formation in 1946, after serving with United Airlines and National Airlines. Prior to this, he attended Dartmouth College and served as a pilot in the Navy Air Corps during World War II.

Mr. Emery started his career with the company in 1946 as a truck driver. He later became a salesman, then Sales Manager, District Manager, Regional Manager, Vice President of Sales, and Executive Vice President, before moving into his current position as President in 1968. In 1975, he became Chief Executive Officer of the company and in April of 1979, he was elected to the additional position of Chairman of the Board.

Mr. Emery is also a member of the Board of Directors of Cluett, Peabody & Company of New York; Pitney Bowes, Inc., of Stamford, Connecticut; and the Hartford National Bank and Trust Company of Hartford, Connecticut. He is a past president of the Sales Executives Club of New York and now serves as president of the Wings Club of New York.

**Willard R. Espy**

# The Princes Serendip Had Nothing on Cordially Yours

*I'll never understand* what moved Mel Hickerson to bring a fiddle-playing grasshopper like me into the midst of all the busy ants in this book. He knows what is going to happen when winter comes: I'll be sitting on the sidewalk in the snow begging for handouts, and the ants will feel obliged to drop in a penny because we all belong to the Mel Hickerson Fan Club.

The moral of the admirable sales stories that surround me here, I gather, is that if you refuse to take no for an answer, and then apply all your ingenuity, you can accomplish the incredible. I am sure that is true; but it has never been true for me. There are two reasons: I always take no for an answer, and I was born fresh out of ingenuity, which I take to mean imagination.

I intended to be a second Shakespeare until a young lady in Paris, generations ago, read my handwriting and said it showed no imagination whatever. Not the veriest flicker. How match Shakespeare without imagination? So as second best I decided to take up journalism, advertising, and a little bit of salesmanship. I figured I wouldn't need imagination in those jobs—I would only need to know how to lie.

Things worked out fine, by and large. Just between you and me, I am even beginning to compete with Shakespeare again. This is because I recently reread *Hamlet*, and discovered that the Bard had no more imagination than I do. He plagiarized every word in that play. I can prove he did; I remember reading those same lines, word for word, fifty years ago; I even memorized some of them. I wish I could think who wrote them.

I laid the groundwork for The Sale That Did the Most For Me—
unaware, to be sure—one summer day in 1967, when I was lying on the
sands in Easthampton. I should not say I laid the groundwork; sandwork
is more like it.

I was working, in my usual practical and systematic way, on the
composition of a verse built around anagrams. An anagram is a huddle
of letters that in different arrangements make different words.
"Endearments," for instance, turns into "tender names," and "panties"
into "step-ins."

My verse that day was built around four anagrams, each a
combination of the letters a d e i p r s. Here is the verse; if you
cannot fill in the coded words in two minutes, admit you are stupid and
look for the solution at the end of this article:


When I ********* to be a father,
You ******* my willingness to bother.
Now you *******; you never knew
I'd leave the ******* to you.


I liked that verse; it seemed to tell me something about the human
condition. So I followed it with more of the same. Indeed, I wrote
anagram verses incessantly—in the bathroom, crossing the street,
flirting, watching television. And when Louise and I visited London that
fall, I carried my collection with me to show to *Punch*, the humor
magazine.

When I opened the door at *Punch*, I found myself in an entryway
with a stair to my left heading upstairs, and a reception window straight
ahead. Behind the window sat a young lady wearing rimless glasses. She
looked surprised to see me.

"I am perfectly respectable," I assured her. "I am just submitting
some verses."

"Oh," she said, clearly relieved. "Very well. The poetry editor is not
in just now, but I will hand them to him."

"I'll wait."

"I am sorry, sir—you can't expect a reply for several weeks."

"I am an American, Miss. We expect quick action."

"Of course. I should have known—that odd accent. A reply takes
several *months* for Americans. Surface mail, you know."

"I'll wait."

"But sir, there are only two chairs in the reception room, and we do need those."

"Look. I'm spending the weekend in Cornwall. If I call back on Monday, will you have an answer?"

"Oh, yes, sir," said the receptionist, clearly relieved that I was not going to set up quarters in the reception room. "Mr. Peter Dickinson is the gentleman to ask for. About ten-thirty, sir."

So I called at ten-thirty Monday. Mr. Dickinson had not yet come in. At eleven-thirty I called again.

"Mr. Dickinson is not here," said his secretary, "but he has telephoned. Are you Mr. Espy?"

That confounded accent again.

She went on, "Mr. Dickinson asked me to inform you that your verses are satisfactory."

I was sure she had said *un*satisfactory. I made her say the word three times in a row.

That afternoon I reached Mr. Dickinson by telephone. I found him hard to understand. He had a curious accent, not clear, like New York.

"Jolly good," he said. "We'll run a verse a week. I suppose we should settle on a screw, too, what?"

I said hastily that that would not be necessary.

"But I must insist, old boy," he said. "The laborer is worthy of his hire, and all that, don't you know? What would you say to four guineas a go?"

I had only a vague notion of what a guinea meant. In any event, I seemed to be getting in deeper than I had intended. "Look," I said, "I'll call you back in the morning."

"Four guineas a screw!" I said to Louise immediately afterward. "Is *that* the way they do business in England? Why, it's positively decadent. I'll have to give up *Punch* altogether."

Louise explained patiently that in London a screw is a stipend, a wage.

"But isn't a guinea a little chicken?" I asked.

She said no, a guinea was a pound and a shilling. Four guineas were four pounds and four shillings. Four pounds and four shillings, at the current exchange rate, came to roughly $16 a verse.

That is how I started my bank account in England.

□

*Up to this point*, you will agree, Mel Hickerson himself could not have improved on my performance. I had been firm. I had shouldered past obstacles that would have deterred many a lesser man. I had obtained a satisfactory screw—four guineas a week.

Matters proceeded comfortably for a little more than a year, until *Punch*'s Board of Directors decided on a new editor. (Peter was only an *assistant* editor.)

"I'll take the job on one condition," said the man of their choice— "that my first assignment, before I even hang up my hat, is to fire Espy."

They were desperate; so, to their disgrace, they agreed.

That cowardly stroke of fate would have finished a lesser man. But not Espy.

I said to myself, why not bring out all those stunning verses of mine in a thin, suede-bound, memorial edition? I rushed to a London publisher and offered him the opportunity.

"I do like your silly things," he said, "but then my friends consider me a strange fellow. Anyhow, we could not sell more than five copies. Haven't you something else?"

So I went back to my hotel room and dug into my suitcase, which contained several tear-sheets from newspaper and magazine articles. I copied off a few puns, like "puberty is a hair-raising experience," and a few malapropisms, such as "I was the suppository of her most intimate secrets."

The additions awed the publisher. "I think we can sell a *thousand* copies," he said.

So, bit by bit, we came to a decision that I would try to assemble within two covers examples of every word game in English. The result was a book called *The Game of Words*. And the rest, as we cliché-lovers like to put it, is history.


*I now return* to my premise. I am a grasshopper, not an ant. The good things that have occurred to me in the past decade—and there have been several—are the result of serendipity.

Oh, I agree that if a batter knocks an easy fly to you, you should be able to catch the ball. But even a grasshopper can do that, if someone lends him a fielder's glove.

A case in point is the fate of *The Game of Words*. After one printing, or maybe two, it disappeared in the United States. The rights reverted to me, so I sold them to Bramhall Press, which by present indications will be selling that book steadily when my name has weathered beyond recognition on my headstone.

When I had finished *The Game of Words*, there was a litter of shavings left over. So Clarkson Potter suggested I do a sequel. I balanced the wordplay with anecdotes about my childhood in the Washington village of Oysterville and called the manuscript *The Oysterville Almanac*.

But just as the book was about to be set into type, Nat Wartels, my friend and publisher, told me he thought I had two books in one. Let's turn the wordplay into one book, he said, and the Oysterville material into another one, with lots of drawings.

That made sense. So *An Almanac of Words at Play* came out, and goes on and on. It was followed two years later by *Oysterville—Roads to Grandpa's Village*, my favorite of the books I have written. If you ever run across it, you will see that Earl Thollander did some mighty fine pictures.

□

One thing has led to another ever since.

Because Oysterville was the retirement home of my Uncle Allie, famed as author of all those anonymous verses you read, I was asked to write *The Life and Works of Mr. Anonymous*. How could I refuse?

Back in 1965, Kathleen Daley mentioned to me that the verb "to lynch" derived from the name of a hanging judge who was notorious in the Revolution for ignoring legalisms. How could I help beginning to drop into a folder the stories of other words that once were proper names—boycott, sandwich, and so on? *O Thou Improper, Thou Uncommon Noun* wrote itself.

Just as *Oysterville* was drawn from notes for a family history I had been filling for more than forty years, and *O Thou* from folders I had been filling for ten, *Say It My Way* summarizes certain conclusions about spoken English that have occurred to me in the writing of other books. *Another Almanac* is the lengthened shadow of *An Almanac of Words at Play*. And so on.

In *Three Princes of Serendip*, Charles Kingsley tells of three princes who "were always making discoveries, by accidents and sagacity, of things they were not in quest of." Cleverness, determination, empathy, self-confidence—such positive qualities are certainly indispensable in attaining the Sale That Means Most.

But never underrate serendipity.

*Note:* As you saw instantly, the anagram verse reads as follows:

When I ASPIRED to be a father,
You PRAISED my willingness to bother.
Now you DESPAIR; you never knew
I'd leave the DIAPERS to you.

□  □  □

Willard R. Espy is pleased if you recognize him from "Today," "Tonight," "The Merv Griffin Show," or any of the many other television programs on which he has promoted his books, but he would much rather have you read the books themselves: *The Game of Words, An Almanac of Words at Play, Oysterville: Roads to Grandpa's Village, The Life and Works of Mr. Anonymous, O Thou Improper, Thou Uncommon Noun, Say It My Way,* and *Another Almanac of Words at Play.*

Though he started verse writing at six, and has been in journalism, advertising, and public relations almost ever since, Mr. Espy's first book on the lighter side of the language did not appear in the United States until he was sixty-one years old. He was graduated from the University of Redlands, California, in 1930, and entered newspaper work in California after additional study at the Sorbonne, Paris. His later writing assignments included stints as Latin American correspondent of *The Nation* and copy editor of Havas, the French news agency. He spent sixteen years at *Reader's Digest*, where he became promotion and public relations manager. In 1957 he established himself as a one-man agency in New York. Among his clients was United Student Aid Funds, which he had helped to organize, and the place where he first encountered the legendary Mel Hickerson.

Mr. Espy is Contributing Editor to *Harvard Magazine* and is featured in leading publications.

**Tina Santi Flaherty**

# *How to Sell 36,000 Legs*

*The Colgate-Palmolive Company* underwrites one of the most ambitious community relations programs in the country, the Colgate Women's Games. Essentially, it is a series of track and field competitions for girls and young women, mainly from the inner city. Every year, more and more girls enter the event. In 1979, 18,000 participated and in 1980, the figure approached 20,000, making the Games the largest track and field meet in the world.

The Games are great for the entrants, opening up their world and teaching them how to compete and win. Of course, it constitutes an excellent corporate identity program for my company, Colgate, and it performs a significant service for our headquarters' city, New York, and our largest domestic plant city, Jersey City, New Jersey.

The top management of our company, myself included, feels that the impact of a sports event is improved if it appears on television. The effect of the event and the audience it reaches is magnified when it appears on the tube, and so we have the "Colgate Women's Games" special—an annual hour-long telecast of the Games on ABC-owned WABC-TV, New York—which appears about two weeks after the Games' finals.

Now comes the real challenge. Because it is company policy not to be second best in anything, our TV special had to result in the high ratings that mean a large viewing audience. In fact, it had to be competitive—on an audience basis—with such sports events as the World Series and the glamorous golf and tennis TV coverage. So we took a cold, hard look at what we had to sell. Stripped of all its auras, the "Colgate Women's Games" is, intrinsically, a group of females running around a track. How could we compete against such sports as the Masters Golf Tournament and NFL football?

**113**

**Ready . . . set . . . go!** A field of young competitors takes off for the finish line in the Colgate Women's Games, and every one of them is determined to get there first. Top three winners get trophies and grants-in-aid for education.

We set out to sell. Our target: the sophisticated New York television audience. The result: we not only got a rating of 10.4, which surpasses even the World Series, but the special was number 1 in its time slot, 7 to 8 P.M., on a Saturday evening in March 1979.

And in addition to the exceptional rating, the share of audience was as high as programs seen in prime time. It was a 22. In other words, 22 percent of all the TV households in Greater New York that were watching TV at that hour had their sets turned to our special.

Trying to sell an audience on watching a particular TV show is something that haunts Hollywood and Madison Avenue moguls alike. What is the magic formula that will make the vast viewing audience turn to *your* program? Is it luck? . . . Great writing? . . . Big names? . . . Is it something that will make them laugh? . . . Make them think? . . . None of the above? . . . All of the above?

We did it through salesmanship. It was an attainment that took five years. Five years of selling our "product," of merchandising, promoting, and publicizing it, pushing for that rating. It was a sales campaign that was honed and rehoned, added to and subtracted from, as we set our sights on that most fickle and elusive of targets—the TV viewing audience—the "channel flippers." And fickle they are—there's little loyalty among viewers. If something on another channel appeals to them, that's what they'll turn to, no matter how hard we try to get them to watch our show. So, luck plays a part too, but we can't look at it that way; we have to make that "sale"!

Every element of our sales strategy was the result of careful study. The setting for the telecast, for example, was of great importance. We chose Madison Square Garden, whose very name signals sports fans that they're about to see a "class act." Only the very best get to play in this sports mecca of the Western World.

And to add to the glamour of the Garden, we book celebrities not only from sports but from Hollywood and Broadway and government.

Our Grand Marshall from the very beginning has been Willie Mays, one of the best known, best loved of all baseball players, whose election to the baseball Hall of Fame in 1979 was by the largest number of votes in the Hall's history. Surrounding him over the years have been such notables as screen star Dina Merrill and "Archie Bunker's Place" co-star Danielle Brisebois. Famed entertainer Pearl Bailey and Tony Award winner Nell Carter. Skier Suzy Chaffee. Hockey star Phil

Tina Santi Flaherty and "MASH" star Alan Alda pose with three Colgate Women's Games competitors after receiving the first "Equal People" Awards presented by the Business Council of the UN Decade for Women. The Award was given to Colgate for the Games' "significant contributions to equal opportunity for women." Representing the Games are (left to right): Jennifer Schmarr, 11; Mary Lynn Nicholas, 13; and Norine Carroll, 11.

Esposito. Basketball great Earl (the Pearl) Monroe. Record-shattering swimmer Diana Nyad. And even Sandy, the canine co-star of the Broadway hit musical *Annie*!

We provide the "sizzle" and they bring the "dazzle"!

But all this is the finished product; this is what the customer gets to "buy." Our sales campaign begins long before we get to Madison Square Garden each year. And even that early on, every element of that campaign is aimed directly at the TV rating.

Every piece of display material, every press release, every poster and flyer is imprinted with a message about the TV show, and each one urges people to watch it. Many of these messages are seen by hundreds of thousands. For instance, this year it was part of a display in that storied store location—Macy's window. Banks displayed the posters at tellers' cages. A New York utility included a flyer on the program in its mailing to customers.

And then there's good old Word of Mouth.

As I mentioned before, more than 18,000 girls and young women entered the Games in 1979.

They all have parents, families, and friends who are told about the show, because every one of the entrants is a possible finalist, which would mean that she'd be seen on the telecast.

And the word is spread, too, by the 60,000 students in the New York City school system who take part in our school plan every year. Several months before the Games begin, we contact 2300 public, private, and parochial schools, offering to send them a film of the previous year's finals, along with a spokesperson who will present it to large groups within the school. They and their teachers are told about the telecast and urged to watch.

And, of course, there are the countless people Colgate deals with by mail and phone every business day; wherever possible, mention is made of the program.

Colgate's Metro sales force gets into the act, too, with ticket distribution as their ammunition. We do not sell tickets to the finals at the Garden. They are given away free to schools, youth and church groups and individuals. Colgate salespersons distribute their tickets among 1000 supermarkets in New York.

And all of them are potential TV viewers, possible rating points.

The purpose of this sales campaign, this all-out push for a high rating, is of course a practical one. We run our Colgate commercials on the show; the more people who see them, the better our sales potential. And the more favorable our cost per thousand. For the 1979 telecast,

It's close—but there can be only one winner! It looks like the competitor on the right is the Champion in her race, at the finals of the Colgate Women's Games in Madison Square Garden.

with its 10.4 rating, our cost per thousand was $4.87, as compared with $12.59 for prime time advertising and $7.09 for daytime.

There's a fringe benefit, too, to having vast numbers of people watch the program. Aside from seeing the commercials, viewers are exposed to a virtual barrage of company identification. Every T-shirt and sweatsuit worn by the competitors, every inch of finish-line tape, the giant scoreboard, the bright red banners—some 20 feet in length—are emblazoned with the Colgate name in a colossal, constant display of company identification.

Another important tool in our campaign to get a high rating is the pointed use of publicity and public relations. In 1979, features on the Games were seen on TV news programs, kiddie shows, special interest and "wake-up" programs, for a grand total of 117 minutes of free time. It would have cost $300,000 if we'd had to buy it. This publicity created so much interest in the Games that it could not help but guarantee us a built-in audience for the TV special when it aired.

As any good salesman knows, you can't exist on one-time purchases. Your customers must want to return to buy your product again and again, or else you've got to rethink your entire sales campaign—or your product.

Similarly, we could not sit back and relax because our program was successful last year. We redoubled our efforts for 1980, adding even more elements, discarding others, all with an eye on that changeable audience, with its hand on the TV switch.

We do everything we can to make them turn that switch to us, and for all the foregoing reasons. But there's even another reason behind our battle for the big numbers.

The Colgate Women's Games is our premier community activities program, the model and inspiration for similar undertakings in nearly fifty countries around the world where Colgate does business. More than 18 million youngsters benefit through those far-flung community projects—programs from the building of new facilities to emergency aid when disaster hits, such as floods or earthquakes.

Colgate is pledged to these activities, with a commitment to social responsibility that begins at the top, with Keith Crane, the company's Chairman, President and Chief Executive Officer. It is important that our showcase in this commitment—the Colgate's Women's Games—is seen on TV by the greatest number of people possible.

Tina Santi Flaherty is a Corporate Vice President and Officer of the Colgate-Palmolive Company, the first woman Vice President in Colgate's 175-year history. She is responsible for all corporate communications activities, including financial and investor relations, consumer affairs, and institutional/financial advertising. She also is responsible for the development and production of major corporate image marketing programs and for the implementation of the company's worldwide public affairs activities, a top-priority project that is fast growing in size and importance. Through these activities, which Colgate sponsors in nearly fifty countries where it does business, more than 18 million youngsters benefit.

The model and inspiration for these programs is the Colgate Women's Games, which Mrs. Flaherty directs. The award-winning track and field series for girls and young women is now the largest in the world.

Before joining Colgate in 1972, Mrs. Flaherty was a Vice President of Grey Advertising. Prior to that, she was a Consumer Specialist for Western Electric, a newscaster for WHER radio and conducted daily TV guest interview programs for WMCT-TV, both in her native Memphis, Tennessee.

Mrs. Flaherty has been the recipient of many honors for outstanding business and professional achievement and public service. *Business Week* and the National Council of Christians and Jews have designated her one of the top corporate women in the United States. Mrs. Flaherty is an active board member of many voluntary and professional organizations. She was the first woman in the consumer products industry to be awarded an honorary doctorate by St. John's University, the largest Catholic University in the country.

**James F. Fox**

# Public Relations: The Nonselling Way to Sell

*Those of us in public relations* like to think that public relations is unique and that it cannot be sold: potential customers must be convinced they need the function before ever seeing a public relations person. Of course, that is not true. Public relations firms compete for business. Only one wins the account. Intangible though the product may be, obviously someone has made a sale. I have now been a public relations counsel for almost twenty years. That whole career has been one of selling in the marketplace of ideas, and it has focused into a single beam every experience of my lifetime, every bit of knowledge I have tucked into my mind.

There's a lesson for all salesmen of tangible products in what I have to say about this intangible service. Hear me out.

How do you sell public relations? We tried listening. One executive said to me, "Mr. Fox, you are the first public relations counsel whose ideas make sense to me." I had not said a word after my introduction; he had talked the whole hour.

Another time we made an elaborate proposal with slides and exhibits, as an advertising agency might do it. We made the sale but later were dismissed for not doing what the proposal promised—they saw our slides, but never listened to the words.

We have made some sales by cold calling and hard selling: they needed to be resold every day.

What we have learned is that the best way to sell public relations is performance. We have tested many techniques of selling and only referrals by satisfied clients have produced good results.

This is my story.

Three men have had major influence on my career. The first was

James W. Irwin, an old-time public relations genius, who (having read my wartime letters to a friend) decided I could write and in 1945 gave me my first job in New York. The second was David Rockefeller, who elevated me to the top of my profession when he picked me to be vice president for public relations of The Chase Bank. The third—and most influential in shaping my life—was Lowell P. Weicker.

If you were to examine the lives of men and women whose names stand out as leaders in public relations, a pattern would emerge. Every public relations career in business is linked with one or more national business leaders who believed in the public relations function and give their staff a stage on which to perform. These three did it for me. The influence of the three men is not unrelated.

In the mid-1950s, I was manager of public relations for the chemical divisions of Olin Corporation. Having just been "merged" as an employee of Mathieson Chemical, I had been told covertly that Mathieson employees were unlikely to be promoted soon. I began to look around.

One day there came a telephone call from a representative of David Rockefeller inquiring whether I would be interested in a vice presidency at Chase Bank. Jim Irwin had told him about me. Some months later, after dozens of skirmishes, I was offered and accepted the job, beginning an intensive five-year relationship with Rockefeller and his associates, a physically demanding and mind-expanding experience, a crash course in corporate affairs.

While I was talking with the bank, I also was examining another option: to become a counselor. That aspiration was so strong that I laid out a complete plan, writing a description of the proposed firm, designing stationery and forms, promotional materials, and announcements.

Five years later I pulled out the file and announced the incorporation of James F. Fox. Younger counselors welcomed my move into the ranks, but one of the most revered of the pioneers, Pendleton Dudley, shook his head and said, "But, Jim, do you know where the clients are coming from?" I admitted I didn't. But I also knew that I had a year to find out.

October ran into November and no one had knocked at my door.

One afternoon in early December, my telephone rang. "Do you remember me?" asked an unfamiliar voice. "This is Harold Weicker." Harold had been a management trainee at Chase the year before, and had spent six weeks in the public relations department. He had left the bank before I had. "Jim," he said, "I didn't enjoy the bank, but the only thing that made sense to me was what you were doing in public relations. Listen to me. My uncle heads a major underwriting firm in Wall Street. My neighbor heads up a giant food conglomerate. My father is chief executive officer of Bigelow Carpets. Which one would you like to meet first?"

I gulped and answered: "Your father, of course."

Lowell Weicker was an impressive man—tall, husky, straight, with a strong face. He had been raised in the aristocratic tradition, and was used to having whatever he wanted, in his business or personal life. He had very little patience with those around him who might not always perform well. There were whispered exclamations by some of those who had encounters with him: Attila the Hun! Louis the Fourteenth!

But he was a "renaissance man" with wide cultural interests and knowledge. He had great loyalty to friends and associates he respected. He could be quick to encourage, praise, or reward.

Weicker had taken over at Bigelow when it was a sick company. He turned it around and made it what it had been in the past—the best known trademark in the carpet industry. It was in the Teutonic tradition that he "willed the thing that must be and by willing made it so."

I had stood in awe of Jim Irwin, the public relations pioneer. I had admired David Rockefeller for the creative opportunities he opened up for me. So, too, I developed inordinate respect for Lowell Weicker, who was to become a father figure, a friend, and a demanding client.

If I had been excited at Harold's call, my first contact with his father was deflating. He simply told me on the telephone that he would be in Europe until mid-January and would I call him later? While this cooled my excitement for a break we needed, it also gave me the time to do my homework.

I talked with some friends at Bigelow to get up to date on internal matters and the status of public relations within the company. I talked with editors of the shelter magazines and the trade journals. I gathered back issues of all those publications and tabulated Bigelow's product and corporate publicity. I had plenty of time and was hungry enough to speculate with it.

One day in January Lowell Weicker agreed to meet with me. He was firm, diffident, and quite specific. I learned he was a friend of David Rockefeller and David had endorsed me.

What he told me was something I hadn't dreamed: he was about to close out his internal public relations staff and to sever relations with two outside agencies. What he asked was this: "Can you be set up in a proper office, and be fully staffed by February? . . . I want you to give me a proposal, Jim, to take over the function here, completely," he said. "You would be responsible for investor relations, community relations, product publicity, and anything else we need in this area."

How long, he asked, would it take to make the presentation?

I could have made it at once, but asked for five days. At the end of the week I put a 150-page proposal on his desk, covering every aspect of the assignment and offering a critique of the company's public relations activities for the previous decade. It had all been written in December.

We proposed a budget in excess of $100,000 with substantial fees. Would he buy it? I thought so, but I didn't count on his sensitivity to his own organization.

The following Thursday morning, I received a phone call from his assistant. "Mr. Weicker would like to see you at 11 A.M. today."

For many years afterward, I was to spend every 11 A.M. on Thursday seeing Mr. Weicker, but I was not prepared for this one. Without any explanation, he walked me into his weekly operations committee meeting. Around the table sat his entire executive group. Without ceremony, he introduced me as someone who had made a proposal to handle the company's public relations. Each executive was asked to quiz me. And they did—one by one around the table, a single question and my faltering, off the top of the head answers. The inquisition over, I left the meeting dejected. I knew I had blown it. Better save my pennies. I took a bus up Madison Avenue and within a few minutes was back in the apartment.

The telephone was ringing.

It was Weicker's assistant again. Would I please return?

I took a taxi and was there in minutes.

The meeting was short. I had made the sale.

We continued to serve Bigelow for fifteen years, under Mr. Weicker and four of his successors. The relationship did not end until a slogan we had promoted (Those in the Know Buy Bigelow) helped induce Sperry & Hutchinson to buy out the company's stock.

A few months after we began work for Bigelow we carried out a joint promotion with American Enka Company, which was introducing its first carpet fiber (Enkaloft) in a Bigelow line. Shortly thereafter we began working for Enka also, and the public relations field buzzed with news of our success.

Lowell Weicker had been the chief executive of Squibb, a family-owned company, and then an officer of NATO. He was unknown in the carpet industry in 1961, but within months he became one of its most widely accepted spokesmen. The sale I made to Lowell Weicker was the most important in my career as a public relations counsel, for out of that sale, and because of his support and belief, came almost every sale we made thereafter. Long after he retired, and up to his death in 1978, Lowell Weicker continued to be the best salesman we had.

Jim Irwin taught me public relations principles and the art of counseling. David Rockefeller added prestige and contacts. Lowell Weicker gave me the chance to put it all into practice.

Now, let me share a secret.

Under a different management in the mid-1940s, Bigelow had been a client of James W. Irwin. For two years, I had been the account executive. I knew some of the employees who were still there fifteen years later. I knew the editors of the trade press. I knew a great deal about the industry.

I never had the courage to tell Lowell Weicker I was not a genius, or how easy it had been to make that written presentation to him, full of insights and facts that even he did not know.

James F. Fox, APR, is a public relations counselor and chairman of Fox Public Relations, Inc., in New York City. He is a past president of the Public Relations Society of America and in 1978 received the Gold Anvil, the society's highest award for individual achievement. He is a trustee of the Foundation for Public Relations Education and Research.

Prior to 1961 when he established his own consulting business in public affairs and corporate communications, Mr. Fox was Vice-President for Public Relations and Advertising of The Chase Bank. Earlier he was a public relations executive with Olin Corporation, Prudential Insurance Company, Congoleum, and Kohler Co.

Mr. Fox is a graduate of the University of Iowa where he is a member of the University's Journalism Hall of Fame. The chapter of the Public Relations Student Society of America at Iowa is named in his honor. He holds an Honorary Doctor of Laws degree from World University, San Juan, Puerto Rico.

He is a life member of Sigma Delta Chi, the Society of Journalists, a member of the executive committee of the Financial Institutions Section of PRSA, and a member of the Society of Consumer Affairs Professionals. He is a past director of the Bank Marketing Association and a former chairman of the Counselors Section of PRSA. Mr. Fox is a contributing editor to *Public Relations Quarterly*.

Also, he is a charter member of the Investor Relations Institute, and a member of the International Public Relations Association and of the World Future Society. He is a frequent speaker and writer on public relations topics, and currently teaches courses in the New York University/PRSA seminar series.

The Fox firm is associated with a consortium of eight European public relations counseling firms which operate as Unipron, S.A., with headquarters in Brussels.

Mr. Fox is married to Sylvia Porter, the widely syndicated newspaper columnist and consumer economics author.

*J. Scottie Griffin*

# *When the Product Is Enough*

*A product with no guarantees*—one that does not appear on supermarket shelves in a bright yellow box, one that is not the focal point of a sophisticated television commercial, one that does not promote instant gratification, one that offers fulfillment only with the cooperation of the customer. Money cannot buy this product. It is not for sale. As a matter of fact, in my twenty years as a clergyman, it has become increasingly clear to me that this intangible product called faith is something that can happen to us when we least expect it. Faith is something that comes to us in various ways, at various times.

Faith gives a person reason to believe that life does have meaning and purpose: it makes a difference in one's ability to live effectively. Those who are guided through life by the belief that God is the source of all that is good and who believe that they are never alone in facing the challenges, responsibilities, or disappointments possess something priceless. People whose faith is genuine can freely admit that they are incapable of handling life's varied demands in their own strength.

□

Several years ago my family and I began to understand the reality of faith in a deeper way and at a time when we least expected it. Had we been given a choice, never would we have chosen to experience faith in such a manner.

A wonderful vacation was drawing to a close. We were returning home to Oklahoma after several weeks in the East. Our two young daughters, ages four and six, were playing in the back seat of the car and my wife was reviewing new materials for her Sunday School class. After a tiring day behind the wheel, I was hoping that the next Illinois

**127**

town would have a comfortable motel with a swimming pool. A refreshing dip in the pool was anticipated by all.

In a split second everything changed: a head-on collision, an ambulance, the emergency room of a small-town hospital. Although dazed and in shock, I was alert enough to know that our two daughters were both bruised and bleeding, and that my wife had been taken to another part of the hospital. She was badly injured; her life was in jeopardy. She would have to be moved immediately to a larger hospital fifty miles away.

It was the most critical period of my life. If ever there was a time for me to test the reality of the claims about which I had been preaching, it was now. On numerous occasions I had quoted the affirmation of the Psalmist to people who were undergoing a personal crisis and reminded them that "the eternal God is your refuge, and underneath are the everlasting arms." How often had I witnessed heartbroken parishioners being sustained by St. Paul's reassuring words: "Nothing can separate us from the love of God."

Could those promises now be true for me and my family? Could we find strength and power to work through this crisis in our lives?

□

My daughters and I were put in the same hospital room. The one truth I wanted them to feel was that God was with us in our time of need. As we huddled together on the bed, not knowing the condition of their mother, the children and I prayed that God would be with us and would help us to face whatever the future might bring. This would be the longest night we had ever spent. Realizing that the situation was beyond our control, we placed our needs in the hands of God.

Early the next morning a man entered the hospital room, introduced himself, and asked how he could help. He explained that he visited the hospital daily, calling on patients who were not local residents. "It's one of the ways I try to say thanks to God for all that He has done for me," he said. This warm and concerned man was just the first of many who would serve as God's special agents in communicating His love and strength and bolstering our faith during the months that followed.

For the first time in our lives, we were totally dependent on others. After years of trying to be a source of strength to others, we were now in an unfamiliar role. We had to learn to rely on and place a trust in people to an extent we had not done before. Faith can become very real when we are placed in such a position.

☐

Two long months after that fateful August day, we were finally able to bring my wife home. It was truly a time of thanksgiving. Now the difficult process of recovery was to begin—one that would stretch over a period of several years. The biblical words that had provided inspiration to generations of worshipers now became an unspoken force in our lives as they directed us to "rejoice in our sufferings, knowing that suffering produces endurance, and endurance produces character, and character produces hope, and hope does not disappoint us." I was to learn personally how true those words could be for the person who allows faith to work in his life. Through the continuing presence of God, my wife gained the determination and perseverance that made her recovery possible.

The willingness to admit a need for a power greater than one's self is a prerequisite to faith. Unfortunately, admitting any kind of need is often perceived in our society as a sign of weakness. How often problems are hidden because people do not want others to know that there is something in their lives they cannot handle. A successful businessman who directs the affairs of a giant corporation may not find it easy to admit that he is unable to keep his family together. A woman who holds positions of importance may not be able to admit a drinking problem. A student whose name appears on the dean's list might be reluctant to admit that he cannot relate to his peers.

☐

Depending on the approach, such difficulties can make a person bitter . . . or better. The person whose life is open to the gifts of faith will know, as my family and I came to know, that some of life's most valuable lessons can be learned in the midst of life's darkest hours.

☐

Faith is taking God at His word and believing that what He has said is true. When we pray, we should do so believing that every thing ultimately depends on God; then we should work as if it all depends on us.

Putting faith into practice is thinking beyond one's self. It is exploration and discovery, love and forgiveness. Faith is the ability to admit needs. It is something that allows us to understand the meaning of unanswered prayer. Faith is learning about control; when to lose it in order to gain it. Faith is recognizing and being grateful for the goodness of humankind—for it is through our fellow man that the work of God becomes a tangible item. Faith is a product that is not for sale. In fact, if it is a genuine article, it must be given away.

□   □   □

The Reverend Dr. J. Scottie Griffin is Senior Pastor, Hitchcock Presbyterian Church, Scarsdale, New York. Born in Brownswood, Texas, in 1935, he studied at Texas Christian University in Fort Worth, where he received his BA in Religion and Philosophy in 1957. He was graduated from Princeton Theological Seminary with a Bachelor of Divinity degree in 1960 and was awarded a Doctor of Ministry degree from Princeton in May 1979.

Dr. Griffin began his ministry as the Pastor of the First Presbyterian Church of Holmesburg in Philadelphia, Pennsylvania, in 1960. In 1966 he was called to be Senior Pastor and Head of Staff of Hanover Street Presbyterian Church of Wilmington, Delaware. In 1969 Dr. Griffin was called to be Senior Pastor and Head of Staff at John Knox Presbyterian Church in Tulsa, Oklahoma. He has served the congregation of Hitchcock Presbyterian Church as Senior Pastor since May 1975.

Over these years of his ministry, he has participated in a number of denominational activities. He served as a member of the Committee on Ministerial Relations, Philadelphia Presbytery and as a member of the Committee on Interpretation and Support, New Castle Presbytery. He has been Chairman of the Ministerial Relations Committee in the Presbytery of Eastern Oklahoma and a member of the Committee on Church Vocations in the Synod of the Sun, while in Oklahoma. He currently serves on the Ministerial Relations Committee in the Presbytery of Hudson River.

Throughout his ministry, his work in community affairs has included Travelers Aid, YMCA and Senior Citizens. During 1976–1977 he served as President of the Scarsdale Clergy Club.

*Jerome S. Hardy*

# A Complete Sale

*Late in the fall of 1959* I left Doubleday to join the book department of *Life Magazine* over at Time Inc. My assignment was to "put us into the book business," and as Andrew Heiskell said, "Don't do anything to embarrass us." By that Andrew meant he would like to have us do something pretty stylish and put together a business that would be ongoing and ongrowing. In fact, before many weeks went by, Andrew said to me that his objective was to have a book business doing 25 million a year at the end of five years. I was the first and only employee for one day. At the end of that day, I had an editor, we each had a secretary, and the editor, whose name was Norman Ross, had hired a chief of research named Bea Dobie. A few weeks later, Joan Manley joined our hectic group. That's important because Time-Life Books is now a half-billion dollar book business, and Joan Manley runs it along with other businesses at Time Inc.

Norm and I started having conversations, but in the environment of a place like Time Inc. it is easy to find yourself attending more and more meetings. Then you learn with some alarm that your associate partner in this venture, who has been trying to get in touch with you while you are in meetings, is himself in conference when you call back.

After a few weeks of this kind of corporate behavior, I took Norm aside and said to him, "Look, let's get out of here. I know a country inn up in Connecticut called Stonehenge. I think if we go up there every Monday and spend our time talking about what it is we want to do, we can spend the rest of the week getting it done."

Norm agreed instantly and we settled on a few ground rules. One was that each Monday there would be one and only one agenda item. If that agenda item was finished before the end of the day, we would go home. If it wasn't finished by the end of day, it would still be the only agenda item for the next meeting.

It was pretty easy to agree on the first thing we wanted to do. We settled on a series of books that would be brief, colorful, pictorial, and

**133**

each devoted to a quick overview of one country. The first country we chose was Russia, since Russia had become important to all of us and most people knew little about the country except what they had learned during World War II. We called the series the LIFE WORLD LIBRARY.

Norm went off to line up a writer, a couple of researchers, a picture editor, and all of the other editorial paraphernalia that it takes to produce the kind of superb work that goes on at Time Inc. I set about to put together a circular that would test the level of enthusiasm among *Life* subscribers for the yet-to-be-published LIFE WORLD LIBRARY. I should note that Walter Weintz, who had spent many years working his marketing magic at *Reader's Digest*, was the principal author of the circular we sent out.

In April of 1960, never the best month for a mail order test, we sent out the first batch of 200,000 test circulars. I sat back and waited for the results, recognizing that if they were terrible, I might not be out of a job, but I was certainly not going to be moving my career forward very rapidly. Within a few days, the results started to come in. And how they came in! Before more than a few days had gone by, we passed a 2 percent response, then 3, then 5, and finally as the last orders trickled in toward the end of the fifth or sixth week, we had a response of 7 percent.

I had been in the book business for a long time at Doubleday, working on a number of their book clubs, and I had never seen a response of 7 percent, nor had I ever met anybody who had seen a response that good. We were pretty sure we had a success. We shot for a full-scale mailing in July, and Norman promised me that whatever it took, the book would be written, edited, researched, illustrated, and ready to go to the printer by early July.

Incidentally, illustrated is not quite the right word. One of the first things I learned during the course of this first book was that the term "picture essay" is a special invention of the people at *Life Magazine*; a picture essay does not decorate the text; it tells a story in another way. Norm was able to transfer that unique way of using pictures from *Life Magazine* to the LIFE WORLD LIBRARY. The full-scale mailing went out and I promised Andrew and the other bosses I was beginning to collect that we could make money at 4 percent. The test had yielded 7 percent, but since I didn't really believe anything could be that good I assumed we would do less when we mailed the whole list.

I was wrong. The full list pulled 7 percent and before we knew it we were sitting on about a quarter of million orders. From then on it was a mad race to meet deadlines, for I had promised the management of

Time Inc. that this new business, which was conceived in the early weeks of 1960, tested in April of 1960, and committed in July, would be in the black by December. I knew we had to get out three books on a very tight schedule of August, October, and December, and I knew that if we met the schedule the business would be in the black and we would be off and running.

For all of the weeks from April, into May and through June, the best and most dedicated people I have ever worked with continued to turn out daily miracles. I can remember parties to celebrate the closing of each chapter. I can remember the day when Charles Thayer, author of *Russia*, stumbled out of the office where he had been working day and night and said, "Norm, it's no use. I can't go on."

Norm may have blanched a little, but he remained reasonably calm. He said, "Charlie, I know you have been working hard. Maybe if you took a couple of days off and just rested, everything would be okay again." Charlie looked at him with a perfectly serious face and said, "Norm, it's no use. I simply can't go on." To Norm's "Why not?" he replied, "I've run out of yellow pads and I can't write on anything else."

I think we had another party after that one.

By the end of July everything had been written, edited, closed, typeset, and sent out to the printer, a large company with a branch plant located in Indiana. Over the next few days proof sheets came in, were okayed, and were sent back. All of the necessary closings that would permit the presses to roll and satisfy those 250,000 orders we were holding began to fall into place smoothly and without a hitch.

Finally, we reached that point where we knew the book was going to go on press. Suddenly, I had a powerful hunch. I picked up the phone and said to Norm, "Norm, we've done everything we possibly can, but something tells me we ought go out to Indiana and see those first books roll off the press. I don't know why; maybe it's just because we deserve the pleasure of being there when the baby is born."

That happened to be the kind of assignment Norm loved, so he accepted delightedly. As fast as we could, we got ourselves airplane tickets, went out to Indiana, and found our way to the printing plant to which we had entrusted our book, our jobs, and our future.

We met the plant manager for dinner and arranged to be at the plant as soon as the first shift started in the morning. It was to be the first day when finished books would come off the assembly line, to be mated up with the envelopes in which the bills had been inserted and a welcoming letter to the new subscriber to the LIFE WORLD LIBRARY told each customer how delighted we were to have him or her aboard.

We arrived there even a little ahead of time the next morning and started the tour of the assembly line. We went first to the big offset presses where the sheets were coming down and being folded. We followed the progress of the printed forms until they were properly assembled and trimmed.

We passed on into another huge room where folded pages were coming from one direction and the printed colorful covers were coming from another direction to be glued together, pressed, inserted into cardboard cartons, labeled, and sent down a long incline toward the waiting mail bags.

Already there were twenty or so mail bags being packed into a railroad mail car on a siding right outside the room where the finished books were coming off the assembly line.

Norm and I looked at each other, and I said to him, "Let's see what one of these is going to look like to the customer when it reaches his house." I reached over and took a book off the assembly line, ripped open the carton and shook out the book. As I riffled the pages, I had one of those flashes of insight that told me why I had had this strong hunch to travel out to Indiana.

The first and last ten or twelve pages of the book were caught in a "squeeze-out." Squeeze-out occurs when there is too much glue between the heavy piece of paper that holds the pages and the actual hard cover of the book itself. Glue is spread on the hard cover—or "case." The case is folded around the pages. Then the book is squeezed or pressed together to make certain that the glue takes hold. If there is too much glue, it seeps out around the edges and flows into the first and last pages of the book. The book I was holding was useless and worthless, since by the time it reached the customer, the glue would be dry and the pages would have to be torn apart.

I looked at Norm, then at the plant superintendent. I reached over for another carton, ripped it open and shook out the book. Again the front and back pages were glued together. We opened two, three, four, a dozen. Always the same, always with pages in the front and back glued together. I turned to the superintendent of the plant and said, "We both know what we have to do, don't we?" He nodded, signaled the stop of the assembly line, and called for the packers to unload the freight car and bring back the books that were already out there.

Somehow, I knew that was the last test of our new project. Norm and I went home knowing the printer would destroy the books that were caught in the squeeze-out and that he would supervise personally the manufacture from beginning to end for the remaining quarter million copies of the edition.

It was the last test of our new idea and I knew that the most important sale of my life had finally been completed.

From that day to this, I have never forgotten that no sale is complete until a wholly satisfactory product is placed in the hands of a customer who receives it with a feeling that he has bought more than he has any right to expect, at a price lower than he has any reason to hope for.

Jerome S. Hardy joined The Dreyfus Corporation on January 16, 1970, as Executive Vice President. He served as President of The Dreyfus Corporation from December 1970 until January 16, 1980.

During the ten years from 1960 to 1970, Mr. Hardy served as a Vice President of Time Inc. and Publisher of *Life Magazine*. Mr. Hardy joined Time Inc. in December 1959. In 1960 he established Time-Life Books, and was its Publisher for four years, during which he developed the division into a worldwide book business for Time Inc. He became Publisher of *Life* on March 1, 1964.

For the preceding thirteen years Mr. Hardy had been associated with Doubleday & Co., book publishers, as Trade Advertising Manager and Director of Advertising before being appointed Vice President for Advertising in 1956.

Prior to World War II, Mr. Hardy worked for several years in public relations for the automobile industry in Washington, D.C., and he served in the U.S. Air Force from 1942 to 1946. He later headed an industrial public relations firm operating in Central and South America.

Mr. Hardy serves on the Boards of Doyle Dane Bernbach, Inc., Direct Mail/Marketing Association, Inc., Encyclopaedia Britannica, Energy Assets International Corporation, The Futures Group, International Intelligence Incorporated, Mahler & Emerson, Inc., National Demographics, Ltd., Reeves Communications Corporation, The Salk Institute, Solar-En, and H.S. Stuttman.

*J. Mel Hickerson*

# On Selling Books House to House

*Many summers have I lived and labored* and the one that I remember most poignantly fell between my freshman and sophomore years in college. I remember the summer of 1916 for its fears, its thrills, its lonely hours, its homesickness, its eye-opening adventures, and its admitted contribution to whatever subsequent success I may have achieved as salesman, marketer, and Citizen. Indeed . . . it was during that oft-remembered summer that I made the sale that did the most for me. No question in my mind about that.

"What are you doing this summer?"

That one question was asked more intently and answered more thoughtfully than was any other in my group, as my freshman year in college neared its end. For on the answer depended much of one's second year in college: how much "dishwashing" he would have to do after school hours and, in many cases, whether or not he could come back to campus at all.

"What are you doing this summer to make enough money to help you get through another year in college?" That was the explicit question.

I chose book selling. Subscription book selling . . . cold canvass, house to house. Why I chose book selling from the score of jobs offered to us undergraduates at the University of Iowa, I don't recall. But choose book selling I did. *People's Home Library* was the volume . . . and it consisted of a medical book, a cookbook, and a veterinary book. "Three books needed on every farm and priced at $10.00, but available in one big volume for only $4.95."

At the time I knew nothing about book selling and very little about selling at all. And the very thought of cold canvass. . . . !

Never will I forget the sales training course conducted by the Field Man for *People's Home Library*! His name was Nelson and he did a

**139**

thorough job on the sizable group of us who signed up to sell for him and The R. C. Barnum Co. We met three evenings every week from late April until the end of the school year in June. Nelson would preside and would sell the book to us for two hours at a time—literally. He would work from the prospectus each of us was to carry in the field and demonstrate to prospects. And, except to hammer home a point, he never deviated from his sales talk. Indeed, he instructed us to memorize the presentation and to follow it to the letter.

As the course neared its end, we neophytes would sell each other, and Instructor Nelson would criticize our presentations. Our opening sentences, our pauses, our questions of the prospect, our reading of selected passages from the text, and our efforts to inject emotion in our reference to the pictures. (Many times I have wondered what became of "Bookman" Nelson. He could have become a great trainer of salesmen for mid-century commerce, and perhaps he did.)

At the last sales training session, Instructor Nelson reviewed the course, "On Selling Books—House to House," in interesting, enthusiastic, and encouraging detail. Just before the final adjournment he admonished his student salesmen on two basic points, then quoted from his Book of Facts. Somewhat as follows:

**1** Stick to your canned sales talk. It is right, it works, it will make sales for you. And . . . warning! If you start fooling with it, as some of you will, you are finished and you may as well come home.
**2** Call at every house! You will make sales where you least expect to find a prospect. And . . . you will make more sales to the obviously poor than you will to the obviously well-to-do.

Never will I forget these pronouncements from his Book of Facts. In essence: "Much as I regret to tell you this, here are the facts on a percentage basis about your performance as a group. $X$ percent of you will never go into your assigned territories. Of those of you who do go, $X$ percent will quit within a week, $X$ percent within two weeks . . . and those of you who work every day for 10 weeks will earn a minimum of $300, up to [I don't recall the figure he used], which is more money than you can earn in any other available job." (Remember, Reader, this was the summer of 1916.)

When the college year ended early in June, I spent a few days with my family at our farm home near Mt. Ayr, Iowa. Daily I reviewed my sales presentation, which I knew word for word, gesture for gesture. And I did a last bit of preparatory work, too. I selected the coat I planned to wear on the job for ten weeks and sewed a special pocket into it. An inside pocket on the left side, large enough to hold the prospectus from which I was to present the merits and values of *People's Home Library*. (In our sales training we had been told never to approach a prospect with book in hand, but to approach him empty-handed "to discuss a matter of business." At the psychological moment, the prospectus was produced from the tailor-made coat pocket.)

All too soon my "few days" at home ended and I caught the morning train for St. Joseph, Missouri, there to change trains and go to Denton, Kansas, in Brown County. All-wise Bookman Nelson had advised me to headquarter and weekend in the little town of Denton (population circa 150) rather than in the larger county seat town of Hiawatha (population perhaps 3000). He had his good reasons, which I did not suspect then nor appreciate for many years.

I had quite a wait in the Union Station in St. Joseph. Also . . . I had my first serious attack of homesickness. And this homesickness was accompanied by fear—the kind of lonely fear every beginning salesman knows. When the train back to Mt. Ayr was announced, my every impulse was to chuck the book-selling job and return home. But I didn't! Just why, I don't know. Maybe it was pride, maybe desperation— maybe indecision.

Strangely enough I don't recall very much about the short journey from St. Joseph to Denton, or about my first impressions of the little town. I do remember my walk with summer baggage in hand from the Grand Island Railroad station to the town's one hotel, a not unattractive "midwest Gothic" structure, two stories high and typical of the locale.

At the registration desk, which was more old-fashioned bookkeeper's desk than hotel registration desk, my host-to-be greeted me. Came the discussion of rates and an easy agreement on a weekend rate (Saturday supper through Monday breakfast). Then the narrow stairway to the room that was to be my headquarters and weekend home for the next ten weeks. By 1981 Hilton standards it wasn't much, but I liked it. It was a haven, and I needed a haven as much as any freshman salesman ever did.

Shortly the dinner bell announced supper, which was served family-style to an interesting assembly of guests. Supper finished, I walked around the town, which was so small that a stranger was spotted quickly—and catalogued almost as quickly. During the tour I called at the post office where mail from my home office welcomed me and encouraged me. Bookman Nelson knew when to write and what to write to his underlings. To top the evening I splurged on a dish of ice cream at the Denton drug store.

Came morning, and a hearty country breakfast—but no morning newspaper. Then . . . my first solicitation. Of whom? Remember . . . I was selling *People's Home Library* (medical book, veterinary book, cookbook). The hotel proprietor's wife, who was the cook at the hotel, was the perfect subject. To make a not-very-long story short, my sales pitch clicked and my first prospect became a customer. Nor did she hesitate to formalize her purchase for delivery in late August by signing her name in the back of my prospectus, following a list of perhaps twenty names I had composed and entered, as instructed. No cash payment was required—only the customer's signature. And when a buyer refused to sign, which was the case frequently, I signed for him as I had been told to do.

Thus began my ten-week-long summer of selling books house-to-house.

Thus began one of the most memorable summers I have ever lived.

And thus continued the summer, with only slight variations. My instructor, Bookman Nelson, had warned me to stick with the canned sales presentation and I was naive enough to do as told. And it worked!

I made the percentage of sales to calls I had been told to expect. Matter of fact, my percentage was somewhat higher. Perhaps because I worked every day, rain or shine, and called on every house—the ones that were rundown as well as the ones that appeared to be prosperous. And . . . the most unlikely appearing farmsteads bought more books than did the apparently well-to-do, just as Bookman Nelson had assured his student salesmen would be the case.

At the end of seven weeks I had called at every farm home in Brown County, Kansas. And . . . because August was still young and I needed more territory, the company assigned me a strip in Missouri, across the Missouri River.

At the proper time I ordered books for delivery in late August, discounting the signed order total by the figure suggested at the sales training course the previous spring. Then the last week in August, I delivered books to the customers whose signatures adorned the last few pages in my prospectus.

For this important job I employed the services of the local taxi driver. We loaded up at my hotel early in the morning and got under way promptly. Most customers accepted their books and made payment in silver dollars. And each book brought in five silver dollars ($4.95 to be exact).

Five silver dollars—ten—fifteen—twenty—up to 100 and 200 or more. Have you ever carried 200 silver dollars in your pockets? Before the local bank closed on the second day we drove in from the country and exchanged silver dollars for a bank draft. But no such opportunity two days later. I was finishing the job on the Missouri side of the river and the country bank was closed when I reached the town, the name of which I no longer remember. But this I remember! I spent the night in the fourth-rate hotel with more money on my person than I had ever seen at any one time. I barred the door best I could, cached the precious silver dollars that were not all mine, and slept hardly a wink. First customer next morning at the local bank was a young book peddler whose business at the bank was exchanging silver dollars for a bank draft.

On Friday of Week *X*, I made the last of my delivery calls, packed up and shipped back to the publisher the few books declined by farmers who had ordered them earlier in the summer, remitted to R. C. Barnum Company their percentage of all books delivered, paid the balance due mine summer host . . . and spent the evening and night in great relief and peace of mind. My summer of hard-for-me work had ended and successfully. I could return to college in September in funds and richer by far in experience—valuable sales experience. Indeed . . . I had made the sale that did the most for me, though I did not fully realize it at the time.

And I took away with me memories and impressions that remain with me to this day:

Mail from the Home Office which reached me every Saturday
Technique of "living off the land"
One week in the wheat fields with the I.W.W.
Breakfast of ginger snaps soaked in branch water
Overnight in a flophouse
How to get leads
Saturday nights in Denton
Making the identical sales talk 500 times
My introduction to distribution costs
Being greeted by barking and sniffing dogs
How a book peddler weekends
One salesman's appraisal of other salesmen
Holding on for the duration

Perhaps "living off the land" is my most poignant memory of my summer selling books house-to-house.

Late each afternoon I would ask the farmer or his wife whom I was trying to sell, "Where around here do you suppose I can get supper and stay all night?" Almost always the answer would be, "Right here!" Sometimes I would be allowed to help do the chores or dry the dishes. Standard payment, if any, for two bountiful meals and a comfortable bed was twenty-five cents, but usually the farm folk of Brown County, Kansas, would refuse money payment.

On the infrequent occasions when I failed to find lodging, I would sleep in a wheat field on a bed made by tearing down a wheat shock and spreading out the bundles. Always, in the morning, I would remake the shock before traveling on. Usually I would not breakfast at all on these occasions, unless it was on ginger snaps dunked in branch water. Not a bad breakfast, either.

One night, after I had bedded down between two hay stacks, a chill wind came out of the North and routed me. I retreated over a five-cent toll bridge across the Missouri River to a ten-cent flophouse in St. Joseph. Under the circumstances, that fifteen-cent accommodation was the best value of the summer.

Early in August, funds became very low. To get some needed cash, I decided to work as an itinerant harvest hand. I bummed a Grand Island freight train into the wheat country and landed a job immediately. It was on this job that I met my first labor agitator. He was an I.W.W. organizer and he persisted with his class appeal until the older man I was assisting chased him away with a pitchfork.

And there are more serious memories, recollections, and opinions that are part of my psyche yet today. Lessons learned "On Selling Books— House to House" way back when. Here are five of them in simple a–b–c– terms.

1   Canned sales talks, delivered word for word, will get orders.
2   Present customers can suggest leads.
3   Personal letters from Home Office sales management are life-savers to people in the field.
4   Selling offers a rewarding career to anyone who will faithfully go through the routine proved by other successful salesmen.
5   The big thing in a summer selling campaign, or in any selling or advertising campaign, is one's ability to hold on "for the duration" . . . to finish the job.

Hail the Salesman and his contribution to a brighter America and a higher standard of living for all!

□ □ □

J. Mel Hickerson, the eldest of eight children, was born on a farm in northern Missouri. When he had been graduated from a single-room country school and was ready for high school, his family moved across the border near Mt. Ayr, Iowa, and later he attended the University of Iowa. His term at the university was interrupted by World War I, but it was enriched by extracurricular work as a student waiter, coal-furnace tender, part-time teacher, typesetter and pressman, college editor, and ad salesman. Indeed, a life in advertising and selling seemed inevitable.

He started his business career with General Electric Company's lamp department when GE's job was selling a philosophy rather than a product—lighting rather than lamp bulbs. Four years later he was transferred to Meriden, Connecticut, to become Advertising and Sales Promotion Manager of a newly formed organization, The Miller Company, whose job it was to sell some philosophy and a lot of product such as lighting fixtures and portable lamps in a fiercely competitive market. For Miller he worked with department stores, distributors, and electric utility companies in each of the forty-eight states, doing sales planning, merchandising, platform work, and actual door-to-door selling.

In 1929 Mr. Hickerson joined A. D. Lasker's Lord & Thomas advertising agency. There he doubled in brass, serving as account executive and copywriter on a group of six accounts. In 1939 he left Lord & Thomas to establish J. M. Hickerson Inc., a general advertising agency, which enjoyed steady growth and became a national agency with branch offices in Washington, Chicago, and Des Moines.

In 1950 he consolidated his organization with Albert Frank-Guenther Law, Inc., which was one of the oldest and best known financial advertising agencies, but the merger came unstuck after a year and J. M. Hickerson Inc. *Advertising* was reactivated. As of December 31, 1962, he sold the agency to one of his talented employees. In October of 1962 he undertook an assignment with United Student Aid Funds, a newly organized not-for-profit, nongovernmental guarantor of student loans. The assignment was for four months and is now in its twentieth year.

*Paul B. Hicks, Jr.*

# Selling a New Point of View

*In the life of each salesman* are a lot of great sales he will always remember—and a lot of near misses he would just as soon forget.

My story involves turning a near miss into the most memorable sale of my life. I sold an idea—a new point of view—to a group of Texaco marketing executives. This sale led to important changes in the way our company merchandised products through service stations. I have to add that it gave my career with the company an important boost.

This story took place in 1957, three years after I joined Texaco's sales organization in Chicago. I was young, energetic, and full of goals, plans, and ambitions. Most of all, I loved what I was doing—selling. I was a salesman and I was damn proud of it.

Young as I was, I had a lot of solid sales experience behind me. My father was an executive with F.W. Woolworth Company, a firm that owes its success to merchandising expertise. I worked at Woolworth as a boy, during weekends and vacations, and after graduation from college. By the time those tough, savvy Woolworth retailers finished training me, I really knew something about merchandising.

One of the most important lessons they taught me, which figures in this story, was: *make use of space, it's valuable. Every bit of space in a store represents a profit opportunity.*

Although enjoying a successful career, I left Woolworth because I wanted to be satisfied that I was succeeding entirely on my own, not because of my father's position.

I also wanted to see if I could bring the merchandising fundamentals I had learned at Woolworth into a different field and make them work equally well there.

If I wanted virgin territory to try out merchandising ideas, the marketing segment of the oil industry was a good place. When I joined

**147**

Texaco's sales organization in Chicago in 1954, I quickly discovered the petroleum industry was not taking full advantage of its many service stations to merchandise a wide range of products and services. Marketing at that time was practically an unknown concept. Except for the names on the signs, you could hardly tell one company's service stations from another. Most gas stations offered gasoline, and maybe a little automotive service, but not much else.

I soon learned that Texaco had procedures and offered advice on these procedures to the independent businessmen who owned and operated Texaco service stations. For example, every "dealer," as the company termed them, was given a desk that was placed in the middle of his "office." All order pads as well as records were kept in the desk, and much paper work was done at that desk in the office. A rack was provided to display a few tires and batteries in the office. Other products, such as waxes and polishes, were arranged on shelves in groups of three. That way, if a can or jar was missing, the dealer could check to see if it had been sold or stolen.

In the lubrication bays, all tools were supposed to be kept in storage containers along one wall. If mechanics had followed that rule, they would have spent more time walking to and from the containers than in servicing cars.

Advertising and promotion on the part of the dealer? There was some but it hardly seemed effective to me.

And that was about it. The real selling of gasoline was done by the car's gas gauge. When it pointed toward empty, the driver pulled into the first convenient station and filled up. A flat tire, a broken windshield wiper, a dead battery—all required instant repairs at the next gas station.

It was obvious to me that we had a terrific opportunity. With the right kind of merchandising, I could help the Texaco dealers in my territory become more profitable and, at the same time, win more customers for Texaco. To do this, I had to establish credibility with the dealers. That meant I had to perform, and perform well, in their interests. These were experienced, no-nonsense people. They weren't impressed by young hotshots, titles, and promises. I was going to be judged solely by what I could do for them.

One of the first things I did was to buy a Texaco service station uniform. I paid for it. A dress shirt, tie, and jacket were fine for offices and meetings but at a service station I felt they created an artificial distinction, a barrier, between myself and the dealer. That uniform helped to create the feeling that I was one of them. It was also cheaper to keep clean when I pitched in to help stack tires or pump gasoline.

From the beginning I felt there was a better term than "dealers" to describe the people who operated these service stations. The word was not an accurate description of their activities. Instead, I felt retailers was more accurate because they were businessmen and salesmen— Texaco's main contact with the public. That was my terminology for them. The company and industry later adopted the term "retailers."

One of the main objectives was to change the way people thought about Texaco gas stations. I wanted customers to look at them as service station–retail stores selling a lot of needed products at good prices. Since Chicago is on Lake Michigan, many people naturally enjoy boating and water sports. So retailers near the lake were encouraged to stock outboard motor oil, life jackets, beach balls, and suntan lotion. Many Chicagoans also like to hunt. What could be handier on the way to a hunting area than to find a Texaco station selling small cooking utensils, flashlight batteries, cigarettes, and snack foods?

Merchandising such items to the public helped attract additional customers. Once cars arrived at the pumps, retailers were encouraged to make a quick inspection of the windshield wipers, tires, and batteries. Just pointing out items in need of replacement often meant added sales.

These marketing ideas were just commonsense ways to serve customers and sell products. Combined with tire sales or special discounts on batteries, they became real profit makers. They gained the retailers a reputation as reliable car care experts.

Most of the retailers in my territory were quick to see the value of this type of merchandising and promotion. Tire sales didn't mean just a few tires. They meant hundreds of tires, vanloads of tires, tires of every size and description, all of them priced at a good savings. A special promotion might include a giveaway of six-packs of soda with each fill-up. Instead of a few cases, in one particular promotion we had 5000 six-packs on hand. People must not only hear or read about promotions, they have to see them in action.

The results started paying off. As their profits increased, retailers started to realize that aggressive merchandising and selling were in their best interests.

Gradually, those useless "offices" were changed into clean, well-lighted salesrooms, places to make a profit. We got rid of the desks, put in chairs for customers, and attractively displayed products on sale. The order pads for service work were taken out of desks and placed where they should be: right next to the cash register.

This was how things were shaping up when I was called into the District Manager's office one morning.

He had received word that the New York headquarters of Texaco wanted two stations in Chicago to be "properly set up" so they could serve as models for the entire Midwest region. One was to be on the north side of the city and one on the south. I was tapped to handle the south side project. I was to select a station and supervise every detail of this model service station. In two weeks, New York executives would come to Chicago to inspect both stations.

This was an opportunity I looked forward to! I assumed that this was a license to set up and show off new merchandising techniques in a Texaco station, making it an attractive outlet for the passing motorist, a dynamic profit center for the retailer—and perhaps a Flagship Texaco station.

A high-volume service station was selected. It was operated by a tough, bottom-line sort of retailer who was interested in serving his customers and making money. I knew he was a good man to work with on innovative programs.

We worked for two solid weeks, including weekends. We cleaned up the entire place, hung banners, ordered and stacked tires and other merchandise, got tire tread measurement gauges and battery testers in place, and set up a smooth traffic flow into and out of the station.

The day arrived and so did the delegation from New York. I was glad they went to the north side station first because I knew it had been set up in line with standard marketing policies. I believed mine would provide a good contrast, showing the terrific potential for every Texaco station.

In this confident frame of mind, I was ready and waiting when they arrived.

The car pulled into the station. But nobody got out. I could see through the windows that the people inside were talking animatedly and peering out at the station.

This went on for some time while I became more and more nervous and concerned. Something was wrong but I couldn't imagine what.

At last the doors opened and some rather distressed looking men got out.

What a picture that station must have presented to that group of oil men! Outside I had a large display of lawn mowers, fertilizer, grass seed, weed killer, and garden hose. More than 100 beach balls were displayed by the front door. The rest of the ground outside was covered with tall, black columns of new tires, hundreds of them. Overhead, in the bright spring air, banners announced a tire sale in progress. The station's employees, working on a bonus system, were talking tires to some interested customers.

But the visitors didn't seem impressed. One gentleman remarked, "The place looks like a circus."

Dismayed, I followed them into the lube bays. There they

encountered still more tires and a lot of batteries. "Why aren't these in the office?" someone asked.

My God, I thought, wait till they see the "office"!

At that moment, one of the men almost tripped over a moveable work bench stationed between the car lifts. "That's dangerous!" he snapped. "And why aren't those tools in their normal place?"

But the biggest shock was still ahead of them: the salesroom. There was no way I could prevent that inevitable confrontation.

When they saw the salesroom, they were speechless. There were large displays of fast-moving impulse items, such as license plate frames, side-view mirrors, wheel covers, flashlights, batteries, gas cans, lighter fluid, light bulbs, soft drinks, and—to top everything off—some colorful beach balls hanging from the walls in nets.

"Where," one of the executives asked, "is the desk? How can this man operate his office without a desk?"

For the first time it became obvious to me that I had misinterpreted the instructions. The station was supposed to have been set up in accordance with the normal merchandising practices of those days. What these men were viewing, with its radical departure from the norm, was most difficult for them to comprehend.

I realized now I hadn't carried out their instructions but obviously there was nothing I could do at this point. Now I was in a position of trying to make them understand my whole approach to merchandising, and I didn't have much time. I also realized I had nothing further to lose, there was only one course of action left, to speak up with all my conviction and defend the directions we had taken.

"Gentlemen, first an admission on my part of missed communications about what you wanted to see.

"Second, an appeal! Let's go outside and start this whole tour again, only this time let me tell you *why* it has been arranged the way it is."

"Fair enough," they said.

We went outside to the pumps. "Whenever possible every car has a windshield wiper check, a tire check, an oil check, and a battery test," I explained. "The employees get a commission on every item they sell, so they look the cars over pretty carefully. That's good for the employee and good for the customer.

"Now look around. There's a lot of space out here. That space can be put to work to properly display good saleable merchandise and create extra sales for this retailer. We happen to be running a tire sale. The banners overhead say so. The stacks of tires prove it. Every tire is priced to sell. As a result, we're selling them. This retailer has made an extra $210 net profit in the last week, just on this tire sale alone. In space he would not normally have used."

Instant interest! These executives all knew very few service stations made that kind of money on tires.

"Now, those lawn products have nothing to do with petroleum products," I continued. "But it's spring and people are thinking about their lawns. While they're getting gasoline or a new tire, they see things they need for the lawn but haven't bought yet. They're buying here, and that's an added profit for this retailer. And again, in space he normally doesn't use."

We returned to the lube bays. "Tires and batteries aren't sold in the salesroom," I said. "They're sold at the pumps if worn tires are spotted there or in the lube bays, when the mechanic has the car up on the lubrication rack and can inspect it. And where the customer can see for himself that he needs them.

"Now that moveable work bench you almost fell over was something this retailer and I built to get around a problem. Tools may be stored over on that far wall but they have to be used right here when a car is on the hoist. What we have done is build a moveable bench so the mechanic can select all the tools he needs. He simply wheels it over to the job and gets to work. It's easier, more professional, and saves time. The mechanics like it."

I could see the point was made. We moved back into the salesroom.

"You asked where the desk is," I said. "It's where we think it belongs: in the storeroom, which is actually more private for bookkeeping. As a result, good salesroom space is freed. This salesroom contains the most valuable space in the station. If it's a *salesroom*, every inch is usable and every single item could mean an extra profit. Our sales records demonstrate that people want and need these products.

"It's obvious why we stocked automotive products. But many of the impulse items may not be so obvious. Look at it this way: most people visit a service station more than any other store, with the possible exception of a grocery store. We want them to know we have many necessities that they can buy here without making another stop. Do you know anybody who has enough light bulbs in his house? Somebody always needs one or two and the people who patronize this station know they can get light bulbs here at night and on weekends. A lot of them get a fill-up while they're at it. As for the beach balls, children are our best sales people. Those balls are inexpensive, but they're profitable."

Our New York people were becoming convinced but the clincher was handled by the retailer himself. "Let *me* tell you something," he said to the entire delegation. "This new merchandising–retailing concept has done more to help my profitability than all the other programs we've ever tried. This might not look like the traditional service station but my customers like it because we're providing a service. My employees like it because it offers them an opportunity to sell. And I like it because I'm making a better profit than I've ever made before."

That did it! Our people were excited and interested. We had made the sale.

That evening as I headed home I had that great feeling of exhilaration that most salesmen experience when they have made a really important sale.

A program had been designed that would be worthwhile—would offer a service and help people—be a money maker for retailers and rewarding to those of us who had participated.

Yes, I am a salesman and then as now I was damn proud of it.

Paul B. Hicks, Jr., Vice President and General Manager in charge of the Public Relations and Advertising Department of Texaco Inc., was born in Norfolk, Virginia, in 1925. In 1944 he enlisted in the U.S. Marine Corps and served abroad from June 1944 until May 1946, winning a Presidential Unit Citation and two battle stars. Returning to civilian life, he was graduated from the University of Virginia in 1950 with a bachelor of arts degree in economics.

Mr. Hicks joined Texaco's sales organization at Chicago in 1953. He served as a Sales Representative until 1957, and then as District Supervisor of Merchandising until 1960, when he was appointed District Sales Manager at Chicago. He was named Assistant Division Sales Manager there in March 1962, and was transferred to New York as Manager of Merchandising in August 1962. He became Division Sales Manager at Columbus, Ohio, in 1963.

In 1965, Mr. Hicks returned to New York and was appointed Assistant to the President. He was named General Manager of the Sales Department–United States in 1966, and was elected Vice President in charge of that department in 1969. He was named Vice President for Worldwide Sales in 1972, and was appointed Vice President in charge of Public Relations and Personnel in 1975. He was named to his present position August 1, 1977.

Mr. Hicks is a member of the board of directors of National Energy Foundation and the Westchester County Association. He is also a member of the American Petroleum Institute's General Committee on Public Relations. He was elected to the board of directors of Texaco Canada Inc. in May 1980.

*Richard M. Hyman*

# *Try, Try Again*

*The organization for which I have worked* for thirty-four years, the Owens Brush Company, is the leading contract manufacturer of high-quality toothbrushes and hairbrushes. Most of these products are manufactured to our clients' specifications. At the time of this story, however, we had a small line of merchandise under our own name as well.

In the early stages of the Vietnam conflict, U.S. armed forces assigned to that area were at a severe disadvantage because the M-16 rifle tended to jam in combat. While it was a fine weapon offering outstanding fire power, jamming was sufficiently frequent and widespread that it significantly impaired the effectiveness of our troops. This problem persisted for many months and was the subject of considerable effort toward resolution: moreover, numerous investigations were launched to determine the source of the problem and to effect solutions.

About this time, we began receiving inquiries, and ultimately a substantial number of orders for toothbrushes, from post exchanges in the Vietnam theater. It was perfectly obvious that the quantities of brushes being purchased could not possibly be used in the normal course of events for oral hygiene purposes. After some digging, we found that these brushes were being used by our troops to attempt to keep the M-16 rifle free of mud, dirt, sand, and other debris that could conceivably cause jamming. When a rifle is used in the field, a certain amount of sand or dirt will almost invariably find its way into the receiver area, and a toothbrush is very useful and effective in removing this material. Thus the use of toothbrushes for this purpose in Vietnam.

Although a toothbrush is not at all appropriate for cleaning the inside of the rifle barrel, it is extremely useful for cleaning the bolt assembly, the receiver, trigger assembly, and many other areas of the weapon. Having been in the Army myself in World War II, I know firsthand that it was a common practice for infantrymen and others in the field,

**155**

armed with small arms, to carry toothbrushes to keep their weapons clean.

I noticed that in a number of cases the brushes that were selected and purchased by the post exchanges in Vietnam that ultimately found their way into the field for the cleaning of weapons were of styles that were not as well suited for this purpose as others that we had available. The thought then occurred to me that it would certainly be reasonable to develop a cleaning tool, made somewhat like a toothbrush, designed specifically to clean the rifle that was having the problem, as well as other small arms in use at the time.

Accordingly, I selected from our inventory perhaps twenty different style brushes and then made arrangements to visit the local National Guard Armory. There I prevailed upon the commanding officer to let me field strip one of each type of the small arms that were being used and try the different type of brushes to determine which characteristics were most effective in cleaning the M-16 and other small arms in use at that time.

As a result of this experiment, certain characteristics became obviously desirable whereas others were less effective. It became clear that there were some special requirements or characteristics in such a cleaning tool, particularly if it were to be used with the M-16 family of weapons, an advanced weapon design that required special cleaning attention. Whatever its design, no toothbrush possessed all these unique requirements.

Considering what the armed forces often call the "exigencies of the problem," the most expeditious approach I could take to provide a brush that would be more effective was to modify a current toothbrush so that it would be better suited for the task at hand. I selected a fairly large, multituft brush, changed the texture to a stiffer version, and cut a large, V-shaped notch across the short axis of the brush head. This notch facilitated cleaning around corners and certain hidden surfaces that otherwise could not be reached.

Even though these modifications must appear rather modest to the reader, the resulting brush was far superior in meeting the need than were conventional toothbrushes. In any case, these modified toothbrushes were sold through the Post Exchange System for rifle cleaning purposes. This was the "wrong way" to reach the market, but it was functional in the sense that it was quick and it promptly made available a badly needed, improved cleaning tool.

The President of our parent organization, then Chemway Products Company, was aware of these efforts, and apparently somewhat amused at the back-door approach I was using to reach this market. We were discussing the subject one evening, and he said to me, "Why don't you design a special brush, one really engineered to do the job optimally, and sell it directly to the Army. They should welcome a special brush if it will help solve their problem." And, of course, he was right. I didn't welcome the idea of trying to sell the U.S. military system a product that was not yet designed, but the President's point was well taken, and I decided to follow his suggested approach.

On the basis of experimentation at the local National Guard, I was able to visualize fairly completely the type of brush that would be needed. This visualization hardly represented the final form of the brush, but the concept was sufficiently well developed that I felt confident it would function effectively. It needed only design refinements and such special adaptation of the concept that would be required to cope with the dimensional limitations of the M-16 rifle.

With the experience gained from the firsthand experimentation, and the interim toothbrush modifications, I became convinced that we could produce an outstanding brush that was optimally suited to the task at hand, specifically to help clean more efficiently the M-16 and other small arms. The next question became one of whom to contact to discuss such a project.

I attempted to work through the Pentagon, our legislative representatives, and specific Army locations, including Rock Island Arsenal. In each case, I was courteously treated but was sent from one office to another in what I am sure was a sincere attempt to try to locate an appropriate entry point to discuss this project.

It seems incredible in retrospect, but this process of being shunted around from place to place, from office to office, from command to command lasted some fifteen months, and finally in desperation and frustration, I wrote the commanding officer of the Rock Island Arsenal a three-page letter, detailing my experiences, and asked him if he could assign someone to listen to our concept.

This letter did the trick, and the next morning I received a call from the Arsenal explaining that the commanding officer was horrified at the delays and shuffling around we had been subjected to, particularly since he was the individual who was ultimately charged with the responsibility of a resolution of this cleaning problem with the M-16.

A few days later an appointment was set up at the Arsenal, and I had the opportunity to review the ideas that we had developed to try to solve the problems of keeping this weapon clean. This in turn led to a series of other meetings, during which ways were explored to determine how we could best work with the Army to develop this brush. While the tool I had in mind was a fairly simple product for which we had the production expertise and capability, the personnel with whom I was working were accustomed to working on developing very technical and highly engineered projects, such as tanks, weapon systems, and other complex and expensive items. It was understandably difficult to keep this small, special cleaning brush in appropriate perspective.

But there was no doubt about the importance of the project, and we enjoyed full cooperation from Army personnel, both military and civilian.

Ultimately, a development contract was granted us. We were issued an M-16, and we set about the task of designing the cleaning brush we had envisioned. We were given a long list of criteria that the brush must meet, including such things as ability to withstand human perspiration, ability to function at a wide range of temperatures, resistance to jet fuel, aviation gasoline, kerosene, vehicular gasoline in the various octanes, cleaning compounds—and a long list of other requirements.

Fortunately, we were able to develop a demanding but suitable list of specifications for the product so that it met all of these criteria. We further improved the design, which finally included a brush similar to a toothbrush on one end, but it was somewhat larger and had a deep notch for cleaning around edges and corners of the parts of the weapon. On the other end of the brush handle we installed a thin, narrow, short-bristled brush designed to fit into certain grooves and channels of the M-16 rifle. We also determined the length so as to make it function optimally, but at the same time the brush had to fit in a butt stock recess along with other cleaning tools.

Since we had been issued an M-16, we could try our designs firsthand, and during the course of the next four or five months, we did come up with a final version that ultimately went into production. As you might expect, it was olive drab, and in the Army vernacular, it was named "Brush, Cleaning, Small Arms."

Once the design was completed, analyzed, and approved, a pilot run quantity was manufactured and tested by the Army. The brush was accepted without a single change.

We have since manufactured millions of these brushes for the U.S. Army and for U.S. allies who have used it with the same or similar weapons. In fact, the brush is efficacious with virtually all small arms.

It was quite interesting to learn from the Army that they considered it very unusual that somebody would bring them an idea from the outside, particularly a specialized concept such as this one, and be successful in convincing the military to use it. The entire episode was used as the basis for a number of speeches that were given around the country, by Army personnel, encouraging small businesses to submit viable ideas to the Federal Government. The story of this cleaning brush was related as a case history of how it can be done.

The experience was extremely valuable to me because it reinforced a

Brush, Cleaning, Small Arms.

lesson that most of us need to relearn from time to time: if one has a good idea, and the idea has sufficient merit to economically justify the time and effort, then we should pursue the concept unrelentingly until we succeed.

In addition to the business that we have enjoyed on this particular product through the years, the experience was also useful in teaching us the importance and the high potential of government business, and as a result of that, we have pursued other contracts with a better than average degree of success. Incidentally, I have found it is also good to know that the product we envisioned and produced for the Army did help our country through a really difficult period of time, and we like to think that it helped our soldiers in the field solve a problem that was literally putting their lives at risk. This is far from the largest sale I ever made, but it certainly was one of the most satisfying.

Richard M. Hyman is a graduate of the University of Toledo. He is Vice President and Sales Manager of the Owens Brush Company, Iowa City, Iowa, the world's largest producer of toothbrushes.

Mr. Hyman is an internationally recognized authority on toothbrushes and toothbrush design. He is a consultant to the American Dental Association, has produced several prizewinning TV films on dental health, is chief U.S. delegate for toothbrushes to the International Standards Organization, and is past President of the American Brush Manufacturers' Association. He has been employed by the Owens Brush Company all of his adult working life.

**Frances Bartlett Kinne**

# Not Only Hope, But Also Benny

*A cheer, hurrah, hooray, and whinny,*
*And even more are due Fran Kinne.*
*She brought, when we were lacking any,*
*Not only Hope, but also Benny.**

*It was April 6, 1972.* The place was Jacksonville University. It was the only time Bob Hope and Jack Benny ever made a joint appearance on a college campus, and in one day they transformed the environment of our university into the center of show business. Everything clicked. Everyone was funny.

The idea was conceived in my mind some years ago, but how to promulgate it was the question. I knew I must practice the same persistence and patience necessary to persuade the various celebrities I had scheduled from the time I had created the College of Fine Arts at Jacksonville University: Arthur Fiedler, on his sixteen visits to campus; Aaron Copland on two occasions; Ann Sothern for three visits; Sir Rudolf Bing; Richard Boone; John Carradine; the late Sir John Barbarolli; Charles Kuralt; and dozens of others. Since Jacksonville University is a private, independent institution, there are no funds to pay "star" fees, so salesmanship must be a viable alternative in attracting celebrities to campus.

I suppose this chapter really goes back to 1948 when my husband and I were married and he was assigned by the Army to China. The Communists occupied the Mainland in that year, and at Christmas we were evacuated and reassigned to Japan, where both of us became

*Ray Knight, *Jacksonville Journal*, April 13, 1972.

members of General Douglas MacArthur's staff during the Korean War. And who should show up but Bob Hope and his great show. Then my husband and I were reassigned to Europe, and everywhere we went we heard comments about the two men who did the most for the morale of Americans assigned overseas, Hope and Benny.

Both men had enriched mankind in many ways. Mr. Benny's outstanding career and appearances for the Services were well known, as were his benefit performances for symphonies all across the country. Mr. Hope's tours for soldier audiences had brought entertainment to more than 10 million G.I.'s in virtually every country and clime, and, of course, he had already justifiably received every conceivable honor. I made it my goal to thank both gentlemen for what they had done and were doing to comfort loneliness, spark inspiration, and touch the lives of millions of people. The obvious answer to me was the awarding of honorary doctorates, but there were many hurdles to overcome before this could be possible.

I first met Mr. Benny when he visited the Jacksonville Symphony. We had supper together with a small party of friends after the concert, and I did what I always do—I approached the subject of a visit to our campus at a later date. He was courteous and charming, but I know he had no concept of the degree of my persistence. He was to learn this over a period of time, since he did give me his telephone number.

Bob Hope came to Jacksonville for a professional show and rehearsed on our campus with our stage band. That little angel who always sits on my shoulder didn't have to remind me twice that this was the opportunity for which I had been waiting. It was then I learned how patient and dear is that amazing man. The students had mixed cement in order to preserve Bob's handprint for posterity. The mixture was inadequately prepared, and Bob tried to make an imprint three different times (finally successfully), each time adding more liquid cement mixture to his French cuffs and handsome sport coat, while laughingly accepting his fate.

"Would you be willing to come back, as I really would like to honor you—but, of course, you would be honoring us."

"Sure, I'll come," he agreed. He also didn't know how dogged was my determination. But again I came up with a valuable telephone number!

So I did what any red-blooded American would do with such priceless telephone numbers—I started to use them.

To Jack Benny: "Would you be willing to share the platform with Bob for an honorary doctorate?"

The immediate answer was, "I'd be honored."

I posed the same question to Bob Hope, and he answered, "I'd be honored."

But then the really insurmountable problem developed: the schedules of both men, our own collegiate schedule, and a "hot-shot" basketball team covering every available date. The schedule almost proved the impossibility of the dream, but I finally gathered all calendars in hand and flew to Beverly Hills for a Fine Arts Deans meeting I was to attend. Of course, the two telephone numbers were in my hot little hand that October day in 1971.

Fate smiled on me, difficulties were resolved, and we came up with April 6 of the following year, 1972, as *the* date.

Back in Jacksonville, work began minutes after my return. There were the details on the doctorates and the manner of presentation, publicity, academic protocol, and regalia. The media were fascinated. There was even a story on the fact that Bob's hat size was 7⅜ and Jack's was 7¼, while their coat sizes were 42 and 40–41 respectively. But seventy-six telephone calls later, we finally made it.

My husband and I met the two gentlemen at the airport with the university pep band and an entourage of admiring fans. It amused the stars when I proposed a minute-by-minute itinerary of what they were to do on the following day, and they asked if I would be supervising their pre-bedtime activities as well. As it turned out, Jack wanted a glass of milk, and Bob wanted to hit golf balls. At 10:00 P.M., I was on the telephone calling local golf driving ranges and saying, "I have Bob Hope with me, and he wants to hit a few balls."

"Sure, Lady, I know you have Bob Hope with you. Everyone does when it's closing time and they can't think of a better one."

April 6 dawned bright and beautiful, and the outdoor Science Green was an appropriate setting for our convocation—an unbelievably beautiful campus, lovely old oaks with Spanish moss framing the setting, azaleas and wisteria blooming in profusion, and the scent of jasmine in the air. Both Bob and Jack were in rare form, undoubtedly touched by the sense of a significant time in show-business history.

We had agreed to do the awarding of honorary degrees in a serious format, and the academic regalia promoted the formality of the occasion.

The Dean of Faculties and I had decided we would present our honorees in alphabetical order. Jack was first, and the formality continued. Bob and I had agreed that after I read his citation and he was hooded, I would reach up and congratulate him with a kiss. We were sure we knew what Jack's reaction would be, and it was safe to predict the outcome. It happened.

As I kissed Bob's cheek and looked from the corner of my eye, I caught the expression on Jack's face. He immediately rose in mock indignation and spoke to the thousands in attendance in a voice only he could muster, with the appropriate Benny pauses,

"*No one* kissed me."

With that I dashed across the stage and planted a kiss squarely on his lips. The Vice Chairman of our Board, a very attractive woman, did the same. And Bob bussed Jack's cheek, while a very historic photo was taken. The audience laughter delayed the continuation of the ceremony for almost five minutes.

The luncheon that followed was equally warm and fun-filled. Mr. Benny said he was pleased to share the day with Bob Hope because they had shared so many things together, but nothing "so cultural." Jack added that this was one of his greatest experiences, the other being "the naming of a junior high school in Waukegan, Illinois, after me. I was thrown out of high school my first year for not studying. I was the most embarrassed honoree at that dedication service. I have always liked history, particularly about Abraham Lincoln, because anyone who would walk barefoot twelve miles in the snow to save three cents on a library book fine is my kind of man." He recalled his experience of visiting one of the classrooms at the school when a little girl asked him seriously, "Mr. Benny, how come they named you after our school?"

Mr. Benny said that Hope came to the United States from England to do a benefit show at Valley Forge, and "after deciding we were going to win that war, he sent for his golf clubs."

Not to be outdone, Bob Hope humorously kidded me about the fact I called him so many times to be sure he wouldn't let me down. He quipped,

"She called me so often and tied up my phone so much that this entire month it was necessary for me to go through her office to make a long distance call."

Both stars were asked to autograph a huge picture of themselves, so that we might frame the photos for students to enjoy. Benny stood back to watch Hope's efforts and exclaimed, "My gosh, he can write." And Hope's retort was, "Not bad for a doctor, eh?" Hope said the picture was big enough for Benny to write out his real name (Benny Kabelsky), and later Benny said, "If I'd known I was going to be such a great violinist, I would have kept the real one."

Hope teased Jack, "He played golf up to three months ago . . . when he lost his ball." After the audience's laughter died down, Hope delivered the final blow . . . "The string broke."

When the Mayor gave each of the comedians a key to the city, Jack bit his and said, "Thank you just the same."

One of the biggest laughs came when Jack mentioned the *Cosmopolitan* centerfold so popular at that time with Burt Reynolds' picture in it, "I didn't think too much of it one way or the other," he said, "I was offered the same kind of a job in *Popular Mechanics*. They wanted me to lie nude on a lawn mower."

From all over the world the newsmen provided coverage for our great day. In fact, seventy-six newspaper reporters and television newscasters made sure millions knew about the two comedians, their doctorates, and the idyllic setting of the Jacksonville University campus. *Newsweek* and *The New York Times* both wrote that Dr. Bob Hope promised to make house calls, while Dr. Jack Benny received a citation saying he was born thirty-nine years ago, quoting Hope, "It is a novelty to think you are honoring two recycled vaudevillians, honoring us in an election year when there are so many comedians to choose from."

The time did arrive for farewells, and we made separate trips to the airport to send each dear man on his way. Bob's turn was first, as he was to fly off for another of his benefits. It was only appropriate that my hero should be flying with an Air National Guard crew who had graciously come to my rescue when a private plane in which Bob was scheduled was cancelled. And as he left, my sad farewell echoed how all of Jacksonville felt.

As we returned to the airport with Jack, he was sentimental and misty eyed, deeply touched by the honor. As we walked down the ramp to the plane my husband paid him the supreme compliment, "Come back, Jack, and I'll take you fishing."

"I hate fishing!"

Whereby I countered, "Come back, Jack, and we'll send Harry fishing."

There was a long pause with that Benny sense of supreme timing, and he responded, with a lifted eyebrow, "That's funny, Fran." And he wrapped one arm lovingly around his Stradivarius and blew a kiss with the other, as he disappeared into the plane.

Fortunately I saw Jack several times after that and spoke to him frequently on the phone. And Bob has returned to do several benefits and even ad libbed one hour and forty-five minutes at a benefit one night in the Jacksonville Civic Auditorium when the lights went out all over the city.

But that's another sales story.

Suffice it to say, Bob and Jack changed our lives—as they have so many others, very much for the better.

□  □  □

Dr. Frances Bartlett Kinne, President of Jacksonville University, began teaching in her native state of Iowa at the age of eighteen while working toward her Master's Degree in Music Education at Drake University. She received the Doctor of Philosophy degree cum laude from the University of Frankfurt in 1957, with majors in music, English literature, and philosophy. Her doctorate was the first awarded to an American woman by the University of Frankfurt since World War II.

Dr. Kinne and her husband, Colonel Harry Kinne, moved to the Jacksonville, Florida, area in 1958 when he retired from the Army and became Senior Advisor to the Florida National Guard in St. Augustine. For the next three years, Dr. Kinne put 47,000 miles on her car commuting to the young, private institution, Jacksonville University, where she had been asked to become professor of music and humanities. By 1961, Dr. Kinne had founded the College of Fine Arts at the University, and served as its Dean until 1979 when she was appointed University President.

Dr. Kinne is listed in more than a score of directories of distinguished Americans including *Who's Who in America, Who's*

*Who in American Education*, and the *Dictionary of International Biography*. She has served on the Boards of over thirty professional and civic organizations and is the only woman to serve as President of the prestigious International Council of Fine Arts Deans. She was the subject of a feature article in *Southern Living* magazine in September 1977.

Dr. Kinne's many honors and awards include Jacksonville University Distinguished University Professor Award, Drake University's Distinguished Service Award, the first annual Governor's Award for Achievement in Arts, and the Jacksonville Area Business and Professional Women's Club Outstanding Achievement Award. She received the Florida Publishing Company's EVE of the Decade Award from among forty-four previous winners of annual awards. She was recognized by the Jacksonville Arts Assembly for the most significant contribution by an individual to the cultural life of Jacksonville. Dr. Kinne was honored by the Prevent Blindness Association of the Northeast Florida area for her unselfish, constant devotion to the people of Jacksonville and their many causes.

*Roger M. Kirk, Jr.*

# Lysol Disinfects
# Its Image

*"Boss, we should have a Lysol Spray!"*

"Roger, why don't you take a few months to familiarize yourself with the marketplace and with the Lysol brand before you make a recommendation like that. Lysol is a declining brand near the end of its product life cycle. We plan to phase it out in the future and milk it for profits which can be used to introduce new products. In fact, a few months ago we consumer tested an aerosol spray disinfectant. The market research clearly demonstrated that the consumer was not interested in a disinfectant aerosol spray. Have Sam show you the market research so you will know why it won't sell to the consumer."

Those instructions introduced me to Lehn & Fink Products Company, the makers of Lysol, in January 1960. To understand the sales challenge of disinfecting Lysol's image, a review and some knowledge of its environment and the image Lysol had is necessary.

The image included our company name, "Lehn & Fink." I have been asked many times why we hadn't changed our name. The standard reply became, "Really, I have never understood why anyone thinks we'd have a problem with the name *Fink*. Besides there hasn't been a *Fink*—I assure you—there hasn't been a *Fink* in our organization for over fifty-five years."

On a more serious note, Lehn & Fink started as a drug wholesaler in 1874, and at one time was larger than McKesson & Robbins. By 1923 the manufacturing and marketing of branded products was thought to have greater potential and drug wholesaling was discontinued. Lehn & Fink was very respected in the drug, hospital and department store field. The company was in a diversified business—franchised cosmetics, industrial products, hospital products, and at the time, consumer

**169**

products under many brand names including Lysol and Hinds Honey and Almond lotion.

In 1960 when I joined Lehn & Fink, I was the only one in the company who had sales and marketing experience in the grocery field. The name Lehn & Fink attracted to the company either cosmetic or drug-oriented experienced personnel including suppliers, agencies, media representatives, and numerous others. When I'd talk to them about the specialized problems in the grocery field, they'd come up with a blank look.

What did this mean to a grocery-oriented person and a product that I felt belonged in the household section of retail outlets instead of the health and beauty aid section?

Before we could service the household product section of the grocery industry, problems had to be identified and then solved over at least the initial objections of the existing bureaucracy.

We had customer service problems including inaccurate billing—approximately 10.0 percent of our invoices were incorrect.

There were delivery problems, for in other businesses customers were satisfied with sixteen days delivery time (from receipt of order to delivery to customer).

Company sales statistics were not in a meaningful, timely format. We had to buy a store audit survey and did buy Audits and Surveys data to give us a feel of what our consumer purchases and sales were in order to manage our business and to make our efforts more productive.

Credit limits had been set as a check to prevent diversion of franchise cosmetics to price cutters. This caused a continuing problem. In fact, when we sold our first truckload promotional order, it was held up for fourteen days in credit because the order was too large. Needless to say we missed the delivery and promotion.

Sales policy—including discounts, promotion, and advertising contracts written for the drug field—had to be modified for food distribution with "teeth" to maintain standards of performance.

We had a problem in sales coverage. Although our forty-two-man force could cover other classes of trade to obtain proper grocery distribution, a food broker network on fixed commission would have to be set up.

Not only hadn't my company heard of *Guidelines for Food Brokers*, but when we appointed seven brokers to test our change in emphasis on Lysol from drug to household, management continued to ask questions and wondered when the broker would take title to the merchandise.

At the time, our own sales force of drug-oriented salesmen were improperly supervised. Many moonlighted and actually had other jobs, falsifying their sales reports. When a new man was hired as sales manager, I gave him the names of five salesmen, one in each region, to run a follow-check on. None of the five were where they were supposed to be on their itinerary. The next week's expenses showed them to be on their itinerary. As a result, we fired five salesmen and then started to build our sales organization and the household positioning of Lysol Liquid.

Even the freight classification under which Lysol was shipped had to be changed from the classification of external medicine to the commodity classification of soaps and detergents.

As we started to make our strategic moves in these areas, I was told that I didn't understand our business, but fortunately conditions were so bad, management was willing to go along on faith. Of course, that logic worked both ways and saved me a lot of explanations because I used the same lines about the grocery business. In other words, you (management) just don't understand the grocery business, and you have to do it this way.

In 1960, we also started to execute plans to improve our position in the toiletry area, introducing Stri-Dex, which is still the number two item in sales for teenage acne problems.

In 1961, we bought Noreen Hair Rinse, which gave us additional cash flow to support our other efforts. Medi-Quik First Aid Spray was introduced. Beacon Wax was acquired in July 1965; this led to the introduction of Mop & Glow in 1972. There were, over the years, other new products such as Wet Ones and many lines were extended. Most have been successful.

Now, getting back to Lysol and how we "disinfected its image." The listed problems and many others in the environment had to be corrected and handled concurrently while we were attacking Lysol Liquid's particular problems.

In reviewing Lysol Liquid, we decided that we knew the advertising was wrong. So we stopped the advertising to save our money. Could anything be more embarrassing than stopping the advertising only to find sales starting to grow? That's exactly what happened. To put it mildly, something was dreadfully wrong. It wasn't just the advertising campaign, either. There was something wrong with the image of Lysol, a seventy-year-old product that was declining in the market. Many younger housewives didn't even know its uses. Traditionally known as a strong disinfectant for killing disease germs or as a feminine douche, Lysol was confined to a hard but diminishing nucleus—the compulsive user segment of the market.

How did the erosion of this brand and its isolation in the market happen? Often in the urge to say something different, to overcome the fatigue generated by repetition of the basic selling idea, advertising will be developed that does not forcibly communicate the basic reasons for the existence of the product in the first place: those all-important core compulsions that were responsible for the initial growth of the brand and caused the consumer to initially purchase the product.

We decided to get down to basic compulsions to find the core again by completely reevaluating Lysol: the product, its markets, its image.*

All advertising was stopped as part of this evaluation, which is how our team found out that advertising was actually blocking—materially and psychologically—Lysol's growth. It was an unpleasant surprise.

Other discoveries were not surprising but equally unpleasant. For instance, although distribution was excellent albeit in the wrong place in the retail outlet, Lysol was invariably classified as an emergency drug item, which automatically limited its household use. Lysol's advertising helped publicize this limitation. Such headlines as "New Killer Germs on the Rise" were used over case history ads full of purple prose about the imminence of disease.

Our old ads seemed to appeal to buyers who had just come through a flood or hurricane or found themselves in the middle of an epidemic. Rejecting the idea of a market bounded by disaster victims, we set out to change Lysol's entire marketing point of view. The result was that the seventy-year-old looked more and more like a new baby.

The prime objective was deceptively simple: close the communication gap between Lysol and the younger housewives, while holding onto the current users of the product (mostly older women who kept getting older every time a Lysol survey was made). Their median age had advanced from thirty-five to forty-five in the ten-year period ending 1957—and by 1961, we felt the median age was well over fifty.

The product image had to be modified. Instead of a special-purpose product, Lysol had to be made over into an all-purpose cleaner—part of the housewife's daily routine. Since advertising was principally responsible for Lysol's market isolation, it received major attention; we rigorously avoided any change in the package or any change in the basic

*In addition to the writer, the original team that repositioned Lysol were Samuel F. Melcher, then Lysol Product Manager, now President of Glenbrook Laboratories; Dr. Thomas Harrison, then Director of New Products, now a consultant to Glenbrook Laboratories and Lehn & Fink Products Co. for new products; the late Edward Gumpert, Senior Vice President, Geyer, Morey and Ballard Advertising Agency.

product. We have had minor changes in package since. The only reason we retained the directions for feminine hygiene for a period of time was for legal reasons. Every person who came in contact with Lysol wanted to change the package. When properly investigated, we found that a change could be harmful. We worked to determine how advertising might project the new image. Copy was tested to discover which themes could make consumers aware of the household need for Lysol, which would persuade them to buy, which would get them to buy again.

Lysol planners and the agency became convinced that television offered the best opportunity for getting across the Lysol story to the young housewife. In fact, it was the only means to properly demonstrate the new household usage concept.

The new commercials, all developed around Lysol's revised "core selling idea," were pretested at Schwerin Research, Inc. The resulting commercial made a new claim: ordinary cleaning might not be effective against germs that cause odors and illness—but Lysol added to regular cleaning water would clean throughout the house.

From its opening line, "Even the most careful mothers can't completely protect families from household germs," the commercial followed the advice of Ernest Dichter, the motivational researcher we hired to guide us around psychological pitfalls. A possible pitfall was averted in the opening line itself: "We did not want to have any housewife think we were implying she was a bad housekeeper."

In the eight-month reevaluation of Lysol, we were faced with old traditions as well as old images. One such tradition was Lysol's summer vacation from advertising, the reason being that the housewife was just not that much concerned with the problems of germs and illness during the summertime. However, the laboratory analysis of Lysol gave a clue to expanding its market. Lysol was also found effective in getting rid of bacteria that cause mildew, mold, and fungus that leads to skin infections, and household odors—and so a "hot weather" commercial was created to show how Lysol could solve these problems.

The break with traditions also extended to the way Lysol used television. In 1961, we pioneered a unique method of purchasing TV participations that permitted a high degree of dispersion of message. It allowed us, a comparatively small advertiser, to enjoy the full scope of television's usefulness, with reach equal to many of the soap giants that seem to dominate the TV scene.

Lysol's strategy was to rotate spot announcements on several programs rather than concentrate on a single show; with this "scatter plan" only one commercial appeared on the same program within a given time period each week. Under this plan, which was carried out with a budget 60 percent lower than former expenditures, Lysol commercials reached more than 90 percent of American TV homes. (However, the old rule of not getting something for nothing still holds true. What Lysol gained in reach, it lost in frequency of reaching the same homes.)

While Lysol Liquid's image was being disinfected, we questioned the original aerosol disinfectant spray research. Dr. Tom Harrison structured a new consumer placement market research project, using the Lysol name with a different positioning from the previous research. When the results came in on April 19, 1961, we thought we had a winner. The new research confirmed the previous research in that only 4 percent would use the product as a disinfectant only. So the original research conclusions that 96 percent did not want the product were authenticated. With our new positioning we found, in addition, that Lysol Spray Disinfectant was used by 49 percent of the respondents as a deodorizer only and 47 percent as a deodorizer/disinfectant. We found 72 percent of the respondents ready to buy the product.

Armed with the results of our $500 consumer placement study, we now had to convince our various publics that the good old Lysol brand could be extended and had a bright future.

Our worst skeptics and toughest sale was to be with our board of directors and management. The personnel within the organization were the most supportive in changing policies and knocking down old shibboleths to permit us to succeed.

My immediate superior didn't want any product that would exceed $2.5 million in sales because he felt we could not compete with the large "soapers." We test marketed at a consumer price of $1.29 with 40 percent drug markup, but in Ohio using Ruth Lyons on daytime WLW-TV we tested a price of 98¢ with a 30 percent trade markup.

As a result of the Ohio test, we predicted first-year sales of $10 million. In presenting our plans to the budget committee of the board (outside directors) we promised only $5 million first-year sales, which could be obtained on a break-even basis. The presentation was made on Black Friday, May 1962 (the day the stock market had a great decline). The retired chairman of the board stated that based on his 45 ½ years with the company, the company had never had a $5 million product, that in his opinion it would never have a $5 million product and if it did the company wouldn't know how to handle it. Although I pointed out that our risk was minimal, the meeting broke up without a decision.

Later I was able to convince the president it was worth the risk and we introduced our product in the fall of 1962. First-year results were just under $10 million—our tests had been on the mark. When the results came in, one of the directors remarked that we were lucky, for we had estimated only $5 million in sales the first year.

Lysol had truly disinfected its image. Now more than ninety years old, Lysol has continued to prosper by introducing further new line extensions and overcoming many challenges and inhibiting theories such as a product life cycle.

Everyone who has had a part in Lysol's success can't help but take great satisfaction out of the new worlds that were conquered. I feel that this type of opportunity exists in many of our businesses today. How many products that were winners in their day have lost out through misdirected changes in advertising appeals, flavor, appearance of product, or appearance of package? How many times has the original reason for success been lost? My message is be slow and careful to make changes until you are certain you have found the correct answer, then prepare yourself, sell hard, and make the change boldly.

□   □   □

Roger M. Kirk, Jr., is Vice Chairman of the Board of the Brown & Williamson Tobacco Corporation in Louisville. Mr. Kirk joined Brown & Williamson in 1977 as President and Chief Operating Officer, as well as a member of the Board of Directors. In April 1979 he was elected to his present position.

Mr. Kirk was associated with Sterling Drug from 1959 until 1977. He was elected a Corporate Vice President and President of Sterling's Lehn & Fink Product Co. Division in 1970, a Corporate Director in 1971, and Executive Vice President in 1975.

During his career at Sterling Drug, Mr. Kirk had executive responsibilities for several of the company's major multiunit interests, including pharmaceuticals, household products, toiletries, and industrial products. He was in charge of reorganizing into a group four principal Sterling businesses: Winthrop Laboratories, Glenbrook Laboratories, Breon Laboratories, and Cook-Waite Laboratories. Products of these companies comprise a wide range of well-known ethical, proprietary, and dental products, including Bayer Aspirin.

While president of the Lehn & Fink Division, Mr. Kirk had total divisional marketing responsibilities for cosmetics (including Dorothy Gray, Ogilvie, Tussy, and Givenchy), consumer products (Lysol brands, Beacon Wax, Mop & Glo, and Wet Ones Moist Towelettes), and industrial products. Also reporting to him were vice presidents of manufacturing, distribution, finance, research and development, new products development, industrial and employee relations.

Mr. Kirk's early background was in sales and marketing. He began his career in 1937 with Standard Brands, gaining experience in sales, distributor relations, and product management. From 1949 to 1954, he was Director of Marketing for John H. Dulany & Sons, Inc., and from 1954 to 1956 he served as Merchandising Manager for National Biscuit Company. He then joined Cook Chemical Company as Vice President of Sales and Advertising. In 1959 he became Sales Manager of Lehn & Fink, progressing to General Manager, Group Vice President, Executive Vice President, and then to President in 1970.

For five years he was a member of the Grocery Manufacturers Association National Marketing Committee of which he was Chairman for three years. In 1972 at the GMA National Convention he was given an award "In recognition and appreciation of the valuable contributions you have made to the Grocery Industry." He was also a member of the GMA Long-Range Planning Committee; director and vice president of the New York Sales Executives Club; director of Cosmetic, Toiletry and Fragrance Association, 1973–1976; member of the National Board of Trustees and the National Finance Committee of the Children's Asthma Research Institute and Hospital in Denver, Colorado, 1972–1977, receiving their Humanitarian Award in 1971.

Mr. Kirk, a native of Chicago, received a BS degree from the University of Illinois in 1940 and served in the U.S. Navy from 1943 to 1946.

*Aubrey C. Lewis*

# The Direct-Honest Approach

*The direct-honest approach* is frequently called the best approach. That certainly has held true in my lifetime and has been my lifestyle. Being a person who cannot say no, I have become a member of the Board of Trustees of many organizations. The main function of these boards generally is to raise funds so that the organization can survive. That is, and was, the case with the United Cerebral Palsy of North Jersey Unit that was about to go bankrupt.

I was invited to a breakfast meeting so that I might see children with cerebral palsy and other handicaps enter the school building for morning therapy. This was a perfect way to persuade me of the importance of not only joining the Board of Trustees but assuming the position of President.

The importance of keeping the facility open was readily understood. The children and the parents of these victims of cerebral palsy had benefited greatly from the services rendered there. The main question was, "How does one generate interest that can be transformed into dollars needed to keep the center open?"

My first order of the day was to rejuvenate a Board that had become a little timid after numerous fund-raising attempts had failed. They had to become believers in the Center and in me if we were to succeed. No matter how you turned it or shaped it, the end result was the same: we needed money now.

It was mentioned that we should have a fund-raising event. I said that we would shoot for a net of $50,000 to $100,000. The Board members looked at me in disbelief. They wanted to know the name or names of people who could generate ticket sales to get the anticipated return. Would you believe they even reluctantly budgeted $1500 up-front money?

**179**

I had read in the papers several days before that Donald MacNaughton, Chairman of the Board of Prudential Insurance Company of North America, had announced his retirement after ten years of excellent service. His name would certainly draw a crowd.

Even though we had an executive from Prudential on our Board, we were hesitant about contacting him, for we had heard that MacNaughton frowned on being the recipient of accolades and honors. I said in a rather positive manner that I would get Donald MacNaughton to say yes, and we would call it a farewell to a giant in the business community.

Because I was a member of the New Jersey Sports and Exposition Authority, I had the opportunity to work with Don MacNaughton on this $300 million plus sports complex housing Giant Stadium and the Meadowlands Race Track.

I reached into my phone book, called him directly and got his secretary, who, in turn, put him on the line, and I popped the question. It went something like this: "Don . . . Aubrey." "Yes, Aubrey?" "Don, we would like to honor you for all that you have done in the New Jersey business community." "Honor me?" He went on to say he had made it a practice not to be involved in these kinds of events, so immediately I said, "Don, we are really not honoring you. We need you to fill the seats so that we can raise funds for children with cerebral palsy." Don kind of chuckled and said, "Give me the date, time, and place."

We "honored" him and raised $66,000, which kept the center open, prevented the unit from going bankrupt, and started what could be considered a remarkable program.

It was a night to remember—governors, both past and present, business leaders, community leaders, and just plain folks came out to share this night with Don and us.

While the affair was being developed, the confidence level of each Board member was raised to such a degree that projects thought impossible earlier became a commonplace expectation. The people to be sold had to be determined first—the Board, the honoree, the cause for which this event was established, and the type of event. Once that was known, the rest was history. Each time we decided on an issue or an item, we would simply ask, "Is it first class or top shelf?" If it was, we did it; if it wasn't, we didn't.

After the affair, we met to discuss our accomplishments and one of the members looked at me and said, "I believe, I believe, walk the water." What he was really saying was, "I am sold on your ability to motivate us and to follow through to see it to a detailed conclusion."

The affair was structured with two points in mind—creativity and elegance—with each guest feeling like a member of one family.

It is my belief that most people do not come close to their potential, intellectually or physically, without some sort of prodding or motivation. This can be an inner or outer motivation: never say die, . . . bounce back when things don't seem to be going your way . . . take a deep breath and push on . . . above all, consider the well being of the other person when making the decision.

As a former athlete, high school teacher and coach, and FBI agent, and now as a businessman, the one sales performance that I consider most gratifying was an early decision that I would not allow myself or my associates the opportunity to say we can't go on. We are tired. By pushing forward one more step, each seemingly unattainable goal has been attained. This works in athletics, it works in community organizations, and it works in our daily business lives.

Characteristics that are foremost are honesty, forthrightness, and the ability to convince business associates—subordinates and superiors—to work with you and not for you.

It is my style to give credit to the initiator of an idea even if it was planted there in the first place.

It is easier to win if you understand the components that make it possible.

□   □   □

Aubrey C. Lewis, a native and resident of Montclair, New Jersey, is Corporate Vice President for Organization Planning, F.W. Woolworth Co. He joined F.W. Woolworth Co. in 1967.

Mr. Lewis is also a part-time television sports commentator for local high school football games on New York station WPIX-11. In addition, he is the commentator for other special events, such as the African-American Day Parade, which are televised on WPIX-11.

Mr. Lewis is an active participant in the National Urban League's Black Executive Exchange Program (BEEP) in which, on his own time, he appears at colleges and universities throughout the country encouraging students toward careers in Business.

Lewis is a graduate of the University of Notre Dame where he received a bachelor of science degree in education in 1958. He then taught English, science, hygiene, and physical education and served as head coach for football and track in a New Jersey high school.

An All-American high school athlete, Lewis went on to become national collegiate 440-yard hurdles champion, breaking the existing record while at the University of Notre Dame. The first black to be elected captain of an athletic team at Notre Dame, Lewis as track captain established another world record in the 60-yard dash. Lewis was starting halfback on the football team for three years, from 1955 to 1957, and was named to the All-Midwest and All-American squads. He was selected to play in the East-West Shrine Game in 1957.

In 1962 Lewis was appointed an FBI agent. He trained in Washington, D.C., and Quantico, Virginia, and served in the territory covered by FBI headquarters in Cincinnati and New York for 5½ years in criminal and intelligence matters. He also taught police science and was a firearms and defensive tactics instructor.

One of Lewis' most significant and far-reaching community-related endeavors involved his membership on the New Jersey Sports and Exposition Authority. For seven years he was a Commissioner of this Authority which had raised the funds and developed the plan for what is now a successful sports complex. He was chairman of the Authority's Affirmative Action Committee. In this position he was the chief coordinator of a program involving the Authority, unions, contractors and the community, which has been cited as one of the best affirmative action packages ever put together for blacks, women, and other minorities in the nation.

In a most significant commitment to national concern, Lewis responded to a call from the U.S. Armed Services for assistance in seeking solutions to human relations problems involving hostilities between black and white servicemen that threatened to erode America's military effectiveness overseas. He traveled to U.S. military installations in Europe and in person-to-person sensitivity sessions utilized his understanding of human nature and needs, and individual and group prides, to get to the root of much of the intergroup hostilities then in existence. His subsequent report and recommendations to the Pentagon were unanimously accepted and incorporated in a military program which has substantially eliminated much of the racial unrest and improved conditions for military men and their families living abroad.

**Seth C. Macon**

# *Planting Seeds That Grow*

*My time and the talents and energy I possess* have been divided over a lifetime among four primary areas of interest: my family, my job, my church, and my college. This story relates to my college, the oldest coeducational institution in the South. It is Guilford College in Greensboro, North Carolina, a city of 150,000 population that has within its city limits three colleges and two universities.

The school was chartered in 1834 and opened its doors in 1837 to 25 boys and 25 girls, all of whom were members of the Society of Friends, a religious movement that began in England in the second half of the seventeenth century. The school grew into a full-fledged college in 1889. It is still a small liberal arts college, the only Quaker college in the South, and one of the few schools in the South, perhaps the only one, that continued in operation without interruption throughout the years of the Civil War (known in the South as the Northern Aggression).

The beautiful and well-kept Guilford College campus is located on 325 acres in the western edge of Greensboro. The college is strong scholastically, well-managed, and sound financially, but has always had something of a financial struggle. Even today, after 142 years, it has an endowment of only about $6 million.

In the late 1950s, a one-sentence, handwritten (penciled) letter arrived at Guilford College: "Tell me about your college." It was signed "Charles A. Dana," and bore a New York address.

If the President of the college, Dr. Clyde A. Milner, had known the author of that terse note, no doubt he would have responded with great enthusiasm, employing his extensive talents to draft a reply that would capture the imagination of this man of wealth. As it happened, Dr. Milner was not involved. There is some doubt as to whether he even saw the note. The request received routine treatment and a small package of printed material about the college was mailed to Mr. Dana. No one at Guilford College gave the matter a second thought.

Charles Dana's second communication with Guilford was another brief handwritten note asking what he could do to help. This time the note got to Dr. Milner's desk and he inquired about the writer. With more information about the identity of Charles A. Dana, Dr. Milner lost little time in getting to New York for a personal visit.

Many wonderful things happened at Guilford College as a result of financial assistance from Charles Dana. Mr. Dana gave sparingly, using his gifts to challenge alumni and other interested people. He said very quickly that he was willing to invest some of his money, or that of the Dana Foundation, if Guilford College people were willing to invest more of their own.

A $200,000 commitment was made by Mr. Dana with the understanding that $400,000 would be raised by the college to match his gift two for one. The funds were to be used to build a religious education–auditorium–music building on the Guilford campus, a beautiful building known today as Dana Auditorium.

Mr. Dana knew how to get things moving fast. His was a challenge gift of $200,000, but he sent the money promptly saying, "Now get busy and raise your $400,000." A solicitor team was assembled quickly by the college, and a meeting of the solicitors was called so that each worker could pick up prospect cards from which to make at least five solicitations to raise money to meet the challenge. Drafted as a "volunteer solicitor," I went to the meeting to select my cards.

A basic principle of selling that should be established early in my story is that *you must believe in your product*. Why do I have such a strong belief in Guilford College?

My great-grandfather was graduated from Guilford in 1850; two of my older brothers were graduated there prior to my enrollment in 1937. I met my wife there, and we have been happily married for thirty-eight years. (That was really the best sale I ever made!) My two younger sisters attended Guilford—one is a graduate and the other left school to get married. Both of our children were graduated from Guilford.

I have been serving on the Board of Trustees for more than fifteen years, am Chairman of the Finance and Investment Committee and a member of the Development Committee, and have served on the Search Committee for each of the last two Presidents. I *do* believe in Guilford College and derive much satisfaction from working to help it become better.

I surveyed the prospect cards to select my five. The names on two of them are vivid in my memory. One C.E. Leak, a retired Executive Vice

President of my company who had been graduated from Guilford College in 1902 and who had met his wife there when both were students. The other card bore the name of Rufus White, who was a Senior Officer, later to become President, of Pilot Life Insurance Company (an affiliate of Jefferson Standard, where I worked), whose home office is also in Greensboro. Rufus White was not a Guilford College alumnus, but was and is an active leader in the First Friends Meeting in Greensboro.

Since my real story is about a "sale" to C. E. Leak, I will tell you first about my call.on Rufus White.

Rufus was a strong supporter of his alma mater, the University of North Carolina at Chapel Hill. His interest in Guilford at the time was not strong. He had not made any contributions to Guilford, but he had some interest in the school because of his affiliation with the Society of Friends. While I won't take all of the credit for fully developing his interest, I did get a pledge from Rufus and perhaps planted some seeds that grew, because Rufus White today is Chairman of the Board of Trustees at Guilford College and is a considerable benefactor in his own right.

Here is the real story. It begins at C. E. Leak's beautiful home on Kirkpatrick Place in fashionable Irving Park, Greensboro's lovely and expensive residential area. C.E. Leak was, at that time, a widower with a son in Detroit and a daughter in Greensboro who was married to the Executive Vice President of Pilot Life, Ted Lind.

Mr. Leak was easy to talk with because we had two things in common—Jefferson Standard and Guilford College. He quickly admitted that he had not kept up his interest in Guilford over the years. He acknowledged driving past the front entrance of the campus almost weekly on his way to the Jefferson Standard Country Club (for employees) without having set foot on the campus for at least twenty-five years.

He soon began reminiscing about his college days, some of his experiences there, meeting his future wife, and other things he recalled from his years at Guilford. I challenged Mr. Leak to let me make plans for him to visit the campus. He readily agreed and we set the date for the following Saturday morning.

Immediately after leaving the Leak home, I called President Milner, explaining the circumstances, and made a date for Saturday morning in his office. I suggested that Dr. Milner and I take Mr. Leak on a tour of the campus ending in the library where, we hoped, the librarian would have available some records of the class of 1902 that might interest him.

Saturday morning found the three of us in Dr. Milner's office, and there followed a tour of the beautiful campus as we had planned. Although we didn't find any pictures, the librarian was very helpful and we were able to get some information about the members of Mr. Leak's class and some of the things that were happening at Guilford in his day.

As the conversation developed, we talked about what Mr. Leak might do in the way of a pledge toward meeting the Dana challenge. Mr. Leak explained that he had given $7500 to the West Market Street United Methodist Church in Greensboro in memory of his wife and that he might consider a gift to Guilford College for the same purpose and of the same amount. This was good news—I had been hoping for a pledge for $1000 (the minimum amount required to get his name on the plaque in the foyer in the new building).

Mr. Leak had retired from his daily duties at the company, but he remained on the Finance Committee, which met each Wednesday to approve investments and make other management decisions. This brought him downtown weekly. On one of his trips, he appeared in my office with a Jefferson Standard stock certificate in the name of Guilford College for a sufficient number of shares to provide a $10,000 gift.

After a brief visit and my hearty expressions of thanks, I rushed out of my office to personally deliver the stock certificate to the Business Manager at Guilford. Subsequent chance meetings with C.E. Leak always resulted in his bringing up the subject of Guilford College. It was constantly on his mind. We continued to talk about it.

Dr. Milner and I made another call on Mr. Leak to talk with him about subsequent contributions. He explained that he did not feel that he could give Guilford College more than he had given the church where he and Mrs. Leak had been active over the years. He was, however, willing to talk. He enjoyed our visits and obviously he had a growing interest in Guilford.

Before many months had passed, Mr. Leak arrived again in my office with another stock certificate in the name of Guilford College . . . and then another . . . and another. His four gifts over a couple of years amounted to $40,000.

As time passed my story advanced not at all. Mr. Leak paid frequent friendly visits conversing about how things were going at Guilford, asking about Mr. Dana's continued interest, President Milner's forthcoming retirement, and other items of general interest at the college.

Mr. Leak's interest in company investments and his personal holdings caused him to keep a close eye on the stock market quotations. On his next visit to my office, I was somewhat disappointed not to see a piece of paper in his hand with a pretty border on it. Instead, he had a question on his mind. He asked: "Did Guilford College sell those shares of Jefferson Standard stock or did they keep them as a part of their investment portfolio?"

I didn't know the answer, but it would be easy to find out. I immediately turned to the telephone and dialed David Parsons, the Business Manager, to relay the question. David explained that Guilford had investments in Jefferson Standard stock in its regular endowment fund and that the shares given by Mr. Leak had been kept—not sold.

Mr. Leak beamed as he received the answer because he knew immediately that his $40,000 gift was then worth $60,000. We talked about this fine appreciation in the value of the stock. Both of us expressed the wish that he could get the additional $20,000 deductible for income tax purposes, but we quickly admitted to each other that this was not a possibility.

Following that visit, I immediately called President Milner to arrange for us to make one more trip to see Mr. Leak at home. We arrived at the Leak residence on a beautiful spring afternoon and sat on the back porch, where the three of us talked further about Guilford.

This call, however, was not made without some important preparation. Guilford's Development Officer, David Morrah, was a graduate in architectural engineering from North Carolina State University. He had drawn for us a sketch of a unique type of Seminar Room that could be built at that time (preinflation) for approximately $100,000.

Our sales talk to Mr. Leak on this visit conveyed the idea that we would be glad to count his original $40,000 gift at its present value of $60,000 if he would give us another $40,000 to complete the $100,000 required to build the "Leak Seminar Room." We then zeroed in on the uniqueness of the Seminar Room designed by David Morrah.

The room may be difficult to visualize, but it is worth the effort because it is unique. Duke Memorial Hall, which was built on the campus in 1897 (with a $10,000 gift from B. N. and J. B. Duke in memory of their sister), was to be renovated. The building had a basement at the back. The building was to have a second entrance added at the rear, so that it would face in both directions with a beautiful entrance at each end.

The new entrance would be at ground level into an attractive lobby area and a foyer to the new Leak Seminar Room. The room would have the appearance of an amphitheater with semicircular seating, each row of seats twenty-four inches lower than the row behind it. The top row was to be at ground level and the bottom row at basement level. The speaker's platform would be at the end of the half-oval at basement level. The room would be beautifully panelled with a unique treatment for perfect acoustics.

The Leak Seminar Room as completed is distinctive in every detail. Each seat is a front-row seat because there is no obstruction of view. It is used frequently. In the foyer hang appropriate portraits of Mr. and Mrs. C.E. Leak.

Another aspect of the "sale" story, one in which Dr. Milner and I had no direct part, is the fact that Mr. Leak kept his word by doing as much for the West Market Street United Methodist Church as he did for Guilford College. As a result, from Commerce Place between West Market Street and Friendly Avenue in Greensboro is the entrance to what is now the beautiful Leak Chapel, an addition to the church built in memory of Mr. and Mrs. Leak.

Until his death, Mr. Leak enjoyed talking about the Leak Seminar Room at Guilford College. I worried at times about what his children really thought of his giving away so much of "their inheritance," but this part of the story has a happy ending, too. His daughter, Elizabeth Lind Smith, later told me how much joy her father received in his later years as a result of these gifts he saw put to such good use.

Perhaps Mr. Leak didn't give *sacrificially*. Maybe he didn't even give until it hurt. But I have the distinct feeling that he gave until it *felt good*.

My success in winning financial support from Mr. Leak for his alma mater gave me courage to accept still another prospect card. This time my call was on a retired Senior Vice President and substantial stockholder in Jefferson Standard. (All the stock is now in the Jefferson-Pilot Corporation—a holding company that owns Jefferson Standard, Pilot Life, and a number of other subsidiaries.)

This man, Joseph McKinley Bryan, and his wife, Kathleen Price Bryan, are substantial philanthropists in the Southeast. They have made their contributions wisely, enriching and enhancing the quality of life for many people. Evidence of this is provided by the Bryan Enrichment Center in Greensboro, a substantial gift to Duke University, gifts to Converse College, Belmont Abbey, the University of North Carolina, and many other well-selected philanthropies.

Joe Bryan's only direct connection with Guilford College that I knew of was the fact that one of his three children was a graduate of the college. My appeal to Mr. Bryan was based on the idea that Guilford College, because of its importance to the greater Greensboro community, should have on its campus something that would connect with the institution the names of Joseph M. Bryan and Kathleen Price Bryan.

A sizable dormitory had been built on the campus, partly with borrowed funds and with a series of small contributions, no one of which was adequate to provide for naming the building. The building was known simply as the 1968 Dormitory.

The Board of Trustees authorized the Development Officer to provide me with a proposal that would name the building for anyone who would give Guilford one-third of the construction cost. The proposal was presented by me to the Bryans, resulting in their gift of a quarter of a million dollars. This met the requirement and changed the 1968 Dormitory to Bryan Hall.

Every time I drive to Bryan Hall, visit the Leak Seminar Room on the Guilford College campus, or observe Rufus White's enthusiasm for Guilford as he presides at Trustee Meetings, I experience a very warm feeling about some special people who had a vision and did something about it. It all began with those three-by-five prospect cards typed with the names of Rufus White, C.E. Leak, and Joseph M. Bryan.

*Salesmen turn ideas into reality.* This is what creative selling is all about!

□   □   □

Seth C. Macon, Senior Vice President–Agency of Jefferson Standard Life Insurance Company, is a member of the company's Board of Directors and serves on the company's Finance Committee. He is also a Vice President and Director of Jefferson-Pilot Corporation. During 1976–1977 he served as Chairman of the Board of the Life Insurance Marketing and Research Association (LIMRA), headquartered in Hartford, Connecticut. Mr. Macon served on the LIMRA Board of Directors from 1974 to 1978 and the Executive Committee of the LIMRA Agency Officers Round Table from 1973 to 1978.

Mr. Macon is a native of North Carolina and a 1940 graduate of Guilford College in Greensboro. He joined Jefferson Standard soon after graduation from college and worked in the company's Raleigh, Tampa, and Asheville Regional Agency Offices. In 1946, Mr. Macon joined the Agency Department of Jefferson Standard. After attending the Institute of Insurance Marketing at Southern Methodist University, he directed the company's training program for agents for more than ten years.

He has been a Senior Officer of the company since 1960. Effective May 4, 1970, he was elected to his present position of Senior Vice President–Agency, with overall responsibility for the Jefferson Standard Agency Department and all field insurance operations throughout the company's territory—comprising thirty-two states, the District of Columbia, and Puerto Rico.

Mr. Macon has served on the Board of the Institute of Insurance Marketing, and as Chairman of both the Management Development Committee and the Executive Development Committee of the Life Insurance Marketing and Research Association (LIMRA). He has held the Chartered Life Underwriter designation since 1949 and is a 1958 graduate of the Executive Program, University of North Carolina at Chapel Hill. He is the author of two books on life insurance agent recruiting, *Action in Recruiting* and *Recruiting—Today's Number One Priority in Agency Management.* He is a member of the Golden Key Society of the American College of Life Underwriters.

Active in civic and church affairs, Mr. Macon is a member of the Board of Trustees of Guilford College and is Chairman of the Board's Finance and Investment Committee. He received the Guilford College

Distinguished Alumnus Award for 1978. In 1974 he completed a third term as Chairman of Deacons of First Baptist Church, Greensboro. He has served as a Director of the Piedmont Sales Executives Club and of the Greensboro Rotary Club. He is a member of Starmount Country Club, Greensboro, and the Greensboro City Club.

[Note. Since this chapter was written, the author has been elected Chairman of the Board of Trustees of Guilford College.]

*Edward A. McCabe*

# A Massive Selling
Effort
That Failed

*This is the story of a massive selling effort* that failed, and of salesmen who somehow couldn't get the message.

Long ago I heard it said—and I hope it's still true—that in that wondrous world of politics a man's word must be his bond, his handshake on a deal a pledge more solemn than any with a wax and ribbon seal.

President Eisenhower used to say that if you made a promise you had no need to remember how you said it. Ike's syntax was often lampooned, but you could bank on his word—because that's the way he was.

I worked as a staff aide in the Eisenhower White House the last five of his Presidential years. We were a small group and I was the youngest of his so-called senior staff. I worked at legal counsel chores and at Congressional liaison. Working with Capitol Hill over those years I became a friend of Barry Goldwater, the affable Arizona Senator whose 1964 Presidential candidacy sold as poorly through the country as Ike's legislative program sold in the 1950s to that partisan Congress.

When Mr. Eisenhower became a full-time Gettysburg farmer in 1961, I returned to private law practice in Washington. Though back at my first calling, my interest in the political world remained strong. I was close to Republican party affairs. And through people in the news media, plus Congressional friends in both parties, I had a general awareness of developments across the political spectrum. My overriding interest, however, was the practice of law, since that's where I earned my living and where the future was.

Like everyone else, though, by the middle of 1963 I could see that my friend from Arizona had caught the public's fancy. Barry Goldwater was by then the man to beat if you wanted to be the Republican nominee for President in 1964. Several aspiring campaigners had precisely that in mind—Nelson Rockefeller chiefly, plus a half dozen others whose hopes were destined to be shorter lived than Rockefeller's. Out of the combat zone and indecisive about running, yet much sought after, was Pennsylvania's Governor William Scranton. And watching from greater distance was the canniest political operative of all, the formidable Richard Nixon.

Fascinating to me was the fact I knew and had worked with most of these people. They all shared an important characteristic. They were what the news media chose to call Eisenhower Republicans—the so-called moderates, regularly contrasted with Senator Goldwater, who made no apology for his conservative label. Later events showed what astute observers knew then—there weren't many differences among Goldwater, Eisenhower, and all these others in their basic approaches to government. However, while Barry was his own man (as was Nixon), the others tried endlessly to position themselves next to the former President, hoping some of Ike's immense popularity might spill over on them. Even more, they sought his endorsement, his blessing. Just a nod from Ike would help them head off the fast-moving rider from Arizona—or so they thought. This is how it was late in the summer of 1963, with the nominating convention set for the following July and the general election just over a year away.

Law practice was exciting too. Among other things, I had been immersed for months in the concerns of a client whose business operations were heavily affected by the Billy Sol Estes case. It was a busy time for me, absorbing and enjoyable. This was where I belonged.

My phone rang. Would I be willing to lend a hand in Barry's campaign? How big a hand? He wasn't thinking of anything full time. Doing what? Would I come over and talk about it? Sure. It was just a ten-minute cab ride to Capitol Hill.

My agreement to help was subject to a final answer I would give in a few days. It would be a spare-time thing and, for greater independence, I wanted no pay and would work from my own office. I could sense something of a general factotum role in the making. No great involvement in any one area for long. First I would organize a program for the Senator to consult regularly with experts in a wide range of public policy areas. Additionally, as a friend of his and a former White House staffer, I would be part of Barry's so-called inner circle. A tempting venture—if I could find time for it.

My law partners and my wife gave it their blessing. That left one more call to make. President Eisenhower. Although no formal announcement was planned, my involvement with the Goldwater campaign would soon be known. There was no news interest in me, but there would be publicity in a "former Ike aide" joining Barry's team. So I wanted The Boss (as we called him) to know promptly what was up, and to hear it first from me. I phoned his secretary and drove the sixty-five miles to Gettysburg the next morning—a journey I would make often in the months to come.

The President was most cordial, as he always was, and we had a long visit. Though I wouldn't for a minute have tried to sell anything to that genial old warrior, there nevertheless was a sale of sorts, a pledge, a commitment, made that morning that had a strong impact on the 1964 Presidential campaign—and possibly on the Presidency itself through the decade that followed.

Ike talked freely about 1964. He regarded President Kennedy as a disaster, and wanted mightily to see a Republican replace him. He had a "minimum of high regard" for the whole Kennedy entourage and their approach to government and politics. Even so, Ike was enough the political realist to know there was a large Kennedy fan club out there, and that 1964 would at best be a hard year for whichever Republican became his party's nominee. He was also enough the political realist to say to me that morning that as things shaped up that late summer of 1963 no Republican was likely to beat Barry Goldwater for the 1964 nomination.

An aside here, as I saw it. Eisenhower liked Goldwater personally. Although Barry said and did things that irritated him, he seemed not to stay annoyed for long. Some things Ike said and did irritated Barry too, but he didn't stay upset for long either. In his 1979 book *With No Apologies,* commenting on the six presidents he has known while serving in the Senate, Barry said, "Dwight Eisenhower was the best of the lot. . . . It was a blessed privilege to know him and to serve with him." They were alike in many ways, these two—friendly, direct, confident, at peace with themselves. Their political and governmental views were not dissimilar; essentially they were those of the traditional orthodox Republican.

Back at Gettysburg that bright September morning, we sat in the General's office, a comfortable room on the second floor of what had been the home of the president of Gettysburg College. Ike was an active man, tending always to animate his surroundings. At one point in our conversation he paused, turned his chair to face his deak, and put those two big hands on the desk top in what was a gesture characteristic of him. He looked squarely at me and said—"Ed, you tell Barry for me that I'm not going to endorse him. I know you're not asking me to do that, but I want him to know I'm not going to endorse anyone else either. When the Convention is over I'll campaign for our nominee as much as he wants me to and as much as the doctors let me."

I told him I would convey that to Senator Goldwater, and I did so the same day. This was important campaign intelligence, because we knew that in a close race for the nomination Ike's stance might well control the outcome.

He extended an invitation for Barry to call on him at Gettysburg any time. There were a number of such visits before and after the nomination, and communication between them was good all the way through. I made many trips to Gettysburg during those next fifteen months—some with Senator Goldwater; more often alone; at times with my friend Bryce Harlow, trusted colleague of White House years and confidant of several presidents. Issues arose in the campaign that needed discussion and prompt clarification. But we never again expressly discussed endorsing or opposing anyone for the nomination. We didn't need to. Ike had told us where he stood. We could bank on what he said—because that's the way he was.

There were others, however, who made a different reading of those signs from Gettysburg.

With Goldwater a clear frontrunner, it seemed that most of the hopefuls decided their best shot at Barry was via Eisenhower—either through Ike's direct endorsement or by getting him to oppose Goldwater. We were confident this wouldn't happen because the General had told us so, but they kept pushing him—and they had every right to try. Their mistake, I believe, came in wanting so much to involve him against Goldwater they convinced themselves he would do it. They should have known better. But political ambition and good judgment are often strangers.

It was quite a drive they put on, over many months. Candidates, emissaries, messengers, supporters, promoters—all beating a steady path to Gettysburg, and many holding press conferences afterward. Typically, each seemed to say: "I'm much encouraged after talking with the President." Did he endorse you? "Well, I'd rather not quote the President, but I am encouraged." Will he join a stop-Goldwater effort? "I'd prefer not to talk about other candidates, but I do feel our campaign is now about to move into high gear." So they came and went, one after another, all of them making news along the way. Meanwhile, from Barry's camp we maintained communication—without too much discordant comment on these Gettysburg efforts of the others.

Early primaries sifted people out. Soon Rockefeller was the only real opponent left. His harsh, hard-fisted attacks and the often raucous response of Barry's supporters would leave much Republican blood on the trail, to delight Democrats in the fall—but when Goldwater beat him in the California primary it was all over for anyone who could count. Barry now had so many delegates his nomination was a formality.

Bill Scranton was my choice for vice president. Goldwater liked him and they knew each other well. Their views—for anyone who would look—did not differ much. A former congressman with a nice touch of the aristocrat, Scranton was a popular governor of Pennsylvania. He was well liked across the party spectrum. I know General Eisenhower liked him. Some well-placed Republicans say that had Ike decided to drop Nixon as his running mate in 1956, Bill Scranton would have replaced him. However that may be, Scranton was in my view the best national Republican to balance the 1964 ticket. That ticket, headed by Goldwater, would have faced an uphill pull in the best of times—more so after the Kennedy assassination—but it was now hurt and limping after the mauling campaign with Rockefeller.

With the primaries done and the convention a month away, time was short for final work about a running mate. I was touting Scranton.

Suddenly—a bombshell. A group of Scranton supporters, in an especially shrill attack on Goldwater, announced that the Governor was getting into the race—going for the top spot. Their drive, it seemed, would be in two parts. Attack Goldwater, Rockefeller style. And the real imperative: count on Ike's endorsement.

Quickly there were predictions, inside and outside Scranton's camp, that the former President would endorse the Governor—this to be the big lift his last-minute plunge was searching for. There were feverish efforts to get Ike to do it. Self-starters from all sides of the question swarmed to Gettysburg. Pressure on the General, already intense, was stepped up. Some came from his own family. Scranton's indecisiveness had long since buried any chance for the nomination, but unwisely Bill had let himself be pushed. The same pushers kept pushing at Ike, harder. Impatient, at times to the point of intolerance that he had his own view of the fitness of such a thing—these Scranton advocates seemed to feel Ike had some duty to do for them what they and their candidate couldn't do themselves. And every time they got too pushy, things backfired. Classic among their efforts to push the old soldier was one convoluted operation where the New York *Herald Tribune* published an Eisenhower statement of principles and trumpeted on page one that it was Ike's endorsement of Scranton over Goldwater. Showing his irritation, Ike publicly replied that was not so; that he did not endorse Scranton.

General Eisenhower's unwillingness to endorse Scranton was a circumstance that surprised many (including segments of the media) but it was no surprise to me. He had told me the previous September he would endorse no one. Through the whole campaign, including the clamor of that frenetic drive for Scranton, I never doubted it.

One lesson Bill Scranton's supporters failed to heed is that essential political intelligence must be assessed carefully. Wishful thinking is not the way. He was badly served by those who pushed him, too late, into a harsh campaign so foreign to his character, and keyed to so major a miscalculation. Had he entered months earlier, and run his own type of campaign, he might well have won the nomination. But getting in so late, and running as he did, he never had a chance. And the bitterness of it all, while delighting Democrats, soured too many Republicans.

Unlike Rockefeller, who sulked and did nothing once Goldwater was nominated, Scranton helped personally in Barry's general election effort, as did Eisenhower and Nixon. Ike said the previous September that 1964 would be a hard year for any Republican. It was. The Goldwater ticket, once nominated, never really got moving. It had inherent difficulties to begin with. To these were added the scars from the Rockefeller campaign. Then came the raw wounds inflicted in the drive for Scranton. Thus it was that, thrice burdened, the Republicans led by Barry Goldwater absorbed a shellacking instead of a conventional loss that November.

Yet the effect on Bill Scranton's political future was by far the more dramatic. Barry still serves colorfully in the Senate, many years later. Scranton was shut out by his own party from further Presidential consideration—and time has now passed him by.

It need not have been so. Had he and those promoting his abortive campaign been incisive in their analysis of available political intelligence, including their inability to make a sale at Gettysburg, his candidacy—I believe—would not have been pushed at a time when he had no chance, betting on an endorsement he should have known would not be there.

But he let himself be pushed, and as it turned out the push was into Presidential oblivion. If the unseemly personal attacks had been left to Rockefeller—if Bill had closed ranks and run number 2 (as Bricker, for example, did with Dewey twenty years earlier)—he would have upgraded 1964 to a tolerable Republican loss instead of the walloping it turned out to be.

Had he gone that route, he would have had first claim on his party's nomination in 1968. And I believe he would have gone on to win the Presidency in 1968 more easily than Nixon did.

And so, I wonder. How would today's pundits—or 1964's political salesmen—now describe what might have been, had those who pushed

Bill Scranton overboard been wise enough to realize that when Ike said he would endorse no one you had to bank on it—because that's the way he was.

Edward A. McCabe is a partner in the Washington law firm of Hamel, Park, McCabe & Saunders. He has been a member of the Bar of the District of Columbia since 1946 and of the Supreme Court of the United States since 1950. He was Counsel and Administrative Assistant to President Eisenhower from 1956 to 1960, and General Counsel of the House Committee on Education and Labor from 1953 to 1955.

Born in Ireland, Mr. McCabe was educated in parochial schools in Philadelphia and attended the University of Maryland and Columbus University in Washington, D.C. Following military service as an Army officer in World War II, he completed his legal education in 1947, receiving his LLB degree from the Columbus University School of Law (now the Catholic University School of Law).

Active as a college trustee and as a corporate director, he has also served on a number of Boards and Commissions concerned with improvements in the administration of justice. He served as a White House Consultant during the transition from the Nixon to the Ford Administration and as a Senior Adviser during the Carter-Reagan Transition.

**Walter R. McCurdy**

# Walt Disney's Dream— And the First Great Sale I Ever Made

*Walt Disney's greatest dream* was to build a park called Disneyland. The two major television networks had turned Walt down on financing this twenty-five-year dream of his. It was considered a high-stakes risk with little chance of success. Finally, Walt convinced the American Broadcasting-Paramount Theaters Co. to help build the greatest amusement center of all time.

Walt had envisioned a Magic Kingdom arising from a sleepy, flat, orange grove in rural Orange County, California. His plan was to carry people over the threshold of this Magic Kingdom, into Fantasyland. No automobiles would be allowed in the Magic Kingdon—no view of the outside world would be possible once inside. Food and drink would be unobtrusive, hidden as far from the visitor's view as possible. Cleanliness would be sacrosanct.

I was a young executive in the New York office of American Broadcasting-Paramount Theaters Co., in charge of Merchandising and Theater Food Service. My assignment was to transfer to California and design, implement, and build a successful food and refreshment operation at Disneyland in accordance with Walt's plans. American Broadcasting-Paramount Theaters Co. would operate as the food concessionaire at Disneyland.

In the Paramount Theater chain, popcorn was a wildly successful and highly profitable item, by far the most profitable item sold in the entire chain. I believed popcorn would be a bellwether at the new fantasy kingdom.

**203**

When I presented my plan to the management at Disneyland, popcorn sales were vetoed. Walt had specifically forbidden popcorn, gum, or liquor at his dream park. The Disney management also planned to locate the refreshment stands in out-of-the-way, obscure places to avoid any clash with the decor of the park.

I requested an audience with Walt. Since Disneyland would share in the profits of all merchandising sales at the park, and because refreshments are vital and necessary to an outdoor attraction, and since popcorn is the highest profit item of all, I felt Walt should reconsider.

It was extremely difficult to arrange a visit but finally it was scheduled. We were to meet in Walt's dual offices at Walt Disney Studios in Burbank, California. As I waited in the outer office, I was overwhelmed by his twenty-odd Oscars and innumerable national and international awards. When I was ushered in, Walt was cordial but he was adamant about banning popcorn, decrying the spillage and general mess it would cause. I countered with the joy that popcorn brings to millions of children and adults when they are on holiday and enjoying outdoor entertainment. Refreshments were crucial to the happiness, well-being, and sustenance of the crowds who would visit Disneyland. The stands would have to be located in high-traffic locations where they were accessible to the public.

Walt finally said that as a boy, he and his brother Roy were very poor and they had worked as "butchers," young men selling refreshments on railroad trains out of St. Louis, his hometown. He had earned his living that way when he was a young man. (This was part of the beginning of his great interest in locomotives and the railroads.)

Walt said that if it were possible to find two or three of the old-fashioned, antique, highly decorated popcorn wagons that used to sell popcorn in the Midwest, he would consider having them in his park. He remarked that he had seen a few such wagons in upper Wisconsin and Minnesota many years ago. He showed me some ancient lithographs of old-fashioned popcorn wagons.

I flew to Chicago and on to Wisconsin, and searched and found two such wagons. On my return, I showed the photos of these wagons to Walt and he was quite pleased. Walt withheld his approval, however, until he saw the wagons. I knew these wagons had tiny kettles and very small capacity. I had to gamble. I had the wagons shipped to Los Angeles at considerable expense. I had new, modern, high-voltage poppers installed and the wagons enlarged and completely rebuilt. They were now twice as large as the originals. They were very beautiful, red and yellow, shining glass, four windows, large yellow wheels. They were magnificent—at least I thought so. The two wagons cost $10,000 each, and I did not know if Walt would accept them or reject them as too commercial.

Two days before Disneyland opened, I had the wagons rolled into Town Square at Disneyland. They were right at the front of the park. A large sum was spent to tear up the concrete to run a 2000-watt line to the two locations that were tentatively selected. I waited until Walt came to the park for his final inspection before the national ABC network television show to open Disneyland. Walt, with a number of dignitaries, walked over to the gleaming popcorn wagon. He said, "Here is a genuine piece of Early Americana—the people will love it!" With that, he saw me and shook my hand and traveled on down Main Street.

On opening day, the popcorn wagons appeared on national television. Popcorn was in Disneyland to the eventual delight of millions of children. The total cost of both wagons was amortized in the first two months. When you visit Disneyland or Disney World today, you will see eight popcorn wagons exactly like the two originals. They will be surrounded by a large number of delighted, contented, happy kids!

□   □   □

Walter R. McCurdy, Vice President and Director of Sales of the Bristol-Myers Products Division, received his AB degree from Harvard College. Mr. McCurdy held the Thomas Slocum Scholarship at Harvard and he was a varsity basketball player and All-New England choice. He received an MBA from the Harvard Business School and was graduated in the top third of his class.

Mr. McCurdy served in the Navy in World War II and the U.S. Air Corps from 1945 to 1947. In the Korean conflict, Mr. McCurdy was recalled as a Lieutenant, Executive Officer of USS PC 1141.

Mr. McCurdy began his business career with American Broadcasting-Paramount Theaters in 1953, serving as Vice President and General Manager of ABC Merchandising Division. One of Mr. McCurdy's assignments was to set up and install the food services at the grand opening of Disneyland in California.

In 1959, Mr. McCurdy became associated with Bristol-Myers Company as Sales Trainee and was named Merchandising Manager in 1960. In February 1962, he became Sales Promotion Manager; in December 1962, he was named Assistant Vice President in charge of Sales Promotion, and in August 1964, he was promoted to Assistant Director of Sales of Bristol-Myers Products Division. In 1968, he became the Vice President and Director of Sales of the Division.

*Virginia Mickunas*

# *From the Cellar to the Sky!*

*My career as a portrait artist* grew out of poverty and personal suppression. Threadbare and lonely at age thirty-five, living on a "dead-end" street with five children in a two-bedroom, leaky bungalow, I felt the first longings for expression. There, on a dining room wall, I drew and painted my family of four sons and a daughter with five small cans of gaudy enamel—more than I really could afford. Riding around in an old station wagon with five children and a thousand pounds of collected old newspapers from nearby apartment houses was the usual routine for adding dollars to our meager income.

At age thirty-five—friendless, moneyless, and without any activities outside the home—I felt uninspired and dull. One night as I hung clothes on the backyard lines, I asked God, "Is this all there is to life?" Little did I know, standing there in the night, what miracles were in store for me and my children.

We moved out of the old lonely neighborhood to a large brick home on a busy street near school and church at the time my sixth child was born.

The scene of my "vocational" birth was a dark, damp, abandoned laundry room in the basement of a newly acquired twenty-four-room monster. We had a leaky tile roof, a cracked brick chimney, and a furnace nearly ready to die of natural causes. Undaunted by the usual financial difficulties, and primarily *because* of them, I acted on a blind impulse to do a gift portrait of my only friend, Katie Snider, who came to my rickety basement room and sat for my first oil portrait since college days, twelve years earlier. Katie sat on a straight, upright chair, precariously poised on an old discarded door, placed carefully on two egg crates. It was Katie's enthusiasm and faith that led to my multi-faceted career!

**207**

□

Thinking back to my meager beginnings in the "cellar" room where my German friend and I spent many hours struggling, I know that the greatest sale I ever made had to be the $10.00 India ink wash study that I sold to a model from Younker's Department Stores, Rae Putney. Rae's unfortunate illness inspired me to give her a study in oil of herself, which led to a wonderful opportunity for me: as a good-will ambassador for Younker's. My advertising promotions grew into a fabulous career as people saw me work in Younker's stores throughout Iowa and Illinois. I soon became a teacher as well. My first students, the two daughters of Iowa's Governor Robert Ray, were driven to my home in a long black limousine once a week. And I became a TV star: Younker promotions led to my being discovered by a local television celebrity, Mary Brubaker. Impressed with my ability to capture a quick likeness on a department store floor, talking, singing, laughing, and drawing with a crowd of people standing at my elbow, she invited me to become "artist-in-residence" on her TV show.

Yes, fourteen years later, thousands of quick pastels later, my God-given gift for making quick portrait impressions relieved me and my children of the paper collecting, yard raking, bottle and metal scraping that seemed necessary to survive on our pittance.

At the beginning of my career, with a disenchanted husband who resented the constant demands on me, I found myself confronted with six children to support, doing what had become the "food" of my life. After a divorce, I accepted every opportunity, from retouching plaster-of-paris stations of the cross, to entertaining and encouraging women in a correctional institution, a halfway house, where every one of the residents wanted one of "them $20.00 specials." These portrait sittings were done in the dining room of the place of their detentions. There, I not only "drew" their unique faces, but "drew out" as well their heavy laden hearts. Girls in trouble for stealing, prostitution, check forgery, and burglary—they all looked sweet and with human potential for good if given half a chance. I arranged to bring one girl home for a studio sitting with special permission. Ironically, this pale, frail young prostitute sat in the same soft chair as the Federal Judge, recently honored by colleagues, who had found her guilty. I paint judges as well as criminals and everything in between and see the best in all of them.

At the start of my unique career, I was visited by the nationally known sculptors Fred and Mable Torrey. Perched wet upon my mantle was my second oil portrait of a neighbor boy. As Fred Torrey stood in my living room that day fourteen years ago, in his long black overcoat, hat in hand, he asked me how much I charge for my paintings. Feeling awkward and embarrassed by this question, I answered, "Oh, I charge $75.00 for one because I am only a beginner." With that humble, almost apologetic reply, the white-haired gentleman who had been a successful artist for fifty years shared a story with me that made me realize that a feeling of self-worth is a prerequisite of successful selling. We must believe *we* are worthy, in order for our idea or product to be worthy. Without this confidence we can *never* make any sale.

□

Remarkable things happen when, as a salesman, you love. When you love someone, it's next to impossible to overcharge or misrepresent. When I love someone, I often follow my impulse to *give* my portrait, and charge only for the frame. This impulse to "give" led to every major event in my career as an artist. An impulse to give in 1966 created the whole portrait idea. The impulse to give to a friend led to further associations with people who have been responsible for programs, portraits, and the opportunity to serve as president of one of the largest hospital guilds in the country, which in turn led to portrait commissions and rich lasting friendships. Carpenters, eye doctors, hog farmers, and TV personalities have traded services willingly for my product. One woman came to the studio one day and shared a thought with me that has changed my life: "Be honest . . . it may surprise some and astonish the rest!" She meant—"be real!" In *The Velveteen Rabbit*, Margery Williams describes, in the exchange between the rabbit and the "Skin Horse," what being "real" is all about. I suggest that if all salespeople were "real people" they would experience vast success—and without a doubt might be a good deal *happier* people.

One of Des Moines' most successful florists impulsively gives away floral bouquets after every one of his own private parties. An owner of a pipe and cigar enterprise arrived at my door one day for a portrait sitting laden with fresh flowers for me. I bought two expensive lighters from him, and I don't even smoke!

The "faith factor" should not be underestimated either. Fourteen years ago, at age thirty-five, I was an unemployed mother of six children with only one friend to my name outside my immediate family. With love and faith and hope, I have learned to do portraits on a department store floor in front of crowds of people, have served as president of two large women's organizations, have been asked to speak at groups of up to 500 people all over the midwest, have appeared on TV monthly for seven years; have supported six children, built a $20,000.00 studio addition at the rear of my home, have increased my gross income from $400.00 the first year to a figure many, many times that size, so that indeed, through being real, loving, and giving I have literally emerged "from the cellar to the sky."

☐   ☐   ☐

Virginia Mickunas, Iowa portrait artist, is the third daughter in a family of four. Virginia was born in a small German farming community of Manning, Iowa; her family moved to the suburb of West Des Moines when she was twelve. After her graduation from high school, she was employed as a typist at Meredith Publishing Co. and then studied fine arts at the University of Iowa for two years. After marriage and the arrival of four sons and two daughters, Virginia, quite by accident, resumed her creative endeavors and in 1966 her career was born.

A woman whose purposes are to know people, to understand them, to enjoy them, to care about them, she is known to have "a love affair with the human race." As a by-product of loving people, Virginia also earns an excellent living.

Virginia Mickunas is deeply involved with the exchange of ideas. She is an expert at taking time for the important things as she goes along, instead of doing them when it's more convenient—and she takes time to listen and really look at everyone no matter who they seem to be. Mrs. Mickunas realizes the importance of replacing fear with faith; boredom with creativity; anger with forgiveness; taking with giving; and doubt with belief. Accompanying this honesty is a compassion for humanity and an "acceptance" that encourages personal insight and growth.

Virginia's success lies in her ability to make others feel and become more than they were. She gives them a base of security they need in order to make decisions that may lead to a richer fuller life. Virginia epitomizes and pursues a way of life that includes love, hope, and concern for others.

*John Milstead*

# A Sales Process

*This sales story* might be called a mini-case study for association executives who are considering the purchase of a headquarters building. Stated another way, it is a case study of the solution of one association's space problem. It is not the typical sales story where a product or service is sold or marketed. It is a true story of the sales process involved in convincing the members of a statewide trade association that they should invest in a larger headquarters building.

The story begins late in 1974, a time when Americans were beginning to believe that economic recovery from the 1974–1975 recession might actually occur. Florida bankers were still feeling the pain of loan losses caused primarily by the depressed real estate market.

If the market is viewed as a purchase, it was indeed the time to buy real estate. Florida bankers, however, were preoccupied with an increasing volume of nonearning assets and shrinking earnings, which were in too many instances sinking into loss figures. In this economic environment and at a time when the market was in our favor, the Florida Bankers Association found itself needing more space in which to efficiently operate. The mental attitude of the membership, however, was negative or at least skeptical toward any real estate transaction, particularly a transaction that could be postponed with little immediate direct impact on the members personally or on their banks.

This sets the stage for a sales process that must take place in any organization deciding to invest in its future by purchasing a headquarters building. In our case, it was somewhat more complex since we owned the headquarters building in which we were located at the time. We had simply outgrown the building and had expanded into a private home we had purchased at the rear of the headquarters building property.

The need for more space was identified by a Building Committee appointed in 1974. Based on the number of people per square foot, the FBA staff was operating in inadequate space. Space for the various work functions being performed was also determined to be insufficient. Parking was identified as a problem, particularly on days when a banker committee was meeting. Frequent committee meetings attended by eight to fifteen bankers often meant the FBA staff had to park on the street or by special arrangement in the YMCA parking area on the next block. It is not unusual for two or three FBA committees to meet in a single week. Thus the building committee recommended in 1975 that the FBA relocate to larger quarters in order to serve more effectively the future needs of the member banks.

In an association with over 700 members statewide, it is important that the need be communicated thoroughly. We described the need for larger quarters as a part of a slide presentation report to the membership at eight meetings around the state. The full report of the Building Committee was published and distributed to all members and a slide and sound presentation was shown as a part of the business session at the annual convention. The reaction was enthusiastic and in December 1975 the Board approved going ahead with a study of the various alternatives. A decision made by the Special Building Committee, appointed year-end 1975, proved to be critical to the ultimate result. We agreed that we should first identify and commission the best professional realtor we could locate in Orlando and request that he help us analyze the various alternatives available to satisfy our space needs.

We were fortunate to acquire the services of Wooda Elliott, a realtor with Tucker and Branham Inc. Mr. Elliott's professional competence, persistence, and deep desire to satisfy our need were a key factor in the ultimate solution to our space problem. My first advice to any executive involved in this process is to carefully select a good realtor, and do it early in the process.

The primary alternatives studied included the following:

**1** Expansion of our present property by purchasing an additional adjacent parcel. This approach was discarded because zoning required an increasing number of off-street parking spaces if our building were enlarged. Expanding on-site would have required us to resort to high-cost multilevel construction. Even though we preferred this approach, our analysis revealed it to be a temporary treatment of the problem rather than a solution. This approach would also have compromised the future marketability of our existing headquarters building.

**2** Leasing space was considered. At the time there existed a surplus of office space being offered at attractive lease prices in Orlando. The leases were short term, however, and the committee concluded that prices would escalate rather rapidly in the immediate future. This proved to be an accurate future estimate. The loss of identity for the FBA in leased space was also a consideration. The bankers appreciated the equity they had built in the existing building and acknowledged that you build no equity when you lease. The idea of leasing was therefore rejected as a solution, but was retained as a possible interim option while deciding whether to build or buy.

Our realtor, Wooda Elliott, did a fine job in helping to analyze the various possibilities. He spent a lot of time screening and showing buildings that were located properly and would fit our needs. Time after time he demonstrated to us that the prices of existing buildings in the market at that time were as low as half the cost of new construction for the same quality building. Existing buildings, however, carry several problems with them. The layout may not fit your needs; the construction may not be complete or the quality of the construction may be poor. Some space in buildings we considered was under lease, which one must assume when purchasing such properties. Our bankers made several trips to Orlando to walk through and personally inspect the properties available. For the reasons stated and others, the available buildings were rejected one by one.

A three-story building at 341 North Mills Avenue, a block from our headquarters building, was the most appealing possibility to members of the committee. We were all convinced that the best solution was an existing building if we could find the right deal in the right location. 341 North Mills was an ideal location and was priced right. The building was, however, larger than we needed, and some adjacent property was part of the package. We were tempted by the possibilities of the 341 North Mills property at the time. Wooda Elliott had also convinced most of us that the building was a good buy, was well constructed, and had low-cost expansion possibilities. Yet the size, estimated renovation costs, and leases to be assumed caused enough concern that we decided to seriously consider a "turnkey" package built to our specifications. This proposal was made by the manager of a highly successful local business and professional park. The opportunity to design and build our own building to fit our specific needs was appealing. The park where the building would be located was first class. We would be in good company in the park.

The park manager along with a staff architect and builder presented several floor plans designed specifically to suit the needs of the FBA.

These plans were based on specifications defined by the FBA managers and staff. The FBA Board of Directors at a meeting in the park office in March 1976 decided to purchase the new building package proposal offered by the park. When the plan was published to the FBA membership, we began to get negative feedback about the timing of the decision. The membership seemed aware of the need, but several bankers expressed concern about going into a building program at a time when member bank earnings were historically low. Acting on this input, the new building deal with the park was canceled and action to solve the difficult space problem was deferred. The staff was disappointed with the delay. The depressed feelings were particularly traumatic following the enthusiasm generated about plans for the new building.

Several months breezed by while our space situation grew increasingly severe and the Orlando real estate market began to show clear signs of new vitality. The FBA staff was beginning to feel as though our space problem with the attendant inefficiency and inconvenience would be with us for a long time. About that time Wooda Elliott again contacted us. He announced that the building at 341 North Mills Avenue was still on the market. He urged us to make an offer on the property because in his opinion the building would soon be sold. Our Building Committee was called together again to take another look at the 341 North Mills Avenue property and to recommend possible methods of financing the purchase. J. W. Crews, Jr., a member of the committee, viewed the property as a good buy and sound investment. He had personal investments in Florida real estate, and the other bankers on the committee respected his opinion and came to the same conclusion based on their own experience.

A financing plan was developed which called for the sale of our current properties, a one-time dues increase, and the use of Association reserves. This plan would finance the purchase of the building, required renovations, and the physical move. The Association would not be required to borrow money and would pay cash for the headquarters building. Paying cash should be the objective of any nonprofit organization planning to build or buy a building. Long-term mortgage financing in such organizations means higher dues over an extended period for all members. Increased dues requirements to pay interest and principal offer no tax benefits to the nonprofit organization. Larger contributions to the building fund immediately before, during, and after the decision to buy or build is the most economical method of financing in the long run. Such a plan helps fix occupancy expense at a lower cost level and reduces the organization's dues exposure to inflation in the future.

The plan was presented to and approved by the Board of Directors in December 1977. On June 30, 1978, we purchased the building at 341 North Mills Avenue that is now our headquarters building.

One might ask why the purchase of the new headquarters building was so meaningful to me. I did not realize financial reward for the final result of this sales process, but it represented my success as a manager. I firmly believe that a good manager has a responsibility to organize an efficient, productive, and comfortable working environment. This is a dual responsibility both to the people for whom he manages and to the people who work with him on a day-to-day basis. Inadequate space for efficient operations frustrates the management process. The frustration is particularly painful when you have a highly capable and highly motivated staff, as we are fortunate to have at the Florida Bankers Association. Solving our space problem, was, therefore, a high personal priority for me as a manager. It is further satisfying to observe the productivity increase now that we are settled in the new building.

Several by-products since the purchase have further enhanced the meaningfulness of this three-year sales process. It was a sound investment. Within a year from the time we moved into our new quarters, we received a written offer to purchase the property under a leaseback arrangement. The offer would have netted the FBA a substantial short-term profit. Our Board declined the offer, affirming once again their agreement that we had, indeed, resolved the space problem and substantially insulated our occupancy expense from future inflation.

There you have it. The story of the sales process that meant the most to me as an FBA executive and as a manager.

Should you be an association manager with a space problem this summary is for you:

**1.** Working with your president and board of directors, select a building committee very carefully. Be sure one of your leaders who is beginning to move through the leadership chairs is on the committee. An active past president should also be appointed to serve on this committee.

**2.** Working with your staff, determine and specifically define current and future space needs.

**3.** Thoroughly communicate this need to the membership of your association. Communication should continue during the search or building process.

**4.** Identify and commission a well-qualified and highly recommended realtor to advise and assist in the search. Spend some time on this and get a competent realtor.

**5.** Be persistent. Don't expect this kind of project to occur overnight. It could take a year or more just to get leadership consensus and come to an initial decision to begin on a specific course of action.

**6.** Begin today if you have a space problem. As a manager, that is your responsibility. You will be glad you did.

☐   ☐   ☐

John Milstead, CAE, has been Executive Vice President of the Florida Bankers Association since 1973. He joined FBA as Secretary in 1965, moved up to Secretary-Treasurer in 1969, and Administrative Vice President in 1971.

He had considerable banking experience prior to his activities in the FBA. Mr. Milstead joined Barnett First National Bank of Jacksonville (now Barnett Bank of Jacksonville, NA) in 1953 while attending Jacksonville University, and he rose to assistant cashier in 1962. He earned his BSBA degree from Jacksonville University in 1960 and received a certificate from the School of Bank Marketing, Northwestern University, in 1963. He has a graduate certificate in Investments from the American Institute of Banking, and holds the professional designation of Certified Association Executive, which he earned in 1976.

John Milstead is currently President of the Florida Society of Association Executives, serves on the Executive Committee of the State Association Division of the American Bankers Association, and is a member of the American Society of Association Executives. In 1977 he was named "Boss of the Year" by the Orlando Chapter of National Secretaries Association (International).

He recently served the American Bankers Association as liaison between the ABA Communications Council and the fifty State Bankers Associations throughout the country. He is Past-President of the Southern Conference of State Bankers Associations, a group comprised of executive managers of fifteen southern Associations.

Mr. Milstead holds the rank of Lieutenant Colonel in the Florida Army National Guard. He is a life member of the national business fraternity Alpha Kappa Psi.

*J. Wilmer Mirandon*

# Use Extreme Caution

*I am not a salesman* but I do recall a "sale" upon which my career, if not my life, may have hinged. Although it has no appropriate relationship to the success stories of the more important contributors to this treatise, it might offer something different. The experience was not a proud one; it seemed unnecessarily dangerous and rather reckless upon reflection only five minutes afterward. You will see, as the story unfolds, that it would never happen in the same way again, if only because of fear.

□

Shortly after my graduation from law school, I spent a rather brief period in the Federal Bureau of Investigation. My first permanent assignment, nine months after training, was that of a resident agent in a predominantly rural area of the Midwest.

A junior high school dropout, who had become a thirty-five-year-old fugitive from a Missouri penitentiary, was known to have relatives living in the community. His sister, residing on a small, unproductive farm twenty miles from town, his mother, and all other relatives living nearby had been visited by me and warned about his escape. They were requested to telephone in the event he should appear. All seemed quite shaken by the news that the family black sheep was running loose again.

While eluding capture, the convict attended a summer carnival where he met a blonde alcoholic about thirty years of age (although she looked sixty) and her thirteen-year-old daughter, who could have passed for eighteen. Around midnight, after the woman drank herself to sleep, he kidnapped and raped her thirteen-year-old daughter.

Several weeks later, in the long twilight of a September day, the fugitive's sister made her way to a pay phone in a crossroads grocery store under the pretext of buying breakfast cereal and called to say that

Dusty, her brother, was hiding in her farmhouse. She said there was a shotgun and rifle in the kitchen, but she did not believe Dusty had a hand gun. I explained that we would try to come directly into the house so that it would not look as though she had informed upon her brother.

An exuberant new agent trainee and I, both with adrenalin flowing, notified headquarters and then drove to the farmhouse. Forty minutes had elapsed before we parked our unmarked car behind the barn. Dusty's sister had returned, but as expected, he was not in sight. We went through the open door and told her to take her two young children and walk some distance from the house. Both guns were found in the kitchen. Apparently Dusty had been too surprised to grab them, or, better yet, he was not the type to use force. The second idea was the more appealing.

Each of the four rooms revealed no fugitive as we drew our firearms and gingerly looked under beds and into closets. Ridiculously it reminded one of playing hide-and-seek. We acted as if we knew someone had to leap out, shouting "boo!" Or maybe Dusty had escaped again, this time to the small patch of woods behind the barn. Instinctively I checked my pockets and felt the car keys.

For a moment a bright glow of sunset fell on the new trainee's face as we peered out the kitchen window. A small radio on the sink was softly broadcasting a twi-night double header from Sportsman's Park in St. Louis.

Finally behind the wood-burning stove, in a break in the wall half-hidden by the growing shadows, a ladder became apparent. It disappeared into a dark opening eight feet above. Although contemplating the hole in the ceiling was frightening, I called out with surprising clarity and authority, "Dusty, this is the FBI. We want to talk with you. Come on down." No answer; no sign of life from the somber hole in the ceiling. How easy it would be to throw tear gas through the opening but such equipment was at least ninety minutes away. After all, it was only one man against two, or twenty as far as he knew. And suppose he was not up there. How silly we would look staring up at an empty hole with tears running down our cheeks.

☐

I called out again, this time somewhat like a salesman pitching his sale. At the same moment, a beer commercial was coming from the radio. It had a subliminal effect.

"We know you're up there, Dusty. You've been on the run long enough. Let's get something to eat—a good steak, corn on the cob, some cold beer. Let's get this over with." No answer. Maybe he was not in the loft after all.

Then with a quick shiver I said I was coming up to talk with him and I started up the ladder with my gun held high above my head, pointed toward the opening. There was still light enough but objects were beginning to take on a less distinctive outline. I thought to myself, what the hell am I doing here at $5500 a year? I had spent my time in the service, almost four years during World War II, and I had come away unscarred. Was I pushing my luck?

More words of encouragement came from my dry throat. "Come on, Dusty, here's a good chance to become friends. We're here to help you." No response. Not even the click of a cocked hammer. The same beer commercial was still on.

Now my extended arm and gun were well through the hole and visible above the attic floor like a puppet manipulated from below. Try to shoot it, I thought; it's only an arm. The attic stillness seemed eternal although the elapsed time since my first plea through the dark hole was less than the thirty-second beer advertisement. I stuck my head above the attic floor, expecting to hear a blast, and saw Dusty hiding in the shadow of the eaves in the far corner. I almost jumped up through the opening, banging my left shoulder on the slanted underside of the roof.

Dusty had a loaded revolver. He slid it across the floor toward me and mumbled that he was through running and that he was glad we had finally come for him. I tried to conceal my shakiness. His revolver had a hair trigger and as I picked it up it exploded. The round went through the attic roof. After shouting to the new agent not to shoot, we all laughed. We bought Dusty a steak and one beer and put him in the county jail. Dusty's eyes were glistening when we left him.

☐

Returning to the office, we heard the phone ringing as we walked down the hall. It gave the impression of having been ringing for a long time in the dark. A clerk from headquarters was on the line. After saying he was glad he had reached us, he rather mechanically recited a teletype sent from the Field Office that had originated Dusty's search. He read that we should be aware that Dusty had killed a bartender ten years earlier in a Kansas City holdup. Also for the first time, we were being notified that he should be considered armed and dangerous. "We should use extreme caution," the clerk went on, but I was not listening to him any longer. All I could hear were prayers of thanks.

□

After all, maybe I was a salesman, stupid but fortunate.

☐ ☐ ☐

J. Wilmer Mirandon is President and Chief Executive of United Student Aid Funds, Inc., a not-for-profit corporation that guarantees loans for college students throughout the country.

He was drafted into the U. S. Army following his third year at the University of Virginia (class of 1943) and served four years, including duty in the Southwest Pacific and Japanese occupation as a First Lieutenant. After World War II, Bill Mirandon attended the George Washington University and received his BS in government in 1947 and his law degree in 1949. He later attended the Stonier Graduate School of Banking where he served briefly as a faculty member. He is a member of the District of Columbia and the New York State Bar, although he has never followed law as a career.

From 1950 to 1959 Bill Mirandon was a resident agent and supervisor with the Federal Bureau of Investigation. In addition to a cross section of investigations in Utah, Illinois, and New York, he was assigned to special cases involving Presidential appointments that offered interesting interviews with Douglas MacArthur, Herbert Hoover, Robert Taft, Thomas Dewey, and other prominent Americans. Then, during a fourteen-year period, he worked for Chemical Bank in both domestic and international operations, rising to a senior vice president before leaving banking in 1973 to become president and chief executive officer of the New York State Higher Education Services Corporation during Governor Nelson Rockefeller's administration. In 1975 he returned to the private sector to head United Student Aid Funds, a nationwide corporation serving fourteen states and numerous schools and organizations in the Guaranteed Student Loan Program.

*Arthur H. Motley*

# The Best Sale
# I Ever Made

*In the summer of 1919* I found myself employed in Ramsay, Michigan, at the Eureka mine, attempting to get together a stake to return to the University of Minnesota that fall. I had missed several months of school during World War I. This was dull, backbreaking work. To save money I spent a lot of my time at a boarding house that served mostly miners. One evening at the supper table (family-style service) appeared a chap who obviously was not a miner. He had on white shirt plus a *tie* and there was no red iron ore under his finger nails. I was intrigued enough to chat with him on the front porch of the boarding house after supper to find out what he did. He was a salesman; in fact, he was a traveling salesman selling zithers to the miners and their families up and down the iron range. He explained to me that he bought the instrument for $5 from a wholesale house in Chicago, sold them for $25, and never took less than $10 down so even if he didn't collect the balance he made a good profit. This sounded better than the pick and shovel so I followed through and with his help became a zither salesman.

It was an interesting instrument. It had two octaves of keys. If you could count to sixteen you could play this zither. The sheet music that was given away with each instrument was scored not musically but numerically. Keys tripped hammers that came down and hit the wires of the zither. It seemed the answer for those who without any particular musical skill or training desired to make music. For a short time, sales were brisk and I was a happy zither salesman. Soon, however, some of the first customers wanted to expand their repertoire. When they came back for more music, more tunes, I found out that the instrument played only in the key of C. To make it possible for the hammers to hit the wires, all the sharps and flats had been removed. This zither could play only tunes transposed into the key of C. I was working to get money to

**227**

go back to college in the fall, and I continued to sell, but I never sold as many per day or week as I had before I found out that the instrument only played music in the key of C. Without knowing it, I had stumbled into one of the great truths about successful selling—you have to believe in your product if you want to sell it successfully.

In the winter of 1931 I was employed as an advertising space salesman for *Collier's Weekly*. Having done modestly well in the southeast, I was transferred to the Detroit office of the company to take the place of a colorful salesman who had died of pneumonia combined with drinking. This transfer, or promotion, as it was described to me, came not so much because of my outstanding sales record, but because of my outstanding ability to hold liquor. Detroit was a hard-drinking town, and in those days prohibition was the law. Management apparently thought I was ideally suited for that environment.

Shortly after we moved into our new home at 89 Taylor Avenue, the neighbors in typical, friendly, midwestern fashion called, and in the course of conversation they naturally asked what I did for a living. My wife showed them a current copy of *Collier's Weekly* and pointed to a beautiful four-color ad for Kelvinator refrigerators. She said, "My husband sells these." "How interesting," the neighbor commented, and then my wife said, "How much do you think they get for these?" The woman asked, and my wife triumphantly replied, "$10,000." The woman replied, "For how many?" My wife said, "For just one." I think the neighbor almost fainted at the thought of $10,000 for a piece of paper with four-color printing on it. This exchange made Motley look like one of the James Boys—a first-rate bandit.

For some time after that I could not get this exchange out of my mind. It rankled particularly because the Great Depression was just settling in and the press and speakers everywhere were publicly attacking advertising and selling as an added cost which, if eliminated, would permit more people to buy more things for less money. In short, Motley and all others engaged in selling and advertising were made to look like parasites living on the goods as they moved from the factory loading dock into the hands of the ultimate user. I liked my job, I was doing well enough to be able to get married, to own an automobile, to belong to a Golf Club. I did not like the idea of being a pariah, but the nagging doubts about the benefits of what I was doing persisted. I finally decided to do something about it. Since I had sold that Kelvinator ad, I decided to start there.

Research of a very sketchy nature revealed that a man by the name of William Thompson, later Lord Kelvin, had discovered the principles behind mechanical refrigeration in the early part of the twentieth century. In the early 1920s in the United States there were a few manufacturers of these mechanical refrigerators—Copeland, Norge, Kelvinator, and the like—selling a total of 500,000 of these contraptions a year at an average price of about $500, and none of the companies was making any money. Then my research showed that something happened in the mid-1920s when two big manufacturers in the United States got in the business: General Motors with Frigidaire, and General Electric. They did not build a better machine, but they did something far more important. They introduced selling, marketing, and advertising into this "new" industry. They appointed retailers in most towns of any size around the country, they taught them how to promote the product, and they began to advertise the virtues of this mechanical marvel. They used billboard advertising, newspaper advertising, magazine advertising, and although it was very early on, some radio. One of the problems they had was the customers' fear of the possible leakage of the refrigerant (freon) and the contamination of the food. The companies in the early days even hired home economists dressed in white who explained the safety of the boxes to the prospective owner.

In a short time they were selling 2 million of these mechanical marvels a year, not 500,000, and the price was no longer $500—it was slightly below $200. In other words, by a process of advertising and selling they were not only fulfilling a *need* for a piece of equipment that would safely preserve food, but were creating a *desire* to own this new and improved "ice box." Volume, as was usually the case, reduced the unit cost. The housewife, who for years had gotten nothing but dirty kitchen floors and bum jokes from the iceman, *needed* a better method and mechanical refrigeration provided that better method, but "nothing happened till somebody sold something."

When I sold that four-color ad to Kelvinator and it was distributed through the 3 million or so circulation *Collier's* enjoyed at that time, I was a part of a "want-creating" process that benefited not only Motley, the company I worked for, and the Kelvinator Company that made the product, it also benefited the user. All of a sudden I realized I was *not* a parasite making a living by adding a cost as the goods moved from the factory loading dock to the consumer, I was part of the *want-creating* process which is the basis of all human progress. Needs were never that important. It is what people want that is important. Here was a perfect commercial example of "want-creating" (selling), producing, at its best.

My employers had taught me how to sell advertising space, but they had failed to teach me the most important lesson of all—why? Why was what I was doing important to someone other than myself or my employer? Why was what I was doing important to some else—in this case the consumer? As a result of this neighbor's question about how I made a living, I had discovered for myself the answer to the important basic question—why? Having discovered my true role in this setup, never again did I feel apologetic about my role as a salesman, and with a belief in my product and myself founded on an understanding of *why* I was important, my sales volume and my success continued to grow over the years. I realized then, as I still believe now, that belief in not only yourself but your product and your profession (in my case selling) is absolutely essential for success. That's why I consider this particular sale, which I made on myself, to be the most important one and the greatest one I ever made. I commend a similar sale to all those who are engaged in the business of selling.

☐   ☐   ☐

Arthur H. (Red) Motley, the future President of the U.S. Chamber of Commerce, graduated from the University of Minnesota in 1922, a Phi Beta Kappa. His lifetime interest in his alma mater was reflected when he became chairman of the University of Minnesota Foundation in the 1960s and later when he received the Regents Award from the University of Minnesota.

Motley began his association with Crowell-Collier Publishing Company in 1928 as an advertising space salesman for *Collier's* in the southeast. In 1941, he was elected Vice-President and Director of Crowell-Collier and appointed Publisher of *The American Magazine*.

In January 1946, he became a partner with Marshall Field III as President and Publisher of *Parade*, remaining as Chief Executive Officer into 1972. During that period, *Parade* went from nineteen newspapers to 100, and from a circulation of 3.2 million to a circulation of 17.8 million.

Red Motley became widely known for his interest in and contribution to selling (marketing). He traveled widely, speaking to thousands of groups in his favorite topic—"Nothing Happens Until Somebody Sells Something." In 1949, he was elected President of Sales Marketing Executives International. In 1950, he headed a group of American Sales Executives who traveled abroad at the behest of the U.S. Government to attempt to show Western Europe how to market their goods in America. The slogan was "Trade not Aid." In 1957, President Eisenhower appointed Mr. Motley chairman of the marketing division of the President's Conference on Small Business. In 1960, Mr. Motley became President of the U.S. Chamber of Commerce.

Mr. Motley retired as Chairman of the Board of *Parade* on January 1, 1978, ending a thirty-two-year association with *Parade*.

*Colonel Barney Oldfield*

# The Saga of the Value-Added Valentine

*As deals go*, the pricetag wasn't all that high. In fact, the range of ticket prices for the Sonja Henie International Ice Show in Omaha's Ak-Sar-Ben Coliseum, February 13, 1941, were listed as $1.10, $1.65, $2.20, with boxes going for the roof of $2.75. With 200 tickets being involved in the $1.65 section, it rounded out neatly at $330.00.

In 1977, CBS's Charles Kuralt on the June 19 version of "Who's Who" described it as "the longest running, open-ended, most enduring publicity stunt of all time." And a small magazine that had been one of many to use the story over the years sued CBS for plagiarism for $1,000,000! If ever there was a case of value-added, a spread from $330.00 to $1,000,000 has to be about as extreme as you can get.

When we add to this that I was *given*—for *free*—the 100-pound cake of bluish-green ice that caused it all, it's pyramiding that would rival a Ponzi or an Ivar Krueger.

It all started so simply. Along with many others, I had received the greetings in 1940 to swap mufti for the uniform of a Reserve Infantry Captain, and report to the First Battalion of the Third Infantry Regiment at Fort Crook, Nebraska. When I reported in, still in my civilian clothes, the frowning battalion commander, Lt. Col. Koger M. Still, studied the card he had on me.

"What did you do in civilian life?" he asked finally.

"I was a newspaperman, columnist, a movie editor, wrote feature stories, gabbed on the radio about Hollywood. . . . " He held up his hand—to know more of such zany nonsense frightened him about what the Army he loved was coming to just to accommodate a rising national emergency.

He was desperate, obviously. "In a job like that," he ventured, "you must have had to see a lot of those B pictures?"

**233**

He was right and I told him so.

"OK," he said, straining for some thread of consistency, "I'll give you command of B Company!" He was pleased with himself, but neither of us laughed. I went on to meet—and be a shock to—the B Company First Sergeant.

Then a hole opened elsewhere at Headquarters of the Seventh Corps Area in nearby Omaha for a public relations type. B Company saw me off, perhaps in relief: Who would want to go to war with a typewriter consort?

I was barely at my new desk when a caller was announced. His name was Ray Gaynor. He said he was the advance man for an ice show that was coming to Omaha's Ak-Sar-Ben Coliseum. The idea had struck him, he said, that people were beginning to think well of soldiers again. He wondered if there would be some gag or gimmick that could be worked to get the star of the ice show in proximity to men in uniform, so that a picture might be taken and printed in the Omaha *World-Herald*.

"Who's the star?"

"Sonja Henie."

"And when does the show open?"

He said it would be for a week's run, starting the night of February 13, 1941. He went back to his original question about whether we could work something out.

"What's in it for me?" After all, one hand often might not know what the other is doing, but it's better if they wash each other some way. What did I mean, what's in it for me?

I told him we were less than ten miles from Fort Crook, and that I knew about 200 soldiers out there who faced an uncertain future. They didn't get nights out on the town much, I said, and if this idea worked and the picture did get printed, could I have 200 tickets so my old company could be Sonja Henie's guests one evening of her run? It was less painful than he thought, and he agreed—immediately wanting to know what we'd do. After all, he had to get his star to go along.

A press agent has to have a calendar and a clock in his head, as timing can make all the difference to an editor. My mention of something in the Valentine line left him unmoved, but I told him I had an idea for an unusual one. Not too thrilled, he left but pleaded that it be something good. A man of little faith, surely.

The day before Sonja Henie was to come in with her skaters, I went to a man named J. J. Gagini. He was the boss of Omaha Ice and Cold Storage company. I told him I had an idea which required a 100-pound cake of his best product. At that moment, blocks were being processed with various colors of dye added. The destinations were major hotels and restaurants where they were sculpted into frigid figurines, initials, or whatever the day and occasion required. At that moment all the specimens coming from the molds were blue-green.

"Take one," Gagini said with a wave of his hand. The noise in the place was considerable as the cakes plopped out on the wet wooden floor and slid down to the pickup points where the trucks waited to make deliveries. With kicks and hand pushes, I got one out of the traffic pattern and beached. As I was looking it over, Gagini handed me an icepick and indicated that I should get to work. Until that moment, I don't believe it had occurred to me that my picture ploy was going to be my work project. But, if Gutzon Borglum could take on Mt. Rushmore with his little chisel, why should I be spared?

It went along easier than I thought. First, some pinpricks to outline, and if there were errors in judgment, the ice had its ability to melt and erase. Then the chipping began in earnest. Fifteen minutes, that's all it took, and there was my Valentine! Gagini stored it for me until we would be ready for the trek to Ak-Sar-Ben. The next step was John Savage, a *World-Herald* photographer I knew. We would have three soldiers make the presentation to Sonja just before she went on for opening night, probably in her dressing room backstage. Was he interested? Sure he was, and said he'd be there. There was the call to Ray Gaynor that the party was on so he could tell Sonja. The three soldiers were easy to come by. It was cold that night, so there was no danger of any meltdown in that open truck we used to get to the outskirts of Omaha—the only hazard would be delay inside the coliseum as that temperature was at a level tolerable to a sitting audience. My trio in uniform and I marched in, they lugging the slippery burden and myself like some unhorsed Paul Revere signaling for the photographer and Ray, who were standing on one foot and the other at Sonja's door. The overture music was on. There was a problem.

Sonja Henie was a star, no doubt about that. Her father had taught her to be a businesswoman as well. She had a piece of the programs, a percentage of the concessions. She said her end of the program sale was too small, and that the popcorn sacks were being filled too full. There was such a thing as a graceful curve in her skating entry, but there was a bottom line that interested her mightily. And now there were these nuts at her door for some silly publicity picture! My warriors' hands were red with cold and bluish-green as the dye oozed forth, a

Technicolor version of dismay. Finally, Sonja Henie came out, took her stance, rigged her dimples, made a pass at trying to autograph the Valentine with a hot nail. That didn't work, but John Savage shot a lot of pictures, more than enough for his purposes. He dashed off. Sonja began to notice the dripping on her dressing room rug, and her face clouded.

"Sonja," I told her, desperate for an exit line. "We'll make you a promise. We're going to keep this Valentine until you come back to Omaha some day. We'll show it to you then, so you know we kept the promise." By now my soldiers viewed the Valentine about the way Sinbad the Sailor thought of the Old Man of the Sea, with his legs locked perpetually around his neck. In the manner of all retreats, ours was not orderly either. Escape was what was important. The Valentine was unceremoniously cast into the truck in the zero weather outside, and we all went in to see the show. If the photo didn't make it into print, at least our foursome would have something to show for the effort. At the finale, we got back in the truck, returned to Omaha Ice & Cold Storage, and told the night man to store the centerpiece of all this commotion and to be sure Gagini had our thanks when he showed up in the morning. He stuffed it in a big pasteboard box, wrote *Sonja's Valentine* on it, and we departed.

There it was the next morning prominently displayed in the Omaha *World-Herald*—Sonja's picture with her icy Valentine, and she looked like the most pleased young lady in Omaha! That night my 200 soldiers from B Company were "Sonja's guests," and they loved it, stood and applauded longest of all the audience on hand. She gave them a special curtsy for their enthusiasm.

Everybody went off to what became World War II.

When I came home in January 1946 making the press arrangements for the Victory March of the Eighty-Second Airborne Division from Washington Arch to Eighty-Sixth Street along Fifth Avenue in New York, there was time to go home to Nebraska for Christmas. Among the people encountered was the photographer John Savage.

"Ever wonder what happened to that old Sonja Henie Valentine?" he asked. I must say I had never given it another thought, but got on the phone to Julius J. Gagini. Did he remember the Valentine?

"Sure do," he said. "We've got it here. What do you want to do with it?" John Savage and I went over for another picture-taking orgy, and dimly remembering the promise I had made Sonja to keep it until she returned to Omaha, it seemed natural to wonder if she had played Omaha during the war.

"Oh, no," they informed me. "She left Omaha so mad at J. J. "Jake"

Isaacson, the Ak-Sar-Ben pooh-bah, she vowed she would never play Omaha again—and she never has!"

The Sonja Henie Valentine, still weighing more than sixty pounds and with recognizable shape, is still there at Omaha Cold Storage Company at 800 Harney Street on the third floor in league with stacks of frozen foods, pork bellies, and the like. It has had two keepers, Wendell Anderson and S. E. "Doc" Chamberlin, and people come from all over the world to ask about it, and to view it.

So much stemmed from that perishable ice block, it is unbelievable. United Service Organizations (USO) was founded on February 4, 1941, just ten days before Sonja did her performance to that mass soldier audience. USO says this was the first Hollywood star routine before troops after its founding, a tradition that was carried on by many stars thereafter, Bob Hope's touching loyalty to the servicemen being the longest lasting. When Sonja died on October 11, 1969, I was a longtime member of the USO Board of Governors and was asked by my colleagues to go to Omaha to place a rose on the old Valentine. J. J. Gagini had died, so Wendell Anderson took me to the old heart. A man's mind does things to him on such occasions, and I chose not to remember the Sonja of program percentages and too-full popcorn sacks, but the diminutive figure on skates who burst out onto the ice, and mesmerized everyone with her grace and beauty. The Valentine which seemed everybody's curse that decades-ago opening night now had an aura about it. The rose we put there began to blacken almost immediately in the 10-degrees-below-zero cold, but the flashbulbs had had a field day again.

That Third Infantry Regiment, whose soldiers had been in the Ak-Sar-Ben seats, is the only regimental-size unit in the U.S. Army that has served unbroken and never deactivated since the American Revolution. The "number" was finally taken to Washington, and this element, now called The Old Reliables, does all the White House lawn ceremonial functions and walks eternal vigil at the Tomb of the Unknown Soldiers! The icy Valentine of Sonja Henie is a part of its long and historic route march to the present.

On February 13, 1981, the Valentine was forty years old, so fragile, so vulnerable, yet so enduring.

A magazine could be so possessive it would sue a national network over it. Yet it is a story that won't go away, and seasoned editors and documentarians marvel at the stamina of this "soft story" which has a warming, emotional impact on many people in different ways, all of them feeling good about it.

Peggy Fleming, reigning queen of contemporary ice-adept, asked me about it one time. When I finished the story, I suggested if she were in Omaha on tour sometime, she might look in on the Valentine. There was a dampness at the corners of her eyes, and she said firmly: "I wouldn't go near it. I would just hope that someone some day would do as nice a thing for me." Not long ago, the management of Shipstad and Johnson's "Ice Follies" was on the phone with a request. Their star, Dorothy Hamill, wants sometime to go to Omaha Cold Storage and pay her respects to the ancient artifact! The sentiment is working on the third generation, you see.

That night Charles Kuralt retold the story on "Who's Who" I had a call from a lady in Cleveland. She was crying. She had just seen the program, she said. I told her I hoped it wasn't that bad, as it hadn't played in my time zone yet.

"Oh, no," she told me in a shaky voice. "It was wonderful. Bear with me while I tell you why. When I was a little girl, my grandfather used to take me to a little shop to buy me new shoes. The shopkeeper put each of our names on a card, put the cards in a bowl, and at the end of each month all the kids who got shoes that month were invited back to the shop for a party—and a drawing. That time, I won—and it was a Sonja Henie skating doll! It was the only thing I ever won in my whole life and I still have it. When the story about your old Valentine came on my TV set tonight, I started to cry—and haven't stopped yet. I have that old doll in my hand right now, it made me so happy. . . ."

The way I look at it, something I had done ten years before that lady was born survived to brighten her days—I may not have made a sale exactly, but I made somebody's heart sail, which isn't bad!

A wide range of civil and military experience has characterized the life of Col. A. Barney Oldfield, a retired U.S. Air Force officer now Corporate Director, Special Missions & Projects, for Litton Industries, Inc., in Beverly Hills, California. He has been a newspaperman, a radio commentator, a Hollywood press agent, magazine and script writer, and author of books. He was the longest timer in military public relations of the more than 5000 officers who served in that capacity in all the services.

Born in Tecumseh, Nebraska, in 1909, he was educated in Elk Creek, Nebraska High School, and graduated with an AB degree from the University of Nebraska in 1933, with a journalism major and military minor. Both these factors had permanent professional influence on his life.

He has thus far lived, worked, done assignments of one kind or another, and traveled in sixty-nine countries on every continent. Part of this was due to his choice of journalism as an initial career field, and the rest to his having been commissioned a reserve Second Lieutenant of Infantry on June 6, 1932. He did not transfer to the U.S. Air Force until July 25, 1949. When retired on September 30, 1962, he was credited with a total of thirty years, three months, and twenty-five days of military service.

As a newspaperman, Hollywood columnist, and feature writer, he set such a movie-seeing marathon record for five years covering and reviewing more than 500 films each year, he was spotlighted in Robert L. Ripley's "Believe It or Not"; in John Hix' "Strange as It Seems" syndicated feature; and on Cecil B. DeMille's pioneer Lux Radio Theater as a principal guest.

He was the first newspaperman graduated in jump training in Class 23 of the Parachute School at Fort Benning, Georgia, after going into service on extended active duty in November 1940. This led to his being given the toughest "sales job" of his life, an assignment in England to talk war correspondents based there into taking parachute and glider training to prepare them to accompany the airborne invasion of Normandy. He eventually got sixteen of them so qualified in the 1943–1944 buildup period. Also, during this pre-Normandy planning phase he had to write the manning and equipment tables and organize the mobile establishments called "press camps" which were geared to follow the ground armies across Europe, providing information, transportation, communications, food, housing, and all the other necessities of life for the accredited war correspondents. One of these, he headed himself—that of the Ninth U.S. Army, which started operations in the Brittany Peninsula and wound up near Magdeburg, Germany, on the Elbe River line where the war in Europe ended.

On leaving the service, he spent two years in the Warner Brothers Studio publicity department (his clients included Errol Flynn, Ann Sheridan, Jane Wyman, Ronald Reagan, Janis Paige, and the twelve-year-old Elizabeth Taylor). Recalled to uniform in late 1947, and given a Regular Army Commission, then transferring to the USAF in 1949, he was given the assignment of introducing the first USAF public relations crews into Korea in July 1950 when that "police action" began.

Withdrawn in October of that year to become the Chief of Information for General Lauris Norstad, who was about to become General Eisenhower's principal Air Force commander when SHAPE (Supreme Headquarters, Allied Powers, Europe) was established, he was loaned by Norstad as General Eisenhower's advance man in his precommand assumption survey of the NATO countries. It was a role he was to perform often on later occasions. After serving as a SHAPE and Allied Air Forces Central Europe "troubleshooter" from Norway to Turkey for three years, he was returned to the United States to become the aerospace defense spokesman, first with the Air Defense command, then the Continental Air Defense Command, and then the North American Air Defense Command in Colorado Springs, a total period of eight years and eight months. He was a prime mover in campaigns for public tolerance for noise, nuisance, and hazards of jet operations and a constant exponent of the requirements for aerospace defense weapons systems as the necessary complement to offensive weapons to ensure the latter's credibility.

Out of his welter of experiences, a book was inevitable and he wrote *Never a Shot in Anger*, a tribute to the 1828 war correspondents accredited by the United States in World War II. Published in late 1956, the book's proceeds were used to set up the Kinman-Oldfield Scholarship Fund (named for his and his wife's parents) at the University of Nebraska. It supports an annual ROTC scholarship there.

Barney Oldfield joined Litton Industries, Inc., on January 2, 1963. He has worked in a myriad of areas on a range of special projects domestically and abroad, including being the firm's specialist in East-West trade, in economic development ventures, in educational liaison, in corporate sociological involvements, and in international public and governmental relations.

He is a Trustee of the Air Force Museum Foundation, is a member of the Public Affairs Advisory Committee of the Air Force Academy Foundation, is the Founder and Treasurer of the Radio and Television News Directors Foundation, is Chairman of the Radio and Television News Directors Association Scholarship and Financial Development Committee, and in 1976 co-editor of a book in German and English entitled *Those Wonderful Men in the Cactus Starfighter Squadron* [*Die aussergewöhnlichen Männer der Kaktus Starfighter Staffel*]. (The income from this book established a Luftwaffe / U.S. Air Force "International Friendship Foundation" whose annual disbursements support Boys and Girls Club activities.) He established the Aviation/Space Writers Foundation, which gives grants to college students who write on or do broadcasts about aerospace subjects.

His latest book, a novel published in 1980 called *Operation Narcissus*, has been a money raiser for four Foundations.

Barney Oldfield is said to be the only "three-way" Colonel: Army, Air Force, and Kentucky!

**David Othmer**

# You May Never Be Together, But You're Never Alone

*On the first Saint Patrick's Day of the decade*, at 1:45 A.M., I stood in front of a Channel 13 camera and asked our viewers not to call and make a pledge for more programming like the kind they had been seeing. As the hard-sell person Channel 13 brings on to pitch when pledging is down, this was quite a change of pace for me: the most important sale I've ever made was paying off. (In fact, the payoff being reflected on the screen was incredible: Channel 13 had set a twelve-month goal of 76,000 new members, had increased that to 80,000 for reasons I'll get into later, and had reached the improbable total of 85,000 in fewer than nine months.)

It was a complicated sale, most complicated, I suspect, because I first had to sell myself, or even more cumbersome, let myself be sold.

A little background. Channel 13, WNET in New York City, is the largest (by a factor of two) public television station in the United States. It produces the most hours of programming for public television, has an annual budget of nearly $50,000,000, and employs over 500 people. But despite its size and outward solidity, nearly all of its funding is year-to-year or project-by-project funding—in other words, there is no security from one year to the next on where the money to run the station will come from. One of our most important tasks, therefore, has been to diversify our sources of funding so that we can go from year to year with the least potential disruption. Funding now is pretty equally divided among foundations, corporations, government agencies, and the viewing public; the viewing public, at 28 percent of the total, is the single largest source.

Looked at another way, however, the viewing public takes on an even larger role. Since over half of our $50,000,000 is earmarked for specific projects, like *Great Performances* or *The MacNeil/Lehrer Report*, and since all of our viewer contributions are for discretionary uses, membership support represents well over half of Channel 13's discretionary funds. And it is these discretionary funds that provide for both the substance and the frosting that make Channel 13 different from any other television station, public or commercial.

Our membership support is, in brief, our lifeline, and we have treated it with the predictable degree of conservatism and risk aversion: you don't, after all, take risks with your air line if you are a deep-sea diver.

This conservatism, however, was gradually strangling us. To carry the analogy another step, a tightly controlled air line restricts your motion—and ability to explore—a lot. We were so afraid of losing public support that we treated our supporters so timidly and so mindlessly that we were running the risk of losing them as a result of the very strategies that we had fallen into to ensure that we keep them. It was, in fact, not unlike many marriages (including my own) in which fear of its breaking up led to behavior that inexorably caused the break-up. And I think that personal realization was the first step in making the sale I'm describing here.

Being able to stand in front of the camera, then, and say "don't call" was the culmination of a three-year effort to—in melodramatic terms—preserve the marriage between Channel 13's viewers and Channel 13, a marriage that we both knew was in trouble, but neither of us knew how to correct.

Although the ultimate sale was, of course, to the viewers of Channel 13, the tough sale was within Channel 13 itself. And, unlike some textbook descriptions, the sale was not made through careful analysis of research data leading to the development of a detailed multiyear plan. In fact, our one attempt to make the sale through such a document got all the proper heads nodding and "nice jobbing," but failed utterly to change the course of our fund raising. The idea of changing the very nature of on-air fund raising on Channel 13 was sold in tiny packages, through indirection and sometimes even secrecy, much luck culminating in an exceptional anticlimax. It was not so much a sale as a process: this is not a tale of intrigue, there were no spies and counterspies, but it does give some insight, I hope, into one process of decision making that, strange as it seems, may be the most effective way to operate in some circumstances. It is important to keep in mind, however, that throughout this process, there was a guiding light, a trust that our perception of what the ultimate consumer—our viewers—wanted was right, regardless of the internal questioning that went on.

Our problem was simple: how to increase the number of members of Channel 13 as a percentage of the people who regularly view Channel 13, and to convince them to give more money for something each of them, individually, could get for free by just turning on the television set. Those of us dealing directly with the problem were confident we knew what to do: the difficulty came in convincing the top management of 13 of the wisdom of our insight.

Our insight was simple: we had lost credibility with our viewers. Our on-air fund-raising techniques—our ability to communicate to our viewers—had not developed apace with the rest of our programming.

In fact, we started off late in the 1960s presenting short breaks with an address on the television screen and "music to write checks by." By the mid-1970s this had grown to what many felt was the direct antithesis of what public television stood for: ten-to-twenty-minute breaks repeated several times a day, for what seemed to be months out of every year, during which either station personnel or celebrities— generally from politics or the Broadway stage—would ad lib pleas for money to the viewing public. By the mid 1970s, long after the excitement of Watergate had worn off, our viewers became disenchanted with our fund-raising techniques, and we ourselves began to understand that we could not in good conscience follow a carefully produced program by Leonard Bernstein, Alvin Ailey, or Bill Moyers costing hundreds of thousands of dollars with a head and shoulders shot of someone standing in front of a bank of telephones ad libbing why you should "call now to support this kind of fine programming." We became, without knowing it, a parody of ourselves, an unintentional Monty Python routine.

One of the greatest difficulties we had in dealing with this problem was that while complaints were piling up, so was the money. We could discern no loss of revenue resulting from our amateurish fund-raising techniques. In fact, revenue continued to grow, and surveys showed that most people were at worst tolerant of our fund raising, feeling that it was a small price to pay for the product they received.

Those of us answering the phones and working with the producers and on-camera people knew that we were basking in the bright light of a bulb about to burn out, but others felt that perhaps we had discovered the eternal ever-brightening light source. Our task was to convince them that the bulb would go out—before we had to suffer through a blackout.

So there we stood: the entire company knew we were making money with a shoddy product and, consequently, was divided on what—if anything—to do. While stuck in this state of animated suspension—we weren't making any progress but we were moving like crazy—we had our first bit of luck: our most loyal and responsive audience, watchers of *Masterpiece Theater,* stopped contributing. For years we could count on that audience above all others to respond to our pitches: they were loyal, they knew us, and month in and month out they contributed out of all proportion to their numbers, calling in and pledging to our amateurish pitches. We even thought for a while that our very amateurishness was our charm: How could anyone resist helping someone so clearly incompetent as we?

But one day they stopped calling. The conventional wisdom inside 13 instantly became fatalistic: we've saturated the market, there are no more people out there in that audience left to give.

I didn't know what to think. With me, in fact, it was clearly a case of feeling very strongly both ways: on Monday, Wednesday, and Friday I felt that the great experiment of voluntary support for something that could be had for free had failed. On Tuesday, Thursday, and Saturday, however, my gut told me that we had but scratched the surface, that our then ratio of one member out of every twelve or fifteen regular viewers was disgracefully low, that if public television were to be an important factor in our society public support had to be its mainstay, and that the failure was our own in not being convincing enough.

The battle raged, both internally and externally. Nonprofessional surveys were taken (we had no money for real ones); statistics were analyzed to within millimeters of their basic unreliability. People became bummed and burned out, some leaving the company in bitter frustration. Finally, after endless debate, the choice of which way to go was gradually shifted so that there was, in fact, no choice: the choice was to go forward and experiment or to accept fund raising as a smaller and less important part of public television.

There were really four sales involved internally: the first was to treat the on-air talent properly by helping them as they sat virtually naked in front of the camera ad libbing pleas for money; the second was to treat the production properly, to give fund raising as much importance as any other program we produced; the third was to treat the producers properly, and give them enough time and support to produce good fund-raising programming; and the fourth was to treat the public properly, by making them true partners in the extraordinary venture of public television.

By 1975 fund raising on Channel 13 had become acutely, boringly predictable. The dilemma was posed as follows: people call only when you ask them to. If you are too entertaining in the asking, they will watch you entertain them, and not call. If you are too boring, they will turn channels. The trick is to walk the fine line of not being either. At first we all took this very seriously, missing the great irony that we were, very seriously, doing exactly what public television had pledged to avoid—producing mild, inoffensive, unthinking programming. So far we had erred dramatically on the side of the boring. This came about because we asked people who knew little about public television (actors, politicians) to come in and lend their names and reputations to our cause. This they did happily, until they found themselves in front of a camera for ten minutes being asked to ad lib why the unseen millions of viewers should support Channel 13. These pitches became painfully embarrassing for everyone: being a great actor or politician was not sufficient qualification to be a good fund raiser.

Our first major step forward, then, was to script the fund-raising breaks. That decision, the first sale, was made with great fear and trepidation: the concern would come back to haunt us throughout the process. "How can we possibly script the breaks?" people asked. "That would lessen the credibility of the talent since it would be obvious that they were not expressing their thoughts in their own words." Some thought it dishonest to tell the performers what to say: it should come from the heart, not a teleprompter. We compromised, and agreed to experiment with scripts but leave plenty of room in every break for ad libbing. Although the experiment was a huge success, it was almost self-defeating. In our caution, we wrote very few scripts, and used them over and over again. As a result, while any individual break looked hundreds of times better than previous ones, over the course of an evening a viewer, hearing the same words over and over again, could go crazy and think that the performer had truly lost his or her mind. The internal critics—basing their case on loss of spontaneity (an argument that would recur and recur)—urged that we abandon scripting. Others felt that what was needed was not less but more scripting.

Corporate inertia came to the rescue. We had hired a script writer and weren't about to fire the person. So we proceeded with more, not less scripting. Within a year, scripts had become an integral part of fund raising, and we had learned that to use the same tone following a Monty Python program, a ballet, and a heavy drama was foolish. Our scripts became specific to each program, and over time not only tried to match the tone and feeling of viewers coming out of the program, but also cut through the boring versus interesting dilemma by discovering that an alternation of a "here's why we're here" pitch with "here's more information about what you've just seen" material kept viewers viewing and made more of them call.

The next sale involved the production. Our fund-raising production suffered in contrast to both our own programming and commercial television programming. We were, in effect, victimized by the economic structure of commercial television (and commercial television, much as we hate to admit it, accounts for 95 percent of the viewing of television in this country). Since commercial networks can receive, for no reason other than supply and demand, as much as $500,000 per minute of advertising time (and they can sell about ten such minutes per hour) the cost of the programs they produce can be very high and still return a large profit to the broadcasters. Being able to spend vast amounts of money on a given half-hour program (the average cost of a half-hour situation comedy like *Mork and Mindy* is in the $300,000–$450,000 range) means that the technical quality of American television production is extraordinary, and as a result American viewers have come to expect all television to have extraordinary (and thus expensive) camera work, special effects, and editing in addition to good performances and writing.

We in public television are caught in the bind that while viewers expect productions as technically expert as commercial television, we simply don't have the extra billion or so dollars to compete. (Which is why we "rent" so much foreign programming—at about 10¢ on the dollar—rather than producing our own.) The most egregious example of this was our on-air fund raising. Operating from a high-ceilinged basement on East 46th Street, on-air fund raising was out of sight, out of mind, and literally underground from the rest of the company, located two miles away on the west side of Manhattan. We were operating from a studio that was Channel 13's original studio in 1962, when the call letters were WNDT, NDT standing for New Dimensions in Television. I think the new dimensions referred to the studio—never had anyone tried to produce anything in so small and odd-shaped a facility—they were new dimensions indeed.

The next sale, therefore, was to abandon studio 46 and get into the big studio, the same studio used by *MacNeil/Lehrer, Dick Cavett,* and occasionally *Great Performances.*

Although it was no secret that the look of our fund raising—a person sitting in front of a bank of phones—was dull and antithetical to everything that we stood for, and although everyone at 13 wanted a better "look," the task of moving out of studio 46 was not easy. What clinched it was getting one of 13's most respected directors to agree to direct the entire fund-raising period in March 1977. This almost insignificant move—bringing in the new director—eventually led to 13's abandoning studio 46 altogether, and was a crucial step in changing the nature of fund raising on Channel 13.

The next major breakthrough was getting out of the ten-hours-a-day, ten-straight-days of live production. The problems were legion: it was a tremendous coordination job of people (production, technical, and above all on-camera talent), it was hard to get on-air talent in the studio at the proper time live hour after live hour, day after day, it was hard to keep the production staff going, and it was impossible to be innovative in terms of the look and feel of the breaks. It was a true marathon, and very soon into it the goal became only to come out alive, nothing more.

And again the bugaboo of spontaneity came up. How could we prerecord a break and still be true to our audience? There was this peculiar thought process that somehow not being live and unscripted was dishonest. The same people who would commit you for suggesting that *La Traviata* be performed live and unrehearsed in our studio thought that our very integrity was questioned if we didn't do all fund raising live, unrehearsed, and unlike *Traviata,* unscripted.

We started by prerecording some of our children's breaks. Caution was once again our first, middle, and last name. We started out with live breaks on Monday, Wednesday, and Friday, and prerecorded ones on Tuesday and Thursday. When, after all the proper discounts were made for weather and the eye color of the talent and we found that the prerecorded breaks did just as well as the live ones, we slowly moved into prime-time prerecorded breaks.

Again, the results were astonishing. With time to actually put together an eight-minute program designed to motivate viewers to call, with time to write scripts, to think through the proper performers and the proper pacing, and to vary the visuals, we found we could get more people to join Channel 13 in a shorter period of time. Step 3 had been accomplished.

But there was still something critical missing. We were treating our viewers honestly in all but one regard, and they knew it, at least subliminally, and we felt they were responding by not calling. No matter how good the breaks were, no matter how well paced, how motivational, how informative, there was still a sense of mindlessness to them. Why were we doing this? Why was it so seemingly interminable? Was there no plan to it all? Did we just come on and ask for money whenever we thought we might get it? Were we really so disorganized that we had to be totally vague and unpredictable in how we went about fund raising? Some of us felt the answers to these questions were clear: we did have a goal, we did know what we needed, and if we were to share that information with the viewers, and make a pact with them that as soon as we reached our goal we would stop fund raising for the year, then we would increase the productivity of our breaks tremendously.

And this proved to be the final, and to me personally most satisfying, anticlimactic (because it was so easy) battle to date. In mid-February 1980, halfway through our fiscal year, we had added about 30,000 new members to Channel 13. Our goal through June (with the biggest fund-raising period still to come in March) was 76,000. We had estimated 40,000 new members in March, and were planning on a June fund-raising week to get the remaining members.

Since the main argument against public announcement of a goal had been that we needed the flexibility to go to the public should a fiscal crisis arise after we'd made the goal, the compromise was to boost the goal somewhat to account for any contingencies, to state a public goal, and say that we would stop fund raising once we made it. The compromise was 80,000 new members, and everybody was pleased because it was generally felt that 80,000 was an unattainable goal.

To me it was a great climax to the long campaign to sell a different way of approaching our public within Channel 13, to establish a true partnership with them. I was so pleased by the progress we'd made to date, so convinced that a goal would succeed in galvanizing support from our viewers, and so tired of the process that we had been going through in making progress so far, that I decided that I would stake my job on the outcome of the decision. I shared this decision with a few people, but held back the threat until it was needed. It was never needed, and thus the anticlimax of that final meeting to set the goal: I was girded to go all out, and found, much to my amusement, that we were able to muddle through that critical turning point just as we had so many times before: scripting, studio, pretaping, pacing.

The internal sales are the most difficult, because, like a marriage, they involve personal relationships, Further, unlike most marriages, they involve many personal relationships. At 13 we had a fairly typical array of people: heart of gold, but very resistant to change; inspirational at the broad level, no interest or ability to deal with detail; good ability, terrible attitude; terrible ability, good attitude; I-could-do-anything-if-only-I-got-a-little-respect; cynical—it-doesn't-make-any-difference-what-you-do-everyone-will-hate-it-and-you'll-still-get-the-money. Trying to get something through all these people, was me, with my own doubts, questions, and personal insecurities. It made marriage look like a cinch. But I learned two things. First, when you have a large cast of characters you may never be together, but you're never alone—there are constantly shifting alliances, and there is great safety in numbers. Second, when doubts and questions are overwhelming you can usually advance and muddle through because although no one is prepared to say "do it" to a major initiative, no one is capable of saying "no" to a minor one. And, at least in this case, many minors made a major.

Symbolic of the whole adventure was Wednesday, March 12, 1980. On that evening we broadcast *On Giants' Shoulders*, a wonderfully human story about a Thalidomide (no arms, no legs) baby. Most public television stations had refused to schedule it on the assumption that such a subject could not possibly be an effective fund raiser. We scheduled it, had scripted, prerecorded fund-raising spots around it pushing the programming and our 80,000 goal, and had one of our most successful nights of the festival. It had all been worth the effort.

David Othmer is Director of Broadcasting at WNET/13, the largest public television station in the United States. This position includes scheduling the programs on Channel 13, making local program acquisitions and productions, and supervising the on-air continuity function (on-air continuity is what happens between the time one program ends and the next one begins), promo production, and on-air fund raising.

David was born in Medford, Massachusetts, but soon moved to Puerto Rico, Guatemala, and Brazil. It was while attending Andover that he was first introduced to television: it was a Saturday night, the program was "Your Hit Parade," and Tennessee Ernie Ford was singing "16 Tons." David was not impressed. He was graduated from Andover, Harvard, and, after a year working and traveling he attended the Harvard Business School. From 1966 to 1968 he was an M.I.T. Fellow in Colombia, where he worked for a local, private development bank in Medellin. David returned to the United States in 1968, bouncing around Washington, D.C., and New York for a couple of years before becoming very involved with an exciting, though ill-timed and therefore ill-fated, entrepreneurial cable television venture.

David Othmer joined Channel 13 in early 1974 as Assistant to the President, and became Director of Broadcasting some eighteen months later. He feels that his major accomplishments, other than impersonating Zorro in a fund-raising drive, have been raising his daughter, Rachel, and helping prepare Channel 13 for the phenomenal communications revolution that is in its first stages.

*Howard D. Putnam*

# The Winning Spirit

*The airline industry* . . . having spent twenty-five of my forty-two years consumed by it, I can't imagine any industry more exciting. And Southwest Airlines, which I joined as President and Chief Executive Officer in 1978, has probably the most colorful, exciting history of any carrier in the entire industry. It's impossible to pick out a single sales story for Southwest and call it the greatest. From our formation in 1967 to our start-up in June 1971, we were beset by endless litigation, problems, and stumbling blocks brought on by the Dallas/Fort Worth Regional Airport Board and competitive airlines contesting our right to become an airline and use Love Field in Dallas. We've been fighting ever since—sometimes for our very life—against seemingly impossible odds.

From its conception in 1967 by Rollin King and Herbert D. Kelleher, a San Antonio attorney, to its stormy birth in 1971 amid heated litigation, it's been one fight after another. But ironically enough, those very fights for existence, for a place among the giants of the industry, are what sent life-giving energy coursing through the veins of the small band of dedicated employees who used their determination and wits as much as anything else to stay alive. For they had more than jobs and money at stake. It was a classic case of the big guy versus the little guy, and our people were determined to hang in there against all the odds. At this point, I could fill this volume enumerating the endless trips Mr. Kelleher made to the courthouse (three times all the way to the U.S. Supreme Court . . . successfully); the price wars (the most notorious of which was the famous $13 war between Southwest and Braniff); the ingenious advertising campaigns which aroused the public's attention and sympathies and made them root for the underdog—Southwest; the experimentation with fares until the magic formula, or pricing strategy, was found (the two-tier fare structure offering Executive Class flights weekdays before 7:00 P.M. and less expensive Pleasure Class flights after 7:00 P.M. and on weekends); and the list could go on and on. But those are oft-told stories that have been lauded in the airline industry, as well as the financial centers, for nine years.

So with one chapter to expound upon one of the greatest of Southwest's sales experiences (we were selling ourselves to the flying public), I'd like to share with you the most recent battle, and oddly enough, it has to do with love. From our inception with three airplanes and three cities—Dallas, Houston, and San Antonio—Southwest has been known as the "love airline" . . . serving "love" potions (cocktails), "love" bites (peanuts), selling tickets from "love" machines (cash registers), handing out "love" lights (matches), serving passengers with professional and "lovely" hostesses dressed in brightly colored hot pants and boots (what else in Texas??), flying through the skies of Texas (and more recently Louisiana, Oklahoma, and New Mexico) on rainbow-colored "love" birds (Boeing 737-200 jet aircraft), trading our stock on the New York Stock Exchange under the ticker symbol "LUV" . . . the list is endless. But the most important "love" of all and the one most vital to public convenience is our service from Dallas' Love Field. That's the one battle we were never able to simply win and walk away from—that's the one that kept rearing its ugly head in a different form after each successful court encounter. And the issue I intend to focus on here is this latest and final chapter in the saga of service from Love Field.

Until December 1978 we had been an intrastate airline within Texas. We were certified by and operated under the jurisdiction of the TAC (Texas Aeronautics Commission), a very progressive and forward-thinking state regulatory agency. The Deregulation Act of 1978 for the airline industry afforded us the opportunity to grow beyond the borders of Texas. We chose to first fly to New Orleans from Houston's Hobby Airport. This interstate route, however, placed us under the CAB (Civil Aeronautics Board). We protested but were denied an exemption to keep our Texas operation under the TAC. We were going from deregulation, it seemed, to considerably more regulation.

For several months it was a constant but rewarding exchange with the CAB. We discussed many issues as we sought on trip after trip to Washington, D.C., to preserve our simple, low-cost, uncomplicated, and profitable company. We're a different kind of airline. We're in mass transit. We serve short-haul markets, mainly 200–350 miles, and draw a tremendous number of customers away from highways, buses, and backyards with our fares, which are 30 to 50 percent below other airlines' standard coach fares. We utilize cash register tickets that carry no name and, if lost, are not refundable. We're highly productive and efficient and thereby make our money on volume.

Under deregulation, every airline may select one route each year for three years, beginning with 1979, as an "automatic entry" choice. We filed to fly from Dallas' Love Field to New Orleans. As the CAB processed our application in early 1979, the Love Field Battle began again. The cities of Dallas, Fort Worth, the D/FW Regional Airport Board, and individual carriers *again* contested our use of Love Field, this time on the basis that all the previous litigation granted us the right for *intrastate* service only. Even some local homeowners' groups, who benefit daily from our convenient service and low prices, were becoming involved, citing environmental issues as a reason to deny us a right given by law. Again, more legal fees, hearings, and trips to Washington were necessitated. Precious time needed to operate and plan a business had to again be utilized to preserve free enterprise.

We brought our customers into the act at the suggestion of Colleen Barrett, a Southwest employee. Petitions were printed in June and placed on every Southwest flight for a week to see if our customers preferred low-fare, short-haul, interstate flights from Dallas Love Field. Also our pilots, hostesses, marketing representatives, and other concerned employees stood on street corners with clipboards of petitions telling our story and getting signatures. The results were astounding. Over 70,000 signatures were received in the air and on the ground. In a CAB proceeding, all exhibits have to be served on every interested party. Forty sets of the 70,000 signatures were made, resulting in nearly 3000 pounds of paper, which we then flew to Washington and delivered by a moving van to the Civil Aeronautics Board. Based on this public

# NOW IS THE TIME

**THE "SPECIAL" AMENDMENTS.** On Monday October 22, the U.S. House of Representatives, by voice vote, passed H.R. 2440, a routine airport assistance bill, but with a special amendment, Section 3, which bans interstate passenger flights from Love Field. There was no public notice or hearing on adoption of this amendment, which is now tied up in a House-Senate conference committee. On Tuesday October 30, the House Public Works Committee approved H.R. 5481, entitled the "International Air Transportation Competition Act of 1979." This bill also contains a special amendment banning interstate passenger flights from Love Field. Again, there was no public notice or hearing on the amendment.

**WHY THE "SPECIAL TREATMENT"?** It's the latest in a series of attempts to circumvent the Airline Deregulation Act of 1978 and the Civil Aeronautics Board (CAB) and to keep Southwest Airlines from providing Dallas with convenient, low-cost service from Love Field to New Orleans and other shorthaul, interstate destinations. It received special treatment precisely so that you, as concerned individuals, would not have an opportunity to speak. If you thought the federal government got out of one industry's economic "hair" with the Airline Deregulation Act—watch out, it's back!

**THE ERRONEOUS CLAIMS:** SAFETY. It has been claimed that Love Field is "unsafe" because of its "mix" of commercial and general aviation flights. The Federal Aviation Administration (FAA), which has exclusive, nationwide jurisdiction over air safety matters, and the Department of Transportation (DOT) completely refuted and rejected this contention in Exhibit DOT-PH-1, filed with the CAB on May 10, 1979 in the Southwest Airlines Automatic Market Entry Investigation, Docket No. 34582.

Every hub airport in the United States of America has a substantial "mix" of commercial and general aviation flights. For instance, according to the "FAA Air Traffic Activity Statistics" for the Fiscal Year 1977, National Airport in Washington, D.C. had 130,417 non-air carrier operations; San Francisco had 87,918 non-air carrier operations; and DFW Airport had 77,214.

If the commercial/general aviation "mix" is a problem, then it's not just a Love Field problem; it's a national air transportation system problem.

**DFW'S FINANCIAL STABILITY.** It has often been alleged that Southwest's furnishing shorthaul air service through Love Field would imperil the financing of DFW Airport. This claim was first made before Federal District Judge W. M. Taylor, Jr. in 1973 with respect to Southwest's intrastate air service. Southwest has continued to furnish such service through Love Field since DFW Airport opened on January 13, 1974. Has DFW collapsed? Quite to the contrary. In 1977, DFW was the third busiest airport in the nation in terms of departures performed in scheduled air service, ranking only behind Chicago-O'Hare and Atlanta-Hartsfield—the two most congested airports in the country!

DFW had more commercial departures (146,297) in 1977 than such major airports as Los Angeles-International and New York's La Guardia

and Kennedy. In terms of domestic passenger enplanements, it was then the fourth largest airport in the United States.

From 1977 to date, DFW has grown at annual "double digit" rates. Under federal deregulation, an ever greater number of air carriers almost weekly receive new national, international, and intercontinental routes into, and out of, the principal hub of the Southwestern region of the United States. The country's largest airport hotel is under construction on its premises, and two of the nation's largest air carriers have moved their worldwide headquarters there. Braniff International and Texas International are substantially expanding their terminal facilities, and, thus, the monumental success story of DFW continues and accelerates.

Southwest provides both intrastate and interstate air service to Houston's Hobby Airport without objection from the City of Houston and without injury to Houston's Intercontinental Airport. After only eight months of service, Southwest is carrying 35,000-40,000 passengers per month between Hobby and New Orleans at generally available, unrestricted fares as low as $22.00. Why should Houston receive these benefits and not Dallas? The oft-repeated tale of a "dangerous threat" to the "big airport" from the "little airport" has been proven a hollow myth in Houston—and in Dallas.

Finally, on the subject of DFW finances, the air carriers serving DFW underwrite all of its expenses—not the citizens of Dallas and Fort Worth. This is what the bond ordinances provide; this is what the written agreements of those carriers with the DFW Regional Airport Board provide; and this is what Federal District Judge W. M. Taylor, Jr. found to be the case in his written opinion in City of Dallas vs. Southwest Airlines Co., 371 F. Supp. 1015, 1021 (N.D. Tex. 1973). As stated by the Executive Director of DFW Airport to Aviation Daily and as confirmed by DFW's Finance Director in his testimony before the Federal District Court: "The Airport Board and management do not have a financial stake in Southwest's presence at DFW. For the cities to be involved in coming up with tax dollars, all of the airlines serving DFW Airport would have to go broke." None of the airlines serving DFW Airport are about to "go broke."

**NOISE.** Love Field has successfully served as a commercial airport for many decades. Contrary to what you have been told, the City of Dallas 1968 Regional Airport Concurrent Bond Ordinance does not ban commercial air service from Love Field. As stated in the opinion of Federal District Judge W. M. Taylor, Jr.:

"... In short, some of the operations to remain at Love Field will use planes larger than Southwest's; some will use planes noisier than Southwest's; some will use planes identical to Southwest's; and, indeed, some of the aircraft operations may be on a scheduled basis and compete in markets which Southwest presently serves ..."

The Fifth Circuit Court of Appeals, in upholding Southwest's right to use Love Field, commented on "this curious and unpleasant feature of the ordinance."

Also contrary to what you have been told, the 1968 Bond Ordinance was not enacted to make Love Field quieter. This is an afterthought, now being used in the twelfth or thirteenth attempt to restrict Southwest's shorthaul service and to deprive you of its benefits. As Section 9.5 of the 1968 Ordinance clearly sets forth and as Judge Taylor found, "... (the Cities of Dallas and Fort Worth) overtly declare their purpose to be the suppression of the competition in pursuit of a purely economic advantage for the Regional Airport ..."

All of Southwest's 737-200 aircraft, and their engines, meet the 1985 "quietness" requirements of the FAA. Ours is, we believe, the only fleet in the country in total compliance. Further, there were 270,000 scheduled commercial operations performed at Love Field, with heavy, far noisier aircraft, in 1973, and there were only 36,000 such operations in 1978. As far as commercial air service is concerned, Love Field has never been quieter.

There is another, thought-provoking issue in connection with noise, which also bears upon the safety allegations of our adversaries. At our last count, there were 97 private jets stationed at Love Field, a fleet more than five times the size of ours. And this figure does not include itinerant jets, operating into Love from other cities.

Many of these private jets are noisier than ours, and many of them do not consistently use noise abatement flight procedures as we do. Some of them are also bigger and faster than our aircraft.

We have no quarrel with general, or corporate, aviation. We are pleased to share Love Field and proud of its national prominence as a general aviation facility. It must be pointed out, however, that if our aircraft operations are to be restricted due to noise or safety considerations, then general aviation jets must also be restricted. There is no defensible legal, logical, or ethical distinction to be drawn between "our" jets and "their" jets.

**"FAIR SHARE."** It has been said that we do not "pay our way" at Love Field and also that we are simply trying to escape the higher landing fees at DFW Airport. Both assertions are unfounded.

The Love Field budget for fiscal year 1978-79 was $5,060,000. During fiscal year 1978-79, based on unaudited year-end figures, we produced for the City of Dallas $1,463,506 in landing fees and space rentals; $1,769,723 in parking fees; $700,547 in rent car and restaurant concession payments and $47,688 in other concessions; and entitlement, based upon our number of enplaned passengers, to receive $1,586,500 in DOT checks to be spent on Love Field facilities. These items together total $5,567,964—$507,964 more than the entire Love Field budget. We are not only "paying our way"—we are paying for Love Field! And the revenues derived from the rest of the many general and commercial aviation activities at Love Field are "gravy" for the City of Dallas.

As to the higher DFW landing fees, we are concerned about higher costs at DFW, but in a different way—and for you, the public, not us, the airline. Every time the government intervenes to regulate the economy—the consumer foots the bill.

**WHY NOT DFW SERVICE?** Southwest Airlines is a highly specialized airline. It is designed, and

# TO FIGHT FOR LOVE.

works, for the benefit of the shorthaul, commuter passenger. That is why, for instance, we have automatic ticketing machines, cash register tickets, and discount ticket books. That is also why we do not interline (exchange passengers) with other airlines, or carry the mail, and why we turn our airplanes around at the terminal in ten minutes.

DFW is a magnificent facility and a tremendously productive economic asset for the Metroplex. But ask yourself whether it is suited for our type of airline operation and our type of passenger? And if your first answer is "yes," then further ask yourself why Fort Worth has requested us to consider, and we are seriously considering, intrastate air service through Meacham Field? And why the Eastern Airlines shuttle service is provided through downtown National Airport, owned and operated by the Federal Government, rather than its outlying Dulles Airport in Virginia?

We don't have to answer these questions. We can let others do it for us:

1. In the CAB's Dallas/Fort Worth Regional Airport Investigation, the City of Dallas strenuously contended that providing service solely through Greater Southwest International Airport, located just south of DFW, would seriously injure the Dallas shorthaul air passenger market. It also presented as witnesses numerous and distinguished Dallas civic and business leaders and public officials to reinforce its contentions.

2. Texas International Airlines in 1973 informed the CAB that its commencement of service from Houston's outlying Intercontinental Airport, rather than close-in Hobby, caused a $2,200,000 loss of revenue in the first year due to the decline in the number of shorthaul passengers it carried and that the move from Love to DFW would have a "violent impact" because the "time for ground transportation from the airport to Dallas will now be longer than some of these (shorthaul) flights, thus making the automobile far more competitive for the inter-city traffic."

3. Judge Taylor found, in his opinion in City of Dallas vs. Southwest Airlines, that:

   "Finally, the attempt to exclude Southwest Airlines from Love Field is particularly irrational and inherently 'unjust' because it removes to a more remote airport the one kind of passenger service which has most need of a close-in airport.... Consequently, this Court concludes that excluding Southwest's strictly shorthaul air service from Love Field, while allowing longhaul flights by charter carriers, corporate jets and others to remain there, is unjustly discriminatory...and improperly grants an exclusive right to the aircraft users who will be eligible to use Love Field after the Regional Airport opens."

4. The United States Department of Transportation limited the use of Washington's close-in National Airport to shorthaul flights and removed longhaul flights to Washington, D.C.'s outlying Dulles Airport because, in the words of the FAA:

   "National—only ten minutes from downtown Washington—is ideally situated to serve the shorthaul market where ground travel time is a significant part of the total trip and often a determining factor in whether a traveler goes by air or uses another mode of transportation.

   "Dulles is especially suited for the international and longhaul markets where ground travel time is a less critical factor. Its long runways, large ramp areas and modern terminal facilities were specifically designed for long-range, heavier aircraft and their users."

   Substitute "Love" for "National" and "DFW" for "Dulles," and none of the rest of the FAA's language need be changed.

   In its last session, the Texas Legislature overwhelmingly passed a 600-mile limitation on non-stop flights into and out of Love Field. But this compromise, acceptable to Southwest Airlines, was vetoed.

## WHAT HAVE DALLAS PASSENGERS GOT TO LOSE?

PLENTY. Literally millions of dollars per year. Look at the numbers — then multiply them by Oklahoma City, Tulsa, St. Louis, and Kansas City! Our roundtrip "Executive Class" fare from Love Field to New Orleans is $100; "Pleasure Class" is $70.

Here are our competitors' prices for roundtrip service from Love Field to New Orleans:

| Braniff | $240 first class | $184 coach |
|---|---|---|
| American | $212 first class | $178 coach |
| Delta | $212 first class | $178 coach |
| Texas International | $168 coach | $102 super coach* |

*Available as Roundtrip only.

Source: November 15, 1979 Official Airline Guide

Southwest Airlines' highest fare is lower than its competitors' lowest fare.

## LOVE FIELD CONVENIENCE MEANS TIME AND MONEY

SAVED. Love gives you an extra half hour for work or pleasure each way. And in a period of rocketing gasoline prices — and fear-inspiring inflation — it would be hard to overestimate the money saved by nearby Love Field service. The economists also tell us we've already entered a severe recession. So don't let the ideas of 1962 — when the Regional Airport Investigation started — rob your 1979 pocketbook. DFW Airport and Love Field have coexisted and enormously prospered for almost five years, just as Intercontinental and Hobby have in Houston for seven years. This will continue.

## WHAT'S IN IT FOR DALLAS? LOTS. Southwest's

home is in Dallas. This year we will pay, out of pocket, some $706,000 in personal property taxes and $1,750,000 in landing fees and rentals to the City of Dallas. We'll also pay $217,000 in taxes to Dallas County, and over $18,000,000 to employees on our Dallas payroll. And how much extra business revenue will we bring Dallas each year if we are permitted to fly from shorthaul out-of-state cities into Love Field? Well, you can get some idea of the magnitude from our New Orleans-Houston experience. Already, we are carrying additional passengers into Houston at the rate of approximately 225,000 per year. If, on the average, each of these passengers spends just $100 for cabs, hotel rooms, meals, and entertainment—that's $22,500,000. And this growth has taken place in only eight months of service—from only one city! Our New Orleans-Dallas nonstop service, partially inaugurated on September 28 with three roundtrips per day and boosted to six roundtrips on November 7, last week carried 60 passengers per flight to Love Field.

IS IT TOO LATE FOR YOU TO SPEAK OUT? NO. Ultimately the Senate must decide whether this anti-Love Field amendment should remain in the bills or not. We know our U.S. Senators to be fairminded men and we feel that they will respond to the needs and wishes of Texas citizens.

IF YOU ARE A SOUTHWEST AIRLINES PASSENGER OR A CITIZEN CONCERNED WITH FAIR PLAY AND GENUINE FREE ENTERPRISE, HERE'S YOUR CHANCE TO FIGHT FOR LOVE — AND MONEY. SIGN THE COUPON, SEND IT TO US, AND WE'LL SEND IT TO WASHINGTON. REMEMBER, IF YOU REALLY BELIEVE IN FREE ENTERPRISE — THERE CAN'T BE ANY STRINGS ATTACHED!

*Herbert D. Kelleher*

Herbert D. Kelleher
Chairman of the Board

*Howard D. Putnam*

Howard D. Putnam
President and Chief Executive Officer

---

To: Southwest Airlines Co., P.O. Box 37611, Love Field, Dallas, Texas 75235

The Honorable John Tower
United States Senate

The Honorable Lloyd Bentsen
United States Senate

Sirs: I want to keep our convenient, efficient, low-cost service between Love Field and New Orleans. I am unalterably opposed to Section 3 of H.R. 2440, and any like governmental interference, as an infringement of my right to a free choice and an unfair restriction on free airline competition.

Signature: _____

Name: _____     Address: _____

# SOUTHWEST AIRLINES

support, the fact that we were not violating any environmental guidelines, and the Deregulation Act itself, we were finally granted the route on Friday, September 28, 1979, at 2:00 P.M. We were ready. I held a brief press conference at Love Field at 3:30 P.M., and we departed on the inaugural flight from Love Field to New Orleans at 8:00 that evening.

As we got back to the business of operating an airline with our faith in the free enterprise system renewed, it happened again. In October 1979, Congressman Jim Wright of Fort Worth, Texas, the Majority Leader of the U.S. House of Representatives, introduced an amendment to a large aviation funding bill that would give to the D/FW Regional Airport Board and the cities of Dallas and Fort Worth the power to prohibit interstate service from Love Field.

History played an important role here. Congressman Wright and business leaders helped plan and create the gigantic Dallas/Fort Worth Regional Airport in the 1960s. Their goal was to force all air traffic into it. D/FW is located some twenty-two miles northwest of Dallas and some twenty-five miles northeast of Fort Worth. A beautiful facility, Love Field Dallas, only six miles from downtown Dallas, was being vacated and wasted by other airlines. Southwest had kept it alive and provided close, convenient, commuter-type service. We had refused to sign the agreement to go to D/FW, and Mr. Kelleher had successfully defended our right to stay at Love over and over.

Now we had a new challenge: how to stop a bill from passing in the U.S. Congress. Herb Kelleher, our Chairman and General Counsel, moved to Washington. We employed additional legal and lobbyist support in Washington and set out on an intensive effort to inform every Congressman and Senator involved with this piece of legislation of the potential danger, not only to us, but to the entire nation, of such an amendment. We also turned again to the people who have always helped us the most—our customers. Again, quickly, petitions were placed on airplanes. In five days 60,000 signatures were received. In every city we served full-page ads headed with "NOW IS THE TIME TO FIGHT FOR LOVE." The ads included a coupon to be mailed back supporting interstate service. These coupons, over 16,000 of them, were delivered to our two Texas Senators, Tower and Bentsen.

Over twenty major newspapers editorialized loudly in favor of Southwest and free enterprise. Thousands of citizens sent telegrams, wrote letters, and made phone calls to various Senators and Congressmen. The city of Harlingen, which Southwest serves, felt so strongly that a delegation, including the Mayor, went to Washington to "fight for Love."

It worked. Enough support and attention surfaced that a compromise became possible. Majority Leader Wright supported reasonable language that allows any airline to go interstate from Love Field to the contiguous states of Texas (Louisiana, Oklahoma, New Mexico, and Arkansas), as long as that airline does not interline (exchange tickets and baggage with other carriers). It preserves our complete intrastate operation from Love Field as well and does not restrict us from flying anywhere we wish from any other city on our system. It also preserves D/FW as the long-haul regional airport and Love as a shorter-haul commuter-type airport. The bill was signed by President Carter in February 1980. We began service to Oklahoma City, Tulsa, and Albuquerque through Love Field in early April 1980.

---

To: Southwest Airlines Co., P.O. Box 37611, Love Field, Dallas, Texas 75235

The Honorable John Tower
United States Senate

The Honorable Lloyd Bentsen
United States Senate

Sirs: I want to keep our convenient, efficient, low-cost service between Love Field and New Orleans. I am unalterably opposed to Section 3 of H.R. 2440, and any like governmental interference, as an infringement of my right to a free choice and an unfair restriction on free airline competition.

Signature: _____

Name: _____ Address: _____

---

We didn't forget those people who came to our defense. After the compromise was reached, another one-page ad was run thanking the people for their help. We've never underestimated the power those folks hold in their hands. These are the grandmothers who fly at Southwest's low fares to babysit for their grandchildren; the children of divorced parents who fly on weekends to visit their fathers or mothers; the businessmen who have found it so convenient to do their business traveling at the times they want on a carrier dedicated to on-time performance; the weekend traveler who, in a time of energy crisis and gasoline shortages, has found it cheaper to fly Southwest than to drive the family automobile. Southwest Airlines is dedicated to serving these people. We're in mass transit . . . it's the way of the future. We're not about to let the public, or ourselves, forget it. We're not perfect, but we're good, and we're getting better. And we'll win . . . because we still have the "winning spirit."

□   □   □

Howard D. Putnam has been President and Chief Executive Officer of Southwest Airlines Co. in Dallas, Texas, since August 21, 1978, his forty-first birthday. He left United Airlines as Group Vice President–Marketing to take on the Southwest challenge.

Putnam grew up on a farm near Bedford, Iowa, and learned to fly from a pasture in his father's J3-Piper Cub. His first airline job at age eighteen was loading baggage for Capital Airlines in Chicago. In 1961 Capital merged with United Airlines, and Putnam held a variety of sales and service jobs, quickly moving through the ranks of United, the free world's largest air carrier.

Putnam has invested twenty-five years in the airline industry, serving at United as a Sales Account Executive (Chicago); Assistant to the Regional Vice President–Sales & Services (Chicago/Midwest Region); Sales Manager (Cleveland); Vice President, Western Region (San Francisco); Vice President–Passenger Marketing (Executive Offices–Chicago); and finally Group Vice President–Marketing from June 1976 to July 1978.

Putnam held one of United's senior management positions and served on the Corporate Policy, Operations Management, and System Marketing committees. He earned an MBA in marketing from the University of Chicago in 1966 and completed the Harvard Business School's Advanced Management Program in May 1978.

*Robert D. Ray*

# *Selling Oneself to the Voters*

*In my business,* the sale that did the most for me obviously has to be "selling" myself and persuading people to vote for me.

Politicians come in all shapes and sizes. They are people with different ideologies, views, and approaches. But to get elected, a candidate must be a successful salesperson. If the candidate is not elected, of course, the failure of that salesperson means his or her programs and ideas may never get sold—and we have another salesman without a product. Selling is exciting, stimulating, and can be most satisfying. In politics and government, that happens only if you are elected—giving you the chance to govern, to lead, to confront problems, propose solutions, and participate in change.

It has been my good fortune in the State of Iowa to have made that sale which has meant so much and to have been elected Governor five times. There have been many similarities in those five campaigns, and yet each one has been different—with new challenges and new opportunities. Each campaign has been a window to let new, innovative, and creative ideas shine through for Iowans to see and judge.

The advancements made in Iowa and the successes and progress Iowans have enjoyed in diverse areas are very gratifying. No matter what the idea might be or its great advantages and potential for improving the quality of life of our citizens, the selling of that idea is rarely free of obstacles and resistance. This was true as we led the nation with a novel school financing plan, in upgrading more miles of railroad branchline than all other states combined, in modernizing our judicial system, and in promoting the sale of gasohol—which makes Iowa the number one state in the country in using this alternative form of energy. And the list goes on and on. These accomplishments, and

**263**

others, have helped to give Iowans an invigorating sense of pride and confidence that we didn't always have.

So you can readily see how difficult it is for me to select a single issue or a single attempt to sell something and say it was clearly the one that "did the most for me."

But there is a sale that I am proud of, not only because it was fiercely resisted and fought, but also because of its strong, valuable consequences for the people of our state. The sale is commonly known as the adoption of the "bottle and can bill."

Although I was convinced this proposal was timely and acceptable and good, my view was not exactly shared by all. Legislative passage was neither easy nor swift. To convince legislators of the value of this bill, it was necessary to reach out and secure the support of the general public, who could, in turn, encourage legislators to vote for a bottle and can bill. To win approval, much time, effort, perseverance, and patience were required—just a few key ingredients to successful selling.

Iowa to Native Americans meant "beautiful land." We take pride in the rich, black topsoil that produces so much of this country's and a good share of the world's food. We are a place where the air is nearly pure and the water fresh. Iowans and visitors had grown careless, doing less than their share to keep the state clean and litter free. Why? Partially, I believe, because of the usual pattern of not caring, the convenience of tossing bottles and cans out of cars, and the great and longstanding freedom to believe we could do whatever we want to do with little or no obligation to protect the beauty and cleanliness of our communities. People felt that it was someone else's responsibility to provide a clean and healthy environment. But perhaps most important, there was no financial incentive to keep the bottles and cans from being strewn around the countryside or tossed onto the streets of our cities and towns. More and more, the bottles and cans sold were nonreturnable—"throwaway"—and they had to be thrown someplace.

In 1976, I was eager to encourage our citizens to control litter in our state. We already had a penalty for littering, which was far from effective. Knowing that a few states had recently enacted legislation dealing with this very problem, my office and I monitored the alternative approaches and learned all we could about the success, or lack of it, in those other states. After deciding on the best concept—one that would reverse the litter trend and would instill in our people a "conservation ethic"—I decided we should propose a plan for the return of bottles and cans that would be recycled and reused. In other words, for each bottle or can of beverage purchased the customer would pay a nickel deposit fee, which would be refunded when the container was returned.

This was practical and positive—a way to get a grip on growing litter and a way to save precious energy. So my product was a deposit bill backed up with statistics, data, and support information—all of which made me feel comfortable with what I had to sell.

This idea cut a swath through many contemporary issues, in addition to energy and the environment. It touched on transportation and the productivity of manufacturing, and it affected the pocketbook of every customer.

It was January 1977 when I proposed the deposit approach to the Iowa legislature. In my Condition of the State Message I said:

Our environment gives us good reason to be proud of where we live. Nevertheless, Iowans say it is not enough to just have fresh air and clean water, and I agree with them. Why not conserve energy and clean up our countryside by making sure that bottles and cans are returned and reused?

The plan I submit is based on solid experience elsewhere. It has worked in other places, and it will work here. Do not delay this simple, but proven idea for two, three or four years. Take action in 1977.

I found the majority of the general public willing to accept a slight inconvenience, because deep within they did have a desire to protect our fragile environment.

But I also found a reluctance on the part of legislators, who were barraged by special interests. Among the opposition were those in business who would be called upon to change their routine of handling the return of more bottles and cans. Also opposed to this concept were manufacturers of glass and aluminum containers as well as distributors and retailers of beverages. They came from everywhere, not just Iowa—they poured in from around the country. We faced a tough battle, and we knew it.

It does not take a salesperson long to discover that even with a terrific, affordable product there may be no sale. During the legislative session we armed ourselves with the facts, we introduced testimony from experts, and we reminded legislators that Iowans use more than one billion beer and soft drink containers every year—three-fourths of which were not being returned. We noted that it takes less energy to sterilize a container and refill it than to mine new ores and convert them to new cans and bottles. Energy savings from this law were estimated to be equivalent to 21 million gallons of gasoline per year—a significant amount at a time when supplies were tight. We pointed out that landfill space was limited and that farmers and highway workers were endangered by flying glass and debris when they mowed the ditches. We also directed attention to the mess caused by the litter in our cities and parks.

Dozens of public-spirited interest groups began moving to support this idea and so did lots of schoolchildren—who were not to be overlooked. Still, whenever we answered one question, legislators were quick to pose another.

Despite our efforts, the bill failed to pass.

To say the least, I was disappointed. However, experience told me not to be disillusioned. So I vowed to be back again the next year.

By January 1978 momentum in our favor was picking up—but so was the opposition, and this time it was organized. Special interest groups budgeted a bundle of money for a blitz of television commercials. These TV spots hit the airwaves just before the legislature convened and continued for weeks. Those elements represented a forceful negative effort to "sell" the defeat of this legislation.

When the legislature reconvened, I told the senators and representatives in my Message:

> We find big-spending lobbyists flexing their "money muscles" and a lavish advertising campaign barraging Iowans with misleading information. The minds of Iowans cannot be bought by this propaganda. The simple facts speak for this bill.

The facts did speak. And so did our Iowans. Seventy-nine percent indicated by survey they would support such a law. Finally, the legislature did too, passing the bill in both chambers and sending it to my desk for signature.

Getting the deposit law approved was the big hurdle. Getting it implemented smoothly was another. So we started what evolved into what I believe was the largest state-wide one-day environmental effort of its kind ever held in the United States. It was called "The Great Iowa Cleanup," and it presented another selling challenge.

The Cleanup was designed to encourage citizens and groups of volunteers to pick up bottles and cans along Iowa's roadsides and in our parks. The goal was to give Iowa a "fresh start" before the deposit law took effect.

Iowa's Energy Policy Council spread the word and local organizations popped up across the state. Young people and adults began planning with zeal for the May 5 Cleanup. And on that bright, blue-sky Saturday, 45,000 Iowans, including myself, joined together to pick up literally millions of bottles and cans. It was fun. We picked up litter, and we felt we were doing something worthwhile—for Iowa and its future.

The Cleanup caused an additional benefit—instilling in our Iowans that "conservation ethic." Those who took part in the Cleanup, and others who soon began living with and accepting the new deposit law, sensed a greater appreciation for our environment.

The deposit law works today. It still sparks some controversy, but most Iowans have expressed their approval of the law—by word and deed. They continue to buy pop and beer. But no longer are Iowans throwing their bottles and cans out of their car windows—as they once did. They bring the containers back to grocery stores and to new recycling centers.

Bottle and can litter in Iowa's state parks has plummeted an estimated 80 to 90 percent, according to our Iowa Conservation Commission. And our Transportation Department reports 70 percent fewer cans in roadside ditches. Other litter has also been reduced. This is the kind of information and ammunition that ought to sell this concept elsewhere.

If the United States is to solve our energy and inflationary woes, other states and Congress would do well to follow the example set by Iowa and a handful of other states. Let's stop wasting energy to produce waste products. Let's increase our gross national product, not our gross national garbage. Let's recycle our American dollars into American labor instead of into imported raw materials.

The main price of mandatory deposits is minor consumer inconvenience. The benefits help point toward consumer economic survival.

Selling this law in Iowa was not easy, but it was accomplished by using the building blocks of any good selling situation: we identified a need. We found a way to meet that need. We decided on a strategy to accomplish our goal, and we marshaled solid information. We went to work and didn't give up after an initial defeat. We listened to people and talked with them—not at them. Then, after the "sale," we kept working with some timely follow-up action.

That is what selling is all about. And, in this instance, approval of the deposit law was not just good salesmanship. It was also good government.

□    □    □

Robert D. Ray of Des Moines is the senior Governor in the United States. Still, Bob Ray maintains a demanding schedule and thrives on the challenges of his job, just as he did when he became Iowa's thirty-eighth Governor. Iowans first elected Bob Ray as their Governor in 1968. He was reelected in 1970, 1972, 1974, and again in 1978—winning an unprecedented fifth term by a wide margin. His job approval rating is still one of the highest of any Governor in the country. Mr. Ray has been chairman of the National Governors' Association and the Republican Governors' Association. Earlier, Governor Ray was chairman of the Midwest Governors' Conference and President of the Council of State Governments.

In 1976, Mr. Ray was chosen by party leaders to chair the Platform Committee at the Republican National Convention, and his work on that difficult task was highly regarded by political observers.

Governor Ray has represented Iowa and the United States on several key diplomatic and good-will assignments. In late 1979, he was one of a handful of Americans to visit both the Soviet Union and the Peoples' Republic of China. He chaired the delegation of Governors on the Russian visit, and arranged for an Iowa trade mission to China while he was in Peking. That mission occurred in September, 1980 and was judged a success by Iowa manufacturers.

The Governor represented the United States at independence ceremonies for the new nation of Papua–New Guinea in 1975. Mr. Ray has visited the Iowa trade office in Frankfurt, West Germany, and was a member of the U.S. delegation to the Special United Nations Conference on Refugees in Geneva, Switzerland.

En route home from China in October, 1979, Governor Ray inspected refugee camps in Thailand. Following that moving experience, the Governor spearheaded a Christmas season fundraising appeal known as Iowa SHARES, which sent $500,000 to feed starving Cambodian refugees.

During his administration, Governor Ray has also met with officials in Austria, Israel, Japan, Romania, Saudi Arabia, and Taiwan.

Governor Ray's pride in Iowa, its people and products, is shown in his active efforts to expand markets for Iowa agricultural and manufactured goods. The Governor has also pursued progressive legislative and executive initiatives to improve the state's quality of life.

Thanks to Governor Ray, Iowa is considered to be a leader among the states in coping with the energy crisis. Good examples of Iowa's efforts include the fuel set aside, coal and solar research, gasohol marketing, and energy conservation and weatherization programs. Most recently, Governor Ray has chaired the National Governors' Association Committee on Energy Emergency Preparedness and an N.G.A. Subcommittee on International Energy.

Governor Ray appointed Governor's Economy Committees in 1969 and again in 1979. Management experts from Iowa companies recommended ways to further streamline state government and save millions in tax dollars, and many of these suggestions have since been implemented.

Iowa and Governor Ray have been recognized by *Time* magazine for efforts to limit rising property taxes. The Governor introduced and expanded tax credits for the elderly, successfully pushed for removing the sales tax on food and drugs, and proposed a $50 million tax rebate in 1979.

While working to bring business and jobs into the state, Governor Ray has also been a strong advocate for agriculture. He has testified before Congressional committees and traveled on "Fine Iowa Meats" promotions. In January 1980, Ray announced a massive hike in funding for Iowa's "first in the nation" soil conservation cost-share program. Numerous farm groups have cited Governor Ray for his efforts, and in 1979 he received the Honorary Master Pork Producer Award from the Iowa Pork Producers Association.

Governor Ray fought for the merger of several agencies into the Department of Environmental Quality and adoption of the bottle and can deposit law to save energy and clean up the environment. The Environmental Protection Agency presented Ray its Environmental Quality Award in 1979.

Iowa's relatively new Department of Transportation is considered a national model, and the state's rail branch-line program has upgraded more miles of track than all other states combined. Both were Ray priorities and helped him earn the 1976 Distinguished Service Award from the American Railway Development Association.

Governor Ray proposed and signed into law a sweeping Urban Revitalization plan for Iowa cities and towns. Earlier, the Governor initiated state revenue sharing with communities, proposed a novel Iowa Tuition Grant program for private college students, appointed an innovative Iowa 2000 futures committee, accomplished reform of Iowa's judicial system, and began the Iowa Citizen's Aide Office.

Actions such as these prompted *Time* magazine to name Governor Ray as one of America's "rising young leaders" in 1974.

Governor Ray was born in Des Moines, Iowa, in 1928, and grew up in Iowa's Capital City during the Great Depression. He was active in sports and captained the Des Moines Roosevelt High School basketball team. Young Bob Ray served in Japan with the U.S. Cavalry and returned home to get a college education. He became a leader on the Drake University campus and earned degrees in both Business Administration and Law. He now holds honorary degrees from several Iowa colleges, including Buena Vista, Central, Cornell, Grinnell, Iowa Wesleyan, Loras, Luther, St. Ambrose, Simpson, Upper Iowa, and Westmar. He also is a recipient of an honorary degree from Drake, along with the Distinguished Alumnus Award and the Order of the Coif from the Drake University Law School.

Ray developed an active law practice in Des Moines and served as a law and reading clerk in the Iowa Senate. While becoming a successful trial attorney, he also moved up the ranks in the Iowa Republican Party. Beginning as an energetic precinct worker, Ray became a member of the Republican State Central Committee and, in 1963, Republican State Chairman. Ray directed dramatic Republican victories in 1966, setting the stage for his election as Governor in 1968.

**William B. Remington**

# Selling British Style

*This memorable and successful sales experience* started in Toronto, Canada, included a trip to the old Midlands city of St. Helens, England, and ended in London. More important to me than the immediate sale were the long-term benefits in terms of lasting friendships and broadened horizons, which have served me well over a period of many years.

In the spring of 1966, I was the Eastern Advertising Manager of the *Architectural Forum*, an architectural journal which for years had been published by Time Inc. At the time of Henry Luce's retirement, it had been turned over to an organization known as Urban America, which was largely funded through the generosity of Mr. and Mrs. Stephen Currier, who were tragically lost several years later flying from San Juan to St. Thomas. Audrey Currier was the daughter of Ailsa Mellon and David Bruce, who later was our Ambassador to England.

About this time it came to my attention that Pilkington Brothers Ltd., of St. Helens, the fourth largest glass producer in the world, had succeeded in inventing a revolutionary new method of making quality glass by the "float" process. Pilkington was the largest privately owned enterprise in the United Kingdom and was nearly 150 years old. The traditional method of making glass was to pour the molten glass on a flat bed and then, following hardening, it would be ground and polished so that it could be seen through and used for windows, doors, automobiles and so on. Alstair Pilkington, after years of research and experimentation, discovered the "float" process of producing glass. By this process the lighter molten glass was "floated" on a flat bed of molten tin. When hardened, the glass came out perfectly clear; the time-consuming and expensive method of grinding and polishing was eliminated. As a result, leading glass producers all over the world obtained licenses from Pilkington in order that they might use the Pilkington "Float Process." United States companies such as Pittsburgh Plate Glass, Ford Motor Company, and Libby Owens Ford, Saint

**273**

Gobain in France, Glaverbel in Belgium, and many other companies throughout the world applied to Pilkington.

There had been an interruption of about eight months when *Architectural Forum* was not published following its separation from Time and its new ownership by Urban America. Obviously, this interruption resulted in the *Forum* losing a large part of its advertising support. I felt very strongly that if we could obtain Pilkington as an advertiser, we would then be in a position to present a very strong case to other leading manufacturers and particularly those who were producing glass by the "float" method.

At this time, I made regular trips to Toronto for the purpose of seeing *Forum* advertisers and prospects. When I called on Pilkington's office there I met Michael Terry, their Canadian Publicity Manager, and John Baldry, now a Vice President of the company but at that time the U.S. Sales Manager. Baldry was a native of Warrington, England, near St. Helens and had started his career with Pilkington there before securing several overseas assignments and then winding up in Toronto. From John Baldry I learned that if the *Forum* was to get Pilkington's advertising we would have to go to St. Helens to see Banastre Tarleton Tinling, the Manager of Pilkington's Publicity Department.

When I returned to the *Forum*'s New York office, I discussed this matter with Lawrence Mester, the publisher of the *Forum*. Although Mester was sympathetic, he was also concerned about the time I would be away and the expense of such a trip. Eventually he gave his approval, stressing the need for minimal travel expenses. This was at a time when large jet aircraft such as the Boeing 707 were just coming into vogue and before the advent of the 747 and other jumbo jets. American tourists by the thousands were discovering the joys of economy fares and low traveling costs in Europe. On the basis of the advice from John Baldry, I wanted to get to St. Helens before September because by that time Pilkington would be doing its media and marketing planning for the following year and decisions would be made.

Unfortunately, it was impossible to get an economy seat on any large American or overseas airline at that time. While visiting a good friend, Paul K. Ray, Advertising Manager of Carrier Air Conditioning Corp., in Syracuse, I mentioned my plight to him. His response was immediate, "I have a solution for you. My secretary, Kay Seaton, is a member of the Clan Douglas and they have chartered a plane which will fly their group to Prestwick, Scotland, late in July." I promptly saw Kay Seaton and with her help, I joined the Clan Douglas for two dollars and then almost immediately obtained a ticket on a British Caledonia charter flight leaving Syracuse on Friday, July 22, for Prestwick. The plane was a refitted turboprop Britannia troop transport and the flight, which had been delayed, arrived nine hours later on Saturday afternoon. After arranging for the rental of a Hillman-Minx sedan, I found an inexpensive nearby hotel and the next day, a Sunday, started my trek to St. Helens, driving on the left side of the road!

Just south of Prestwick in the town of Ayr, I passed the cottage where Robert Burns was born and later on historic Cuzlean Castle, which the British gave lifetime use of to General Dwight Eisenhower in appreciation of his wartime service. Because of my interest in these and other attractions along the way, I did not arrive in Carlisle, an old border town on the western end of the Roman Wall, until about nine o'clock in the evening. Carlisle was about ninety miles from St. Helens and at that time there were no motorways. I decided to find a hotel and then start for St. Helens at dawn the next morning. At a little hotel called the Carrow House I arranged all my papers in a folder for my presentation to Mr. Tinling, which was scheduled for 10 the next morning.

I was up at 5:30 A.M. and I came down the staircase of this little hotel very early, to be sure of being on time for my appointment, and as I did so the folder of papers slipped from my hand along with an address book. I picked up the address book, put it on the reception desk, and then retrieved the papers that were strewn all over the lobby, putting them into proper order in the folder. I walked out the front door and was about two miles south when I discovered that I had left my all-important address book with numerous addresses and names and telephone numbers of people I was going to see in England. I immediately turned back and arrived at the Carrow House a few minutes after 6 A.M. to be confronted with a locked door and a sign that read, "ring the bell!" At that hour of the morning, I did not think that the proprietor would appreciate being awakened so I walked around to the side and then to the back of the hotel finding no open doors. A rear window was open, but it was out of reach. Luckily, on the ground and near the window was a ladder. There were also several houses nearby. I carefully surveyed the situation and concluded that everyone who could see me was asleep. I put the ladder up to the window, climbed through it, and stepped in on the kitchen sink. I pushed the ladder down and then worked my way out the kitchen through the dining room and back to the reception desk where I retrieved my address book and then continued my journey to St. Helens.

Well before 10, I arrived at the head office of Pilkington located in an impressive twelve-story high-rise tower building surrounded by numerous other factory buildings in which 25,000 Pilkington employees produce glass and other related products. I was promptly ushered into Tinling's office, introduced to several of his associates, and next came the tea wagon along with some pleasantries concerning my trip including the recounting of my departure from the Carrow House. Then we got into the reason for my trip, which was to persuade Pilkington that it would be appropriate to run an advertising program in America's leading architectural journal, the *Architectural Forum*.

Tinling, who seemed to have a soft spot in his heart for Americans, was receptive to the presentation and obviously the effort that I had made to get from New York to his office in St. Helens made a favorable impression. He let me know almost immediately that our chances were good and he asked me to go to London to see Pilkington's advertising agency, Pritchard Wood and Partners. I made a similar presentation on behalf of the *Forum* to Jim Ambrose, the Media Director, and Robert Scarlett, who was then Account Supervisor on the Pilkington account. About six weeks after I returned to New York, we received an order from Pritchard Wood for eight four-color pages in the *Forum*.

From that time on, I made annual trips to St. Helens to see Pilkington and Banastre Tinling. Our business relationship ripened into a very good friendship with many tips and suggestions coming from him as to where I could go in England and in Europe for additional advertising for the *Forum*. As a result, we did carry additional advertising from glass producers in France and Belgium.

The news of Pilkington's success and importance spread. Numerous stories about the company and its float process of producing glass appeared in all media. One of the best and most comprehensive of these was a ten-page story called "The Eccentric Lords of Float Glass" which appeared in *Fortune* in July 1968, more than two years after my initial contact with John Baldry of Pilkington in Toronto. Obviously, it gave me a great deal of satisfaction that my efforts were contributing to Pilkington's fame and fortune.

Pilkington's Banastre Tarleton Tinling is one of the most fascinating men I have ever met. Before joining Pilkington in Canada, he had worked in the United States for the Hoover Company and thus had some exposure to American advertising, merchandising, and marketing methods. After many years in Canada, Sir Harry Pilkington (now Lord Pilkington), Pilkington's Chairman, asked Tinling to return to St. Helens. Tinling was named for a distinguished forebearer, Banastre "Bloody" Tarleton, who was a young British General under Cornwallis. Today there are many signs in Virginia and the Carolinas attesting to the exploits of Tarleton's raiders and the fact that Tarleton almost captured Jefferson at Charlottesville. After the American Revolution, Banastre Tarleton returned to England where he continued his career as a Member of Parliament. It is also interesting to note that Tinling's younger brother is Teddy Tinling, well-known as a designer of women's tennis apparel.

As a result of this initial trip and those that followed, I became acquainted with many leading personalities in the British and European press, all of whom proved to be useful contacts for me when I started a new career in 1972 as Director of Public Relations for the St. Louis-based architectural firm of Hellmuth, Obata & Kassabaum, now nationally known and also internationally known for important assignments in Saudi Arabia and Egypt.

In looking back on this adventure which took me to Banastre Tinling's office at Pilkington in St. Helens on a Monday morning in July of 1966, I have had ample reward and satisfaction for this effort. First, I got the order I sought as well as many renewal orders and orders from other companies. Second, I was able to expand my knowledge and contacts with British and European publishers. Third, I made many friendships which have lasted through the years. Every time I go to England and Europe, usually with my wife, we always try to spend a day or part of a day with Joyce and Banastre Tinling as well as many other good friends in a variety of publishing enterprises.

In short, the real and meaningful rewards of selling are not only the satisfaction of successfully persuading your customer and prospect that your product or service is of value to him but more important are the friendships and personal growth that are generated by such contacts.

William B. Remington is Senior Vice President, Director of Public Relations for the architectural firm of Hellmuth, Obata & Kassabaum. This firm is known for such projects as the National Air and Space Museum in Washington, D.C., the Dallas/Fort Worth Airport, the Galleria in Houston, Texas, and the University of Riyad in Saudi Arabia.

Mr. Remington has held a variety of advertising sales positions with leading publications. In the summer of 1966, and at the time of this story, he was the Eastern Advertising Manager for the *Architectural Forum*, a professional magazine for architects.

*David P. Reynolds*

# My Most Satisfying Sale

*For a salesman who has spent over four decades in selling,* success stories abound—it's that way for any salesman. But for each there is a special order, a special sale that sticks in the mind and comes back time and again bringing with it feelings of satisfaction and accomplishment.

Every individual has different reasons for calling a favorite sale "special." It may have been the biggest order in a sales career. It may have been the sale that opened a whole new market. Or it may have been a sale that had ramifications far beyond the writing of an order. My greatest sale had all three of these elements.

In 1959 I was Vice President of Sales for Reynolds Metals. One day I went to a board meeting where I heard one of our vice presidents present a request for several million dollars to build barge docking and unloading facilities on the Tennessee River. These docks would be used in the transport of raw materials from our operations in Texas to our aluminum refining plants in Alabama. The Southern Railroad, which was doing this hauling, had just presented us with a substantial rate increase and it was felt in some parts of the company that it would be cheaper to barge the material than pay the new freight rates.

I wasn't too happy about spending that kind of money on a capital investment that wouldn't make one additional ounce of aluminum that I could sell. And knowing the management of Southern Railroad—my father had been on the Southern board some years back—I couldn't believe that they would let that amount of business get away without a struggle.

So I asked that our board postpone the vote. I wanted to talk to Southern about that rate increase. I felt something could be done to reduce that new rate.

I made an appointment with the Chairman of Southern and we had dinner together at the St. Regis Hotel in New York. And when I told him we were thinking about barging our raw materials because of his high rate he was stunned. After he agreed to renegotiate the rate, our conversation ranged over other topics, including the aluminum business. I asked: "How is it that you don't use aluminum freight cars? Aluminum would be perfect for gondola and hopper cars to carry bulk cargo."

Reynolds had been trying to get the railroads to build aluminum freight cars for years. But we just couldn't crack that market.

We had done market studies that showed that an aluminum freight car had a distinct advantage over the steel freight car, both in weight savings and low maintenance. But we were just unable to convince the railroads that there was an advantage in using aluminum for bulk cargo cars. The railroad market was almost an obsession with us. We knew that if we could just get one railroad to use aluminum cars, we could open a substantial new market.

Reynolds had always been an innovator in the aluminum industry. We were the first to print in four colors on aluminum foil, and we introduced Reynolds Wrap in 1947, and we pioneered the use of aluminum siding and the aluminum can. Aluminum was being used in truck building and in aircraft fabrication. And we had some business with the railroads in extrusions and doors. But we knew we were just nibbling around the edges of a large potential market.

The problem was that the railroads were tradition bound. Steel cars were good enough. The railroads had told us that weight savings weren't significant. Fuel oil was cheap then, and we just couldn't make an impression on the railroad industry.

And here I was at dinner with a very attentive chairman of the board of one of the nation's leading rail carriers. Gradually as I talked about the virtues of aluminum for freight cars he became increasingly interested. Finally he agreed to set up an appointment for me with the vice president in charge of the engineering and mechanical departments.

□

Then our work really began. We finally had our entrée to the right person. I had stirred up some initial interest. Now it was up to Reynolds to close the sale.

But first there was the problem of finding someone willing to build the cars—no one had ever done it before on a mass production basis, and no one wanted to. We called on the major car builders and after long explorations, the Magor Car Corporation in New Jersey and the Pullman-Standard Company in Alabama finally agreed to build the cars. But they were used to working with steel and were somewhat uneasy about tackling aluminum.

We agreed to supply technical assistance and to teach them how to work with aluminum.

Meanwhile our engineers and the engineers and design people from Southern were working on the design of the cars. Simultaneously the financial and marketing people from both companies were working on return-on-investment and cost comparison studies.

At this point Southern was listening hard and had an open mind, but the railroad wasn't entirely convinced. The management wasn't sure that the extra $6000 per car was fully justified.

□

We did more studies that showed that because aluminum bodies were so much lighter than steel, bigger cars could be built without exceeding the weight limitations of the track. These bigger cars could carry more bulk cargo and each car could carry six to eight tons of payload for literally nothing. We also showed that over the life of a steel car an average of $3000 was spent correcting corrosion problems that would never occur with the aluminum bodies. These savings could be used to offset the higher initial cost of the aluminum car.

Well, the railroad agreed with our studies and our cost analysis, and yes, there were advantages to the aluminum car, and yes, Pullman-Standard and Magor would build good railroad cars, but. . . . We still didn't have an order.

Finally I told Southern that aluminum had a scrap value far above the value of scrap steel. I said that when the useful life of the railroad car was finished we would commit to buy back the cars for scrap at 25 cents per pound. "Put that into your cost analysis," I said. Now 25 cents per pound was what we were getting for our primary aluminum ingot at the time and I was offering an outrageous scrap price. But I knew that the cars would last many, many years and that scrap prices could go nowhere but up over the long term.

That tipped the scale in our favor.

We wound up with an order for 1205 hopper and gondola cars to be used for hauling bulk cargo. The Reynolds order was for 20 million pounds of aluminum plate—the largest single order in the history of the industry.

□

There is an epilogue to this sale. For Reynolds, it opened the door to the rail transportation market—a door that had been closed to us for many years. We eventually sold other aluminum cars to many other railroads. I think it is safe to say that these cars resulted in a technological breakthrough in the business of building bulk freight cars.

A couple of years later, when use of aluminum bulk freight cars was an established practice on the railroads, D. William Brosnan, president of Southern, who was by then a great believer in aluminum freight cars, built an aluminum hopper car called "Big John." These "Big John" cars were huge, covered hopper cars built to haul grain from the Midwest to the Southeast at a 60 percent rate reduction over conventional freight charges.

In fact when Southern lowered these rates, its competitors fought the reduction all the way to the Supreme Court—and lost.

The reduced rates for grain shipments to the Southeast were instrumental in the development of a beef cattle and poultry industry that went a long way toward making that section of the country self-sufficient in meat production. At the court hearings it was said that the lower-cost grain had added $1 billion to the economy of the Southeast.

In 1963, Mr. Brosnan and I presented a one-third scale model of the "Big John" hopper car—made of aluminum by Reynolds, of course—to the Smithsonian Institution Museum of History and Technology as a tribute to the role of aluminum railroad cars in changing the way bulk freight was hauled on American railroads.

□

As a salesman I have had many "great sales" in my career. But the aluminum railroad car always stands out because of the way our company persisted for many years in the face of opposition. We persisted because we knew we were right and we were not discouraged by rejection. And we were able to seize on an opportunity when it presented itself. I am very pleased when I think of the dedication and teamwork that came into play when we were making our case for the first aluminum freight car.

Oh yes, as for the scrap prices on those original cars—the cars are still in service and in 1980 the price of that kind of aluminum scrap was more than double the 1959 price. In the interim, through Reynolds pioneering efforts, recycling has become a major factor in the aluminum industry.

□   □   □

David P. Reynolds is chairman of the board and chief executive officer of Reynolds Metals Company. In his forty-one years with Reynolds Metals he has earned a reputation as one of the aluminum industry's most innovative executives and as a constructive environmentalist. He has sparked the company's reputation for marketing—in building and construction, in the automotive market, in containers and packaging, and in pioneering Reynolds Wrap aluminum household foil.

Mr. Reynolds is responsible for launching consumer aluminum recycling on a nationwide basis as an imaginative solution to the problems of litter and solid waste. He is a founder and a director of The National Center for Resource Recovery, Inc., and in 1973 directed construction of the first home built of recycled materials— to prove the market potential for such materials in residential building. For two consecutive years he was chairman of National Boy Scout Keep America Beautiful Day, and has served as chairman of the Aluminum Association's Clean Air, Water and Land Committee and its Board Resources Committee.

For his work in the environmental field he and his company have received the Phoenix Award of the Philadelphia Metals Association, The Environment Monthly Award, the Keep America Beautiful Business Award, the Recycling Award of the National Association of Secondary Materials Industries, and citations of commendation from federal and municipal governments.

In 1978 he received the Institute of Human Relations Award of the American Jewish Committee. His achievements in the packaging field won him recognition in 1971 from the Packaging Education Foundation as Packaging Man of the Year. In 1954 he was honored as Light Metals Man of the Year.

In 1974 he was elected for a two-year term as Chairman of the Aluminum Association, which includes seventy-seven companies representing all primary producers, principal secondary smelters, and most fabricators of aluminum.

He joined Reynolds in 1937 as a salesman. Immediately prior to United States entry into World War II, as assistant manager of the Aircraft Parts Division in Louisville, he helped set up facilities to blank out aircraft parts, returning scrap to the plants the same day. It was an important aid in war production.

During the war, Mr. Reynolds became sales manager of the company's Aluminum Division and director of advertising and public relations. He was named a Vice President in 1944.

Four years later he was named Director of the General Sales Division, which included sales of aluminum foil products and mill products as well as aluminum powders and pastes. In 1949 he reorganized Reynolds sales force along market, rather than product lines—an innovative move since followed by other basic materials producers. Under his direction, Reynolds Metals became the first basic materials producer to advertise on network television.

He became Executive Vice President of Sales in 1958, and assumed the position of Executive Vice President and General Manager with added responsibility for production operations, when the company was reorganized on a division basis in 1969. In 1975 he was elected Vice Chairman of the Board, and in 1976 was elected to his present post.

Mr. Reynolds has been a member of the Prime Aluminum Products Industry Advisory Committee of the federal government since 1951. President Carter in 1977 named him to the board of directors of the National Alliance of Businessmen (NAB) and appointed him regional chairman, NAB region III.

He is also a member of the Board of Directors of Reynolds Metals Company and various subsidiaries including Eskimo Pie Corporation, Reynolds Jamaica Mines, Ltd., Reynolds International, Inc., Canadian Reynolds Metals Company, Ltd., and Reynolds Aluminum Company of Canada. He is Chairman of the Board of Reynolds Metals Development Corporation, chairman of the board of Robertshaw Controls Company, and serves on the Board of United Virginia Bankshares, Richmond, Va.

A native of Bristol, Tennessee, Mr. Reynolds attended Lawrenceville School and Princeton University.

**Milton R. Scheiber**

# The Very Tangible Intangible

*I am a salesman,* and sometimes—surrounded by clients or relaxing after a long day—I get the feeling that I have become fairly good at it. Oh, I've had my ups and downs—failures and successes—but I wouldn't trade away any one of them.

Thinking back over those many sales experiences, there is one in particular that stands out in my memory. As great sales stories go, perhaps it wasn't very much. But it sure meant a lot to me.

☐

The year was 1967. I had just joined Lone Star Cement Company (later to become Lone Star Industries) with the specific assignment of organizing a corporate management development and training program. This was right down my alley, as I had acquired a good deal of experience in "troop training" both in industry and in the Army, going back over a lot of years.

After the usual short tour of corporate headquarters, I was told to please get out in the field and "make something happen." The first training session I was to conduct was for a group of supervisors in one of our cement plants located in Bonner Springs, Kansas. In preparing for the session I learned that the folks at Bonner had participated in a number of programs of various types and, in fact, just a couple of months back the company had sent out a well-known behavioral psychologist to do a training needs analysis and conduct a seminar on professional management. I knew the man they sent. He is very good and knows the subject thoroughly. However, our psychologist did not make a big hit. In fact, he "bombed." This group considered the visitor to be both abrasive and insulting and would have physically thrown him out—but old-fashioned gentlemen don't do that to a guest.

Enter the expert from the home office. I was introduced to the group and found them quite friendly. My lecture was about modern management techniques and I poured all I had into it—flipcharts, slides, the works. At the end of my two-hour stint, I asked if there were any questions or comments. One of my new associates raised his hand and said, "Mr. Scheiber, sir, that's all well and good back East, but this is a very basic business we're in and it just wouldn't work for folks like us." There it was—the client asking the "killer" question.

As I cleared my throat to attempt a response that could turn imminent defeat into victory, I had quick visions of a lot of things— including looking for another job and wondering how I had managed to get myself into such a predicament. This old New York boy was not going to make it—certainly not if I should fall flat on my face the first time out.

□

Visions of my first job out of college. It was 1936 and there weren't that many good jobs around for a kid with no specific profession or salable skill. Remington Rand was looking for salesmen. The sales manager was an old-timer with much experience in bringing on new salesmen. He gave us a quick training program that included a reference to how lucky we were to get any kind of a job at that particular time. He said that he had taken a lot of young guys with no talent and made them into star salesmen. He said that selling is the ultimate career. It is the "be all to end all." But we must remember to always sell *tangibles*. Anything we could feel, demonstrate, work with. . . . But above all else, we must sell only *tangibles*.

Well, in the Army of 1940 there was a lot that was tangible. And some of the fellows became experts. Perhaps some of the skills we learned could not be carried into civilian life, but boy were they tangible. As 1945 was drawing to a close, one of my Army buddies was trying to get me to join him in the life insurance business. He said that I was a natural life insurance salesman. He had been a district manager for Prudential and was going to take over a large territory in a southern state. He talked me into visiting their home office in Newark, New Jersey, and taking an aptitude test. I passed with flying colors. One big problem—I had long been convinced that I absolutely could not sell anything that was not tangible.

□

I did go back to selling, though. I sold appliances, kitchen cabinets, and plumbing products, and finally wound up with the giant American Radiator-Standard Sanitary Corporation, where I went from Sales and Product Management and Sales Training to a brand new job called Management Development. This was an entirely new area. They had never before done this kind of training. However, they knew just where to get the members of this new department—from the Sales Department, of course. Then, eventually, I made the fateful move from American-Standard to Lone Star.

Like a drowning man reviewing his life, I saw all of this as I listened to my Bonner Springs compatriots and pondered a way to respond—and to hold on to this new job. Well, you're familiar with the old bromide: I was going to return to the home office either with my shield or on it. I decided to tell it "like it is." My response, quoted as accurately as I can remember, follows.

□

"Gentlemen, I certainly can understand what you are saying and I think that one of the problems is that I have neglected to tell you about myself and fill you in on my background. Before joining Lone Star, I spent many years in the Army and then with major industrial companies. Just prior to coming here, I spent several years with American-Standard—world famous manufacturers of plumbing and heating products, some of which are installed right here at the Bonner Plant. Among other things, they are the largest manufacturer in the world of toilet bowls. You talk about a basic business. Well, I certainly understand the concept of basic and I cannot think of anything more basic than toilet bowls. In fact, from where I sit, moving from toilet bowls to cement is a step up."

They looked a wee bit startled. Then much laughter and friendliness and real warmth. We understood each other. I was one of them and welcome at any time to talk about even such an arcane subject as management development.

I have reflected on this incident many times. It may have been the best sales talk I ever gave. And that's exactly what it was—a sales talk. My product: management excellence.

So, as I move along toward retirement years, I'm proud to say that I am still a salesman—and I'm still with Lone Star. Talk about selling intangibles. But then again, look at it this way—you can *feel* management excellence, you can *demonstrate* it, and you can *work with it*. Perhaps management excellence cannot be felt directly, but the profits that result and the dough in the wallet can be felt. Oh, I can assure you that it is a very tangible intangible.

□

Yesterday someone asked me what I do for a living. I told them simply—I am a salesman.

□   □   □

Milton R. Scheiber is Director of Corporate Management Development at Lone Star Industries, Inc., which is the western hemisphere's largest producer of cement. He is also Dean of the Lone Star Management Institute, which conducts intensive career development programs for upper-middle and senior management. Between stints in the U.S. Army covering the years between 1938 and 1976, Mike had time to develop a civilian career in sales and product management, sales training, and eventually in human resource and management development.

Mr. Scheiber is a graduate of New York University's School of Commerce in New York City, where he also pursued graduate studies in economics, marketing, and psychology. He is also a graduate of the U.S. Army Command and General Staff College at Fort Leavenworth, Kansas.

Prior to joining Lone Star, Mr. Scheiber had a succession of very satisfying assignments at American Standard, Inc., and Avco Manufacturing Corporation. He also had his own marketing company where he was "afflicted with big eyes and a small wallet."

He is a frequent lecturer on his favorite subject, "Objective Performance Appraisal in the Real World" or—"When Was the Last Time Anybody Ever Gave You an 'Attaboy Charlie'?"

He is a member of the American Society for Personnel Administration, which awarded him the designation of Accredited Professional Diplomate (APD).

He is also a long-time member of the American Society for Training and Development, which presented him with the prestigious National Torch Award for "dedication and outstanding contribution to the field of human resource development."

*David L. Scott*

# The Starvation Factor

*Since my early childhood years* I have been totally immersed in the private club industry. People change, as do economics and the world's taste in general, and so have the private clubs of America, although some have been strong in resisting change. This chapter deals with how one change was sold and implemented.

As any salesman knows—and we are all salesmen—ingenuity and planning are two of the most important facets of any sales plan. The executive who has the ability to look at a market and use ingenuity to find a need and come up with an idea will be successful.

In our "hospitality industry," which incidentally is the second largest industry in the nation, a good place to start looking for that need is to determine what I call a "starvation factor." A starvation factor is something your members or customers have been looking for that you don't provide. This can be illustrated easily with the following experience. I was manager of the Scarsdale Golf Club before taking on my present position at the Pinnacle Club in New York. I instantly saw a need for new and fresh ideas to bring a badly stagnated club back to life. The mean member age was over sixty and no effort was being made to lower this statistic. No young members could be attracted to a club so deeply entrenched in yesteryear. A new dawn was needed; this was how we attained that new sunrise.

First, we had to design a plan to pump new life into the organization. The first step was to create a new social program that would get the close-knit community of Scarsdale, New York, talking. We started with a "Salute to W. C. Fields." The reason for this was to make a night of nostalgia for the older members and bring the younger people in to see this truly gifted comedian at work. We arranged a nice dinner, checkered table cloths, bowls of popcorn, and about twelve of W. C. Fields' shorts shown through the evening with the use of two projectors and screens. The night was a smash. The sales of food and liquor far surpassed our expectations. This started the talk and it did travel fast.

Step two consisted of a "Battle of the Bands." This was calculated to not only attract the oldsters with a society-type band but to bring in the youngsters to enjoy a fine local rock band. The bands alternated—a half hour on and half hour off. The party turned out to be such a success that the rock band was extended an extra hour and a half past its scheduled ending. Everyone was happy, both young and old. Again, we were on our way.

Now we were ready for a push on membership. A membership drive was formulated and we began a personal pitch and set up a meeting with local civic groups to tell them what we had to offer for both the young and old families.

Our success surpassed our wildest dreams. Requests for applications kept our committee hopping for months.

Now was not the time to stop our programs. It was time to show our members and prospects that this was not just a flash in the pan but a carefully conceived program to increase their enjoyment at their club. Part of this was our Beef & Burgundy nights. A beautiful full-course prime rib dinner with all the wine you could drink, at a very competitive price. We were mobbed. Again, we met a need.

Another Battle of the Bands was held, even more successfully than the first. Reservations had to be closed for dinner but that didn't stop them. After dinner we were inundated. We did it again. We couldn't stop now—our sales campaign was in full swing.

October rolled around and what better time for a classic "Oktoberfest." Wow—did the members love it! Suckling pigs, bratwurst, headcheese, sausages, all the beer they could drink—the works, presented on a large buffet complete with hanging sausages, travel posters, and a real oom-pah-pah band. Not only was our treasury growing but our membership was growing at an astounding pace. We were fulfilling a need—we had found the starvation factor.

We were making people happy; a trend had been reversed. It was now the time for our members to start helping with their own suggestions. They were telling us at this point what their needs were. They were stimulated. One said, "We can't get a light meal and a few drinks late on a Saturday night." Aha! We had found another starvation factor. Now we filled the need again: pub night was born. Every other Friday evening a piano player, salad bar, and minute steak from 10 P.M. to midnight.

These are just the highlights of a sales job in the private club industry. They have been admired and copied, but never as well or as successfully. There were many ideas that followed—fireworks, splash parties, trick golf parties, zany bowling parties, a trip to West Point for football.

We were successful because we recognized the starvation factor and we sold the solution to the membership.

□   □   □

David L. Scott, currently General Manager of the Pinnacle Club of New York, also serves as a hospitality industry consultant. Mr. Scott has been General Manager of the Fenway Golf Club as well as the Scarsdale Golf Club.

Mr. Scott is a graduate of the University of Denver and holds a BSBA degree in Hotel Restaurant Management.

*J. L. Scott*

# Remember the
# Little Things

*These reminiscences bring to mind* one sale that I made so early in life I had almost forgotten it. We were living in Kemper County, Mississippi, in the small town of Scooba. This particular summer I had developed an ice route of some thirty miles to outlying farms and one small town. In building this ice route, I visited each house along the road, contacting each person and making my pitch as to the desirability of having ice in the home during the summer. I noticed an older house sitting a little further off the road than most of the other houses. This house, for some unknown reason, seemed to be a challenge from the time I noticed it until I first knocked on the door. The door opened and there stood an average farmer's wife who asked, "What do you want, young man?" I started my sales pitch about ice and its many uses. I explained that you could use it to preserve food and to cool drinking water or ice tea. This lady exclaimed that she had never seen ice and that she would like to have some delivered each trip I made, but what on earth would she store the ice in and how could it keep her milk cold. This, of course, gave me the opening I wanted. I then explained that I could deliver her ice and an ice box on my next trip. When I told her that the cost of the ice box would be eighteen dollars, but it would hold fifty pounds of ice and had ample storage space for milk and meats, a smile came over her face and she replied, "Bring it; I can't wait." For a fifteen year old this ice route became big business and turned out to be very prosperous.

The sale that did the most for me was only the first in a series of sales that have been occurring since March 15, 1947. The most successful people just happen to be in the right place at the right time. My success was no different, except that I sold my services to a very fine educator in the field of higher education.

The State of Mississippi has a twelve-member Board of Regents that

**297**

is responsible for all public higher education in the state. The executive secretary of the board was authorized to interview and recommend the employment of an auditor. I was invited for an interview for this position. I was somewhat familiar with the community colleges in the state and was a graduate of the University of Southern Mississippi in the field of business education with emphasis in accounting. This was the big moment and the sale I made in this interview has lasted for thirty-three years.

This was the beginning of a series of assignments that led to sale after sale. The first assignment was to install in all institutions a uniform accounting system that could compare institutions with other institutions, thus giving the presidents of the colleges a good management tool and providing each Board of Trustees an insight into the financial operation of the colleges. So what, you ask? Remember this is 1947, with enrollments increasing and G.I.'s returning with veteran grants. Each business office had only one or two people employed. There sat the chief accountant at a plantation desk with a pen and ink writing students' names in a three-foot-wide ledger known as the Students Accounts. This is where the supersale began. I had to convince this person that there was a better way of keeping records. When I started explaining my new chart of accounts and talking of ledger sheets, machine posting with fewer errors, I could see his eyes glaze over his head. It would have been easier to sell him a one-eyed pig. Remember, there were seven of these business officers to convince that I had the latest, simplest system and if they would just listen and use the material I could give them, it would be easy to convert from the old system to this new and modern one I had to offer. Some just stood and looked dazed; others shook their heads; and one took off his green eyeshades and picked up his hat and walked out of the office. During one visit, I remember being extraordinarily patient with this older man, explaining in great detail how the system worked and how easily it could be installed. He looked me in the eye and said that I was going to fire him and that he needed this job. After that statement, he started crying. This really upset me and I promised that he would have his job as long as he wanted it and of course he stayed until retirement.

These were trying times at the institutions and enrollments were increasing by leaps and bounds. This was really the turning point and by this time my sales pitch had been polished, changed, proofed over, and rearranged several times. But with the retirement of older employees and the hiring of younger employees, my work was made a lot easier. We soon had our system working as it should and the reports were rolling in on time.

The second assignment was to canvass the armed services and make application for excess personal property under the federal surplus property account. This proved to be most interesting to me and profitable to the state and the universities. I requested property such as 500,000-gallon water tanks, airplanes, vehicles, typewriters, and buildings. This was a new ballgame in selling. Have you ever driven up to a security gate of an army camp and asked for a visitor's pass to see the property officer whose name you did not know? Usually the property officer did not know the disposal regulations and you had to educate him first and then convince him that you were the authorized agent representing your state and public education. Then the selling begins. Usually when closing time came you asked him out to dinner. You'd be surprised what a tender steak can do to soften a tough sergeant. These were most interesting forays into camp after camp with every one a new challenge.

I also had the good fortune to sell a uniform set of meat specifications to be used by the purchasing agents of the State of Mississippi. These specifications were furnished to the packers or bidders on meats and poultry products. This saved writing a long list of products for bidding when all meats could be referred to by item number of the specification (Item 7—100 pounds).

The most interesting sale turned out to be a purchase: the purchase of insurance (fire and extended coverage) on student housing. We were told that the published rates were the rates that all companies would charge. According to the insurance representatives, all bids would be the same. After many visits to the rating bureau and talking with insurance representatives, I wrote an insurance specification and advertised for bids on $60 million insurable value package. This started the wheels turning and on bid opening we received over a hundred bids with two deviating from the published rates. This saved the institutions over $32,000. I might add that this was a breakthrough that has continued over the years.

These are just a few of the experiences that one is faced with in carrying out the wishes of a Board of Regents and eight college presidents. Selling becomes a day-by-day and hour-by-hour job during the legislative session.

Public higher education depends largely on state appropriations for its operating budget. Since the executive secretary and I were the only ones to present this budget to the Legislature for funding, we were faced with a very important selling job. Appearing before the Senate and the House Appropriations Committee was a real selling experience. My advice to anyone who has this responsibility is to study your lesson, know every conceivable answer, anticipate the questions, and have good answers ready. If you are lucky you will answer fifty percent of the questions satisfactorily and the other fifty percent you will promise answers to in a few days.

These hearings are just icing on the cake and provide a place where the Board may be taken to task by a sorehead legislator who has received two field tickets near the end zone to the Slippery Rock football game. Thank goodness we only have a few of these people around. However, there are enough of them to give everyone at these hearings the impression that you misspent your last appropriation and misrepresented every figure that was submitted to support your appropriation request. This is the supreme test for a salesman. We have survived thirty-three years of this type of selling with the appropriations increasing from a beginning appropriation of $5 million in 1948, and this was for a biennium. In 1979, the appropriation for one year was in excess of $100 million.

In addition to the support funds requested from the Legislature, we also asked for Capital Improvement Funds. This was a different sale completely, requiring personal contact with the members of the Legislature living in the district in which the institution is located. They immediately understand that they can point to a certain building and say to their constituents, "I voted for that building." This type of sale requires knowledge of the statewide budget, the latest estimate of revenues, and the total estimated expenditures of the state budget. With these figures in mind and the ability to recall and quote what the budget director will quote the next week, you will have credibility you will need when you talk to that legislator again. We apparently did a good selling job on Capital Improvements because we had over $160 million under contract at one time.

The point I would like to pass along is that there is always good, sound information that you can receive for the asking. You might have to cultivate friends in different areas and offices, but this is selling your personality and friendship. Remember the little things; a kind word to your neighbor will make both of you feel better.

Our office is like everything else in this day and time; inflation has eroded funds that would have been used for salaries. Utilities have increased to the point that we dread opening a new facility because of the additional drain to pay for heat, lights, and water. In spite of this inflation we have grown from a three-person staff to some thirty people at this time. The paperwork has increased one hundredfold and continues to do so. I would like to make one last sales pitch before I retire and that would be to reduce the tons of paperwork that cross the desks in our operation. The requirements for filing will soon equal the total office space required for one operation. It would really be nice if we could revert to the days when we had six people doing the work that thirty are now doing.

These years have been most gratifying for me. I have had the good fortune to live and work with some of the most highly recognized educators in this country. We have been through the war-baby boom, civil rights protests and forced integration. Very few people have had the opportunity for such a variety of experiences.

J. L. Scott was born in Kemper County, Mississippi, and attended grade school in Scooba. After graduation from high school, he enrolled in East Mississippi Community College, transferring after three semesters to the University of Southern Mississippi, from which he was graduated in the spring of 1939. While at the university, Mr. Scott won letters in football, basketball, baseball, and boxing, which aided him early in his career.

After graduation, Mr. Scott accepted a teaching and coaching job at St. Martin High School, Biloxi, Mississippi. In 1940–1941 he accepted a position as coach and head of the business department at Bay High School, Bay St. Louis, Mississippi. Returning in 1941–1942 to the University of Southern Mississippi, he became head of business education at Demonstration High School, the practice teachers' training school. The next four years were spent on the East Coast helping in the war effort.

In 1946, Mr. Scott returned to Pearl River Junior College as head of the business department and as coach. This was a productive year for athletics, as Pearl River won eight football games, losing two and tying two. In 1947 Pearl River won the State Championship for basketball.

On March 15, 1947, Mr. Scott accepted the position of auditor with the Board of Trustees of State Institutions of Higher Learning. He has continued in this position to the present, although his title has changed many times during the last thirty-three years.

**Muriel Siebert**

# The Day I Made the Stock Exchange Coed

*The damned phone was insistent.* Groggily, I reached over and lifted the receiver. A pert and all-too-cheerful voice said, "Good morning, Miss Siebert, it's 5:45. The temperature is 63 degrees, and room service is sending up your breakfast." A helluva way to start the day.

It was the way I would start many days, every time I traveled to California from New York. I was on the telephone to Wall Street by 9:00 o'clock, New York time, to talk with my customers. It was one of the things I had learned. These good customers would go along with me, but only so long as they got the services they were used to. They were used to having the results of yesterday's digging and picking in the aerospace industry. They wanted new information the first thing in the morning.

My customers need recommendations on whether to buy, sell, or stand fast. And I needed the commissions on those sales to pay for what I had done—something I had just bought.

A few months before, in December 1967, I had become the first woman ever to buy a seat on the New York Stock Exchange. That shopping spree had cost me $445,000.

Looking back now, the steady climb could only have led in one direction, up from research trainee in a brokerage house to chairman and president of my own company thirteen years later. While it was going on, all I knew was that I was good. I also knew I had to work harder than men to go as far as I wanted to go.

I arrived in New York in 1954 to seek my future. It was the farthest I had ever been from my home in Cleveland. It would take some doing, I told myself, for a college dropout, even a bright one, just to get a good job. I toured the New York Stock Exchange soon after my arrival and decided on Wall Street as a career. Well, I did have top grades in accounting in school.

Bache and Company offered me a job, either in the accounting department for $75 a week or as a trainee in research at $65 a week. I took the trainee job. Eventually, I became an analyst and then an industry specialist, responsible for several industries.

"Plump, smart, happy, and lucky." That's how I have described myself. All but the first have stood me in good stead. My first real good luck came at this time at Bache.

Working with senior analysts, I learned by doing. One of these seniors covered all the industries that move: railroads, shipping, buses, and airlines. He was allowed to "dump" one industry on me, the trainee, to lighten his load. If you remember, in 1954 the airlines were nothing like they are today. This senior analyst didn't believe there was much future in the airlines, that they could not even finance the next round of equipment, so he "gave" me that industry to learn and cover.

The following year, turboprop aircraft were introduced. It was only a few years before jets revitalized the industry, and eventually the commercial jet industry came into being.

I was in at the beginning of a major chapter in the nation's economic history, and I became one of the aerospace industry's first experts in the Street. Aviation and aerospace were not all he gave me, however.

As an old-line analyst, whose heart was really with the railroads, he knew every mile of track, every rail line, and where every boxcar could be found. He knew the people and the history and the statistics in his industry, and he could make a shrewd guess as to the future performance of every rail line in the nation. He taught me to learn everything there is to know about an industry, and he taught me how to look at the numbers and let them tell the story.

My "first sale" came without my making it. I had never become registered, not believing that analysts should be registered representatives. By now, I had moved to another large brokerage firm. The manager of a major investment fund called to say he owed me an order, having made money on one of my reports. My firm sent me over to take the order, and that's how I started selling securities.

To keep growing, I had to keep going. As a salaried analyst, I was paid half the firm's regular commission on my sales. I soon found I was earning my salary for this company several times over each year. Over the next few years I moved through several smaller firms, where I could get full credit on my sales—as a partner, increasing my productivity as I climbed. Finally, in 1967 I decided I was ready to move to a major firm, this time as a partner with my own accounts.

One day, after a meeting with the creative and brilliant Jerry Tsai, head of the Manhattan Fund, I asked him which major brokerage house he would recommend I consider. He was walking me to my car, I remember. He turned and said, "Why don't you buy a seat on the New York Stock Exchange?"

"Don't be ridiculous!" That was my first reaction.

Jerry pointed out that there was no law against a woman being a member, that many people knew the work I did, and that this was the only way to get the kind of return I was looking for on my productivity. I knew he meant it, and I knew he respected me. But I thought he had gone off the deep end.

That night I took the Stock Exchange Manual home with me. Indeed, there was no law that said a woman could not buy a seat. You had to be over twenty-one, be able to finance the purchase, and you had to have a definite business reason for wanting to buy the seat.

I soon discovered women were discouraged from applying, so no woman had ever actually tried. I could find no good reason I should not pursue it. Certainly, I was over twenty-one. I was pretty sure I could finance it. I would have no problem proving I had a business reason. When you are with a small firm you easily can show that the business you do is your own, not just the firm's.

Maybe Tsai's suggestion wasn't ridiculous.

It took me six months to get up the nerve. On one hand, I really wanted this. But I was doing well, I had plenty of income, life was good. In fact, I had everything I wanted—except a seat on the Stock Exchange. I wanted to meet this challenge.

The planning was completed, and the day came for me to meet with the two men in charge of Exchange seats. I had memorized a detailed speech, going into all the reasons why I should be allowed to buy the seat. It didn't work that way. When I got before them, my great speech went down the drain. I began: "Is this a club, or can I buy a seat on the New York Stock Exchange?"

In all fairness, I never was faced with having to change an old-boys-club kind of thinking. That was not the problem. They only wanted to be certain I was doing this for purely business reasons and not for publicity. However, with the price of a seat then at $445,000, which represented a considerable portion of my net worth, I would have to do a great deal of business to make this purchase. They were convinced I had a business reason.

There's no denying they were very cautious. They even required an extra letter of financial support from my bank. At first, I resented this, but I realized I represented a new situation for them. Yes, I had already learned some of the problems of being a woman in business in the 1950s and 1960s.

Being a woman has worked for and against me in business. I learned that if, as a woman, you stay a nice person, then people want to do business with you and even help you out. However, I also learned that it usually took me an extra year to develop an account—prejudices did exist.

The women's movement came along about then, and it helped. By that time I had developed patience. I had seen some of the prejudice, and I had learned how to handle it.

From the beginning I knew I had to deliver more than my male counterparts, and I was doing just that. One of the reasons I had five jobs in thirteen years was that I saw men earning 50 to 100 percent more than I was earning for the same work and results. I even worked for one company that said it would not allow me to represent them outside New York City, because I was a woman. Fortunately, in my business I could pick up my pencils and move to another game, if I had to.

However, the problems facing me in Decmeber 1967, when *Muriel Siebert & Co., Inc., Member, New York Stock Exchange*, came into being, were not strictly because I was a woman. I had made the New York Stock Exchange coed, but my main concern was whether my customers would continue to do business with me.

After all, I was making many times more than some of them were earning. A $20,000-a-year person in a bank could give me over $100,000 worth of business in a year. Would their feelings about me change, now that I was management and no longer the small, independent person they'd worked with? The answer, I knew, lay in continuing to do what I had done to reach this goal.

I had to give them more and better advice, information, and service than they could get from anyone else. I had to make those predawn phone calls from California.

I said I have been lucky. This is especially true of some of the people I have been associated with. I remember a marvelous and crusty old man, who not only taught me how to trade blocks of stock but also taught me how to master all those four-letter words that nice girls from Cleveland know but wouldn't dare to use.

I shall always be grateful to those outstanding senior analysts who taught me how to play by the numbers. I believe in taking the Big Chance when it comes along. I follow my hunches, but before I act, I look at the numbers—inside out and upside down. Before I bought that seat—my biggest gamble—I knew exactly how much volume I would have to do to meet the cost of the interest and pay my expenses.

As my firm grew, I always looked at those numbers to know just how much office space, new personnel, and increased business we could afford. We grew slowly, and it was a time of great happiness for all of us, because we grew together. We had great camaraderie as we played out that string, just as far as it would lead us.

I've been lucky, too, because I haven't grown cynical. I still have the same great faith in people that I had when I moved to New York, in 1954. Generally, people have not let me down. I will always back up once, even twice, but then I'll come out swinging, if I have to fight.

It's the philosophy I was raised with, and I can remember my mother telling me to suppose "if I were he, and he were me." I couldn't even be angry when I tried to join the all-male luncheon club at the Exchange.

The floor representatives who had promised to support my application all backed down. One of them put it flatly, "Good Lord, Mickey, if I support your membership, I won't have a friend left." I did get into the luncheon club, by the way.

Although I have never been a militant member of the women's movement, I have tried to do my share by helping with career counseling to young college and professional women. I urge them to get to know themselves, honestly and fairly. Where prejudice exists, they must fight it; but I caution them against counting their own lack of ability or unwillingness to work as prejudice.

I ask them to fill in the blank: "I'm really being stopped because_____." I ask them to consider this: "Am I being treated unfairly, or am I not suited for what I'm doing? Once you firmly believe in yourself, after this kind of examination, and you honestly find prejudice against you because you're a woman, then move on. But remember, it's very easy to blame your own shortcomings on something else."

Being a woman these days does not have to be a disadvantage in business. I am confident I was appointed Superintendent of Banks of the State of New York not because I was necessarily the best person for the job, but because I was the woman whose name came up most often to the Governor. After all, he was committed to filling a certain number of posts with women.

Fortunately, I have always surrounded myself with a sufficiently loose structure to be able to go after whatever I wanted. When I was tapped as Superintendent of Banks, I was able to leave my firm behind me. I wanted to pay back some of the obligation I feel for my good fortune. I could do that by devoting some time to public service. One drawback to accepting a job in the public sector, however, was that when I divorced myself from my firm, I also had to resign from the New York Stock Exchange.

For nine and a half years I held that seat on the Exchange, and for nine of those years, I was the only woman. As far as I know, I am the only woman ever to buy a seat with her own money.

With the risk and work behind me I knew it was worth it. Why? Because that, after all, was the sale that did the most for me, and because I'm the one in the record books for making the Stock Exchange coed.

Muriel Siebert was sworn in as Superintendent of Banks of the State of New York on July 7, 1977, following nomination by Governor Hugh L. Carey and confirmation by the New York State Senate. Prior to joining the Banking Department, Ms. Siebert was Chairman and President of Muriel Siebert and Company, Inc., Members New York Stock Exchange.

Born in Cleveland, Ohio, Ms. Siebert attended Western Reserve University. Among other distinctions in her business career, in 1967 she became the first woman member of the New York Stock Exchange.

Ms. Siebert began her Wall Street career as a Research Trainee with Bache and Co. in December 1954. She became a Security Analyst and Industry Specialist. Specializing in the analysis of the aviation industry, she subsequently served with Selig Altschul, a leading aviation consultant, and Shields and Co. In 1960 she became a Partner in Stearns and Co., and subsequently served as a Partner in Finkle and Co. and Brimberg and Co., all Members New York Stock Exchange. In 1967 she became a Member of the New York Stock Exchange and organized Muriel Siebert and Co., Inc., where she served as Chairman and President until 1977.

Ms. Siebert has also served as a director of several corporations and as a Trustee of Manhattan Savings Bank. Among many civic contributions, Ms. Siebert has served on the Board of Women's Forum and the New York State Economic Development Board. Ms. Siebert is currently a Trustee of Manhattan College and is on the

Executive Committee and Board of Greater New York Council of the Boy Scouts of America. As Superintendent of Banks she is on the Boards of Directors of the Urban Development Corporation, New York Job Development Authority and the State of New York Mortgage Agency. Ms. Siebert has been a frequent lecturer on economic and financial topics at various colleges and universities, and she has received honorary doctorates of commercial science from St. John's and St. Bonaventure universities. Ms. Siebert has received an award from The Business Council for the United Nations Decade for Women for Outstanding Contributions to Equal Opportunity for Women, presented to her in October 1979.

*William E. Simon*

# Protecting Our Liberty

*This is an unusual sales story.* It involves a deal of immeasurable volume that requires no cash transaction and cannot be closed in the normal way, yet demands the most sophisticated marketing techniques to fight the powerful competition. The value of this ongoing sale far exceeds the billions of dollars of bonds I used to underwrite at a Wall Street investment bank. It is, quite simply, the selling of free enterprise ideals to the American people.

We Americans have the unique privilege and opportunity of living in a country that was organized constitutionally for one overriding purpose: to protect the individual's freedom of thought, choice, and action. Our Founding Fathers were determined to leave the new Americans free to seek their fortunes with a minimum of state interference—to discover, to experiment, to succeed, to fail, to profit, to consume, to risk everything or nothing—all on a voluntary basis. They knew that individual liberty entails the individual's economic freedom as well as the freedom to speak and worship without government constraint. They understood that economic and political liberty are inextricably related, and that the former is a necessary condition for the latter. For a government that controls a nation's means of production is capable of compelling conformity, suppressing dissent, and stifling democratic rule. The Communist understands this perfectly: by seizing private property and prohibiting profits, he places the entire production/consumption mechanism under state dominion, which means, of course, that the physical life of each individual is at the mercy of the state. This is the essence of tyranny. As Alexander Hamilton said, "Power over a man's substance is power over his will."*

*Federalist 79.

**311**

The current crop of economic planners in this country certainly do not see themselves as tyrants. They act most frequently in the name of "the public interest," "equality," and, ironically enough, even "freedom." It seems to me that these central planners, for all their high-flown, do-good rhetoric, reveal an alarming and dangerous degree of hubris. What qualifies this handful of individuals to substitute their judgment for the millions of decisions that transpire in a free market? Whence derives their wisdom, wisdom that somehow tells them what people should pay for a product, how many should be manufactured and by what means, how much profit is justified, how strong the competition should be, what rates of interest should be charged on loans, all this among myriad other daily decisions formerly left to the market? Moreover, the "equality" they claim to promote is hardly the equality of the individual before the law guaranteed by our Constitution; rather, it is a pernicious twisting of the word to mean equality of result, a frightening assault on justice and the freedom of the individual to strive to better his lot according to his ability. Ironically enough, these egalitarians are really superelitist—they credit only their select number with insight into "the public interest"—and they are keenly concerned with power, the power to mold our civilization as they deem fit. So what the bureaucratic regulators and Naderites are really doing when they pound their fists on the table denouncing the evils of capitalism is expressing their own class interests as a kind of dispossessed aristocracy that has lost its mandate to rule. They are, as Robert Nisbet writes, "The New Despots."

These people provide keen competition for those of us trying to revitalize free enterprise in this country, for they are citizens who hold positions of influence and respect in universities, the law, medicine, foundations, and social service organizations, and they permeate the media industry. Furthermore, their motives appear so noble on the surface as they extol health, safety, and a clean environment that it is extremely difficult to challenge their assumptions without sounding heartless, evil, and self-serving.

But let's take a look at what happens when a society becomes overregulated in the name of "the public interest," when leaders try to "correct" free market processes, manipulate the money supply, determine prices, profits, and interest rates, to redistribute the wealth. Excessive government intervention in the private sector involves heavy costs economically, politically, and socially, and frequently ends up exacerbating the very problems it purports to solve. Such overregulation retards innovation, impedes the capital formation so crucial for economic growth, increases unemployment, diverts crucial manpower from research and development to meeting essentially bureaucratic requirements, and increases the costs of products to the consumers in whose interests the regulators claim to act. The Federal Drug Administration, for instance, is so overcautious in approving new drugs that lifesaving advances are significantly delayed or even foreclosed, while the minimum wage law has priced many young minority job seekers right out of the market.

In other words, excessive government regulation impedes progress. Economic growth and technological and scientific innovation are the cornerstones of progress, the engines that keep this country running. Progress is, of course, a very difficult word to define and means something different to each individual. One thing is clear, however, and that is that we cannot afford simply to maintain the status quo. Without economic growth, there is no hope of generating the jobs to enable the slum-dwellers to better their condition, of developing new energy sources to meet our domestic needs and provide for national defense, of fighting disease, or of engendering enough wealth to share with the needy in the Third World. Most important, the United States cannot remain the beacon of freedom and hope to the world if it lacks the resources to preserve the precious liberty that sustains its leadership role.

The Capitalist system, like any human institution, is not perfect; Irving Kristol gives it two cheers rather than three. It can be wasteful, and the market is not always the best judge of equality. No, it isn't perfect, but to paraphrase Churchill, it's the best system we've got. It's an extraordinarily efficient engine that has conferred unprecedented wealth on its adherents, wealth that has liberated countless millions from poverty and the daily grind of just keeping body and soul together. Capitalism is also the system that best supports democracy. An economic order founded upon respect for individual market decisions and property rights against encroachment by the state lays the groundwork required for the development of a democratic political order. There are, of course, Capitalist authoritarian regimes, but I cannot think of a democracy today the seeds of which did not spring from a liberal Capitalist past.

There, in a nutshell, is my sales pitch for the free market system. It's a pitch I've been making fervently all my professional life, from Wall Street to the Treasury Department, through my book, *A Time for Truth*, and the many articles and speeches I write today. The selling is very different from what I learned as a bond trader; not only does it concern the extremely sensitive area of ideology, but until recently the competition has virtually held a monopoly in the opinion-making arena, in our universities and the media where the balance of cultural power lies. My persistence has been fueled not only by an immutable dedication to the principles of our Capitalist system, but also by a firm faith in the integrity of the American people and their inherent love for liberty. On a more personal level, I want my children and their children for generations to come to enjoy the same freedom and opportunities I have been privileged to experience in this great country of ours. Most Americans, I think, value our free market system as highly as I do, but the rhetoric of the left is powerful and seductive, and its methods subtle. It is easy to be coopted by the false morality and and perverted righteousness of the so-called liberals if one doesn't scrutinize their arguments and motives with meticulous care. As Justice Louis D. Brandeis said, "Men born to freedom are naturally alert to repel invasion of their liberty by evil-minded rulers. The greatest dangers to liberty lurk in insidious encroachment by men of zeal, well-meaning but without understanding."*

Happily, there is reason to believe, as I write, that the sales on the side of freedom are rising again. The spreading of the tax revolt, the emergence of the neo-conservatives from the womb of the left, the success of Milton and Rose Friedman's *Free to Choose* television series and book—all suggest that the tide is turning. It is critical, however, that our sales force not become complacent but redouble its efforts if this trend is to turn into a more substantial commitment, for the day we take our freedom for granted is the day we begin to lose it. If I have helped in any way through what I have said and written to sell the American people on the importance of protecting our precious heritage of liberty, then this is without doubt the greatest sale I ever hope to make.

□    □    □

William E. Simon has had long experience in public service and finance. His financial career began in 1952 with Union Securities in New York, after which he became associated with Weeden and Company. He joined Salomon Brothers in 1964, heading the Government and Municipal Securities Departments. He was also one of seven partners serving on the Executive Committee of the firm.

In January 1973, Mr. Simon was appointed Deputy Secretary of

*Olmstead v. United States*, 277 U.S. 479 (1928).

the Treasury. As such, he supervised the Nixon Administration's program to improve and restructure U.S. financial institutions. Later that year, Mr. Simon was named Administrator of the Federal Energy Office and assumed the overall responsibility for the government's energy policy during the Mideast oil embargo. Mr. Simon was appointed the sixty-third Secretary of the Treasury in 1974. In this capacity he served as the chief economic spokesman for the Nixon Administration. He was also designated Chairman of the East-West Trade Board.

Mr. Simon is the author of *A Time for Truth*, published by Reader's Digest Press/McGraw-Hill Book Company in 1978.

Deeply committed to the American free enterprise system, Mr. Simon assumed a number of new responsibilities in the business community upon leaving the Cabinet in 1977. He is Senior Consultant, Blyth Eastman Dillon & Co., Inc. and Consultant, and Chairman of the Advisory Committee for Brazilinvest. Mr. Simon is a member of the Board of Directors of Citibank/Citicorp, the INA Corporation, the Xerox Corporation, Dart Industries, Inc., the Halliburton Company, and the Power Corporation of Canada.

William Simon serves as President of the John M. Olin Foundation, Treasurer of the United States Olympic Committee (USOC), Co-Chairman of the Board of the Institute for Educational Affairs (IEA), Member of the Board of Trustees of the U.S. Council of International Chamber of Commerce, Member of the International Chamber of Commerce (I.C.C.) International Panel on Extortion and Bribery in Business Transactions, Member of the British-North American Committee, Member of the Board of Trustees, Chairman of the Financial Policy Committee, and Member of the Executive Committee of Lafayette College, Member of the Board of Overseers, Hoover Institution on War, Revolution and Peace (Stanford University), Member of the Board of Trustees of the Hudson Institute and of the George C. Marshall Research Foundation, Member of the Board of the Heritage Foundation, and Member of the Board of Directors Damon Runyon–Walter Winchell Cancer Fund.

*Robert C. Sinnaeve*

# Promises

*There is a Latin word*—apologia—meaning defense. What is written here could be so considered. And it qualifies as a remarkable sales story, too. When one feels strongly about a cause, a position, a belief, there must be an inherent responsibility to make a corresponding defense—just in case a situation arises that might question an individual's resolve. This is especially true when it is a matter of one's convictions and beliefs. Although sometimes it is not evident to others, each person understands and knows what must be done to uphold individual dignity and honor. I paraphrase Blaise Pascal, the philosopher: the heart knows things the mind does not understand.

February is always one of the coldest months in the Midwest, and 1967 was no exception. At night the Golden Dome of Notre Dame du Lac is always brightly lighted. Flight captains use the landmark for visual guidance. The gold dome tops the university's administration building where my office was located. Inside on that cold night, the old steampipes hissed and occasionally clanked. I sat at my typewriter staring at the keys almost afraid to begin. Maybe the radiator noises were trying to distract me. More likely, I noticed the thumping because my heart was keeping pace with the sound. A deep breath and finally I began *the letter*.

> Dear Reverend Father Provincial: After many months of deep and intensive thought and prayer, I have reached some decisions concerning myself and my future.

My heart was now running ahead of and stronger than the hissing and thumping steampipes in the room. I'm sure I then felt it was much too hot in the room—or was it just me?

This was to be one of the most important letters I had even written. My thoughts and emotions swept quickly back to a day nine years and six months earlier when I lay prostrate on the sanctuary floor of the

**317**

Sacred Heart Church on the university's campus. I believe there were fifteen or so others also solemnly prostrate with me. My sacred words joined those of my companions and rose to commingle with the beautiful Gregorian chant of the Moreau Seminary choir. The Catholic Church accepted our perpetual vows of poverty, chastity, and obedience. We were dedicated as Brothers in the Religious Life in the Congregation of Holy Cross. The vows were a culmination of six years of training, studying, and testing whether a dedicated full-time religious life was for us or not. There had been three years of temporary, one-year-at-a-time vows, but this was for life—perpetually! The *Te Deum* was sung.

And now, almost ten years later, I was about to petition to the Reverend Provincial Superior for a dispensation from my three vows. My fingers moved again at the typewriter.

> . . . and so, Dear Father, it is only after much time and evaluation of my motives . . . that . . . I have decided to request a dispensation from my vows.

I remember that night well. It had taken me two years to be sure my decision was right. I do not perspire easily, especially in winter, but that night I recall a trickle ran down my side. Writing the letter was difficult for me; it must be written correctly. I must explain and defend my decision, and the Church must approve it. For my conscience and my own satisfaction, I knew it had to be done right. I rejected any thoughts of what the alternatives might be. It was a matter of my own peace of mind and soul. I wanted to depart with the same strong convictions and faith that brought me to the solitary life in the first place. Others might have turned sour and even rejected their beliefs. We'd all heard about some of *those* scandals. The whispered stories of a priest, nun, or brother going "over the wall" were only fantasy and mostly malicious gossip in certain non-Catholic communities. Nevertheless, rumors and gossip have a tendency to be cruel and destructive. The truth was, the door was always open. Anyone could walk out at any time. There were no locks or restraints. This was a voluntary and free-giving life of service and dedication. Anyone could simply pick up and be gone. No, I refused to entertain those alternatives. My challenge was to petition correctly, convincingly, successfully. I had come a long way since that day fourteen years earlier when I stripped off the clothes of the "old man" and "put on the garments of a new." I was not now about to reject what all that meant. What I had learned, discovered, come to love, to respect, to be in awe of, was much too valuable to compromise.

It was late that February night of 1967 when I finished the letter. I trembled; not outside, but inside.

I assure you of my wholehearted appreciation for all that the Congregation of Holy Cross has given me, and done for me. These I will always treasure and be most thankful.

Very sincerely yours,
Brother Robert Sinnaeve, C.S.C.

The letter was signed with a firm hand. I sealed the envelope. It was now very late. The campus had quieted down for the night.

I can't remember the long walk across the campus to where I lived. I knew the path well and it knew me, for all the years I had made the trip. My mind and heart were someplace else, I'm sure. It was a momentous night. And I still had the letter in my overcoat pocket. There was the last minute, the last second of hesitation before it dropped into the mail slot.

Days, weeks passed. The office was busy. Students were coming and going in a constant stream. It was that time of year to award scholarships and financial aid for the incoming freshman class. We were a popular office; almost as much as the campus snack-shop, the Huddle. It was good to keep busy. I'm sure that made the weeks of uncertainty livable.

A month had passed since the letter was mailed to the Reverend Provincial Superior. I knew the feeling of the prophet Job. Had I failed to adequately present my story, my request? Horrible doubts worked their way through my thoughts. No: "A patient man shall speak of victory."

Immediately after dinner was the best time to make a phone call to the provincial headquarters in South Bend. The person who answered informed me that the Father Provincial was out of the country, but his assistant was in. I knew Father Craddick well. He had been the Director of Novices during my year of novitiate in Jordan, Minnesota.

I was never sure whether he liked me. In those early days of my seminary training, I was assigned an "obedience" of keeping the seminary's carpeted floors clean. One day, somehow, I accidentally mistook his best hairbrush and used it to vigorously sweep clean all the carpet corners and edges. It was his "*very best* brush," he told me afterward. But we were friends and could talk easily. My letter had arrived, but he wanted to talk of other matters, that was obvious. "We're pleased to hear you've been appointed by the Governor to the Council for the new College Student Loan Plan of Indiana."

I wasn't really listening to him. My mind raced. Apparently, I had not been convincing enough in *the letter*. I interrupted him. "But, Father, tell me, has any action been taken on my request of over a month ago?" I had never spoken so firmly to a religious superior before! That might have been disrespectful, I thought; maybe even a fault. But not now, not now! The phone was silent. Finally, a very changed voice told me that I must write specifically requesting a petition be made to the Holy Father in Rome for a dispensation. I knew that my friend was not pleased with my decision; that it was uncomfortable for him to advise me on the proper protocol. Perhaps he thought I was experiencing the "dark night of the soul" and that it would pass. We were taught to have hope and pray that all temptations would pass and we'd persevere.

I lost no time. A second letter was composed. First in my head, finally on paper. It was dated March 18, 1967.

By this letter I am petitioning the Holy Father, through the Sacred Congregation of Religious, to grant me a dispensation from my perpetual vows.

I carefully explained that my decision was based on two years of efforts to dispel the thoughts I no longer had a religious vocation. I continued:

During this time I have sought proper counsel, prayer and intense thought.

I'm sure those that came in daily contact with me at that time noticed I was somewhat distracted, quite pensive.

The Vatican was notoriously slow with its red tape. Everyone knew that. The Procurator General would submit my petition to the Sacred Congregation of Religious. No one can bypass the procedures established, or hurry them on. But patience is a virtue. I knew it would just be a matter of time.

All during this difficult process I was concerned about how those I was so close to over all these years would take the news of my departure. The hundreds of associates, students, companions, families, and friends that were so very much part of my life, my training; how could I ever explain to those that loved me that a major change was to occur in my life? Perhaps they had put me on a horrible pedestal. I was a highly visible person in the university's administration. Treasurer, Director of Student Financial Aids, Residence Hall Prefect. The fourteen years of service had been greatly rewarded with numbers of friends, close friends.

So many thoughts ran through my mind. How shall I publicly explain my decision and actions? Would the public compare what I had done to a divorce? A rejection of the tenets of religion, of God? Divorce probably results because of a breakdown of the marriage and the vows given. Would my family, friends, students, and associates put me in that lot? I couldn't let that happen! The Second Vatican Council had just finished its work of renewal and updating of the Church's entire outlook. Good Pope John's effort to "open the windows of the church to let in the fresh air" had just begun to work its way. Early 1967 was still a time of rather introverted spirituality. Formality still ruled in our private and public institutions generally. I had made up my mind much earlier that I could not leave without attempting to assure my friends and family that I had not suddenly changed or lost my faith and convictions. I wanted no part of scandal or disillusionment. It was important to me that the faith and love I deeply believed in not be lost or diminished. It was not a question of fear that I would lose the respect of others. It was a matter of conscience and the fact I indeed had not lost my faith. I knew I had one more letter to write. Perhaps even more difficult than the other two. And time was not on my side now because Rome responded sooner than I expected.

The Rescript granting my dispensation was written in Latin. Cold, official . . . *"Beatissime Pater . . . benigne adnuit . . . saecularizatinionis . . . nullius roboris esto si ab Oratore non fuerit. . . ."* I almost expected to feel different somehow. Of course, I didn't. But an inner peace was mine. In retrospect, these were hard decisions for a young man to make. For a Catholic to appeal to Rome is not done every day, after all.

I carefully wrote that farewell letter to be mailed on the day I last wore the black cassock and roman collar. My convictions, my faith, my beliefs were unchanged, I assured all; in no way did I leave behind any value I had learned, any friendship I had made, any insight gained during these intense years in the religious life. I was now stronger than before in my faith. The garments were changing, yet I remained the same person with the same goals and desires. I used a weak example. I was simply changing vehicles, the mode of transportation. But I was still on the way to my destination.

A friend drove me to Indianapolis that May of 1967. It was a new beginning for me. A new career, a new life.

Robert Frost is one of my favorite poets. In the seminary I sometimes used his material for daily meditation. Even today I do. He wrote what so many felt:

> The woods are lovely, dark and deep.
> But I have promises to keep,
> And miles to go before I sleep,
> And miles to go before I sleep.*

☐　☐　☐

Born and raised in Detroit, Michigan, Robert C. Sinnaeve attended public and private schools there until 1951 when he entered the Holy Cross Seminary at Notre Dame, Indiana. From 1951 through 1956 he studied at Notre Dame and entered the religious life in The Congregation of Holy Cross in 1954 after completion of an intensive year of seclusion at The Sacred Heart Novitiate in Jordan, Minnesota. In 1956 he was appointed Treasurer of the newly opened Notre Dame High School for Boys in Niles, Illinois. During that time he continued studies at Northwestern and Marquette universities specializing in school business administration and finance in The Graduate School of Education.

In 1963 he was appointed Treasurer/Head Cashier at the University of Notre Dame, where he also served as a residence hall Prefect. In 1965 he was designated as The University's Director of Student Financial Aid and Executive Secretary of the Scholarship Committee. During this time his interest in assisting financially needy students expanded as he served on various panels developing principles and practices for the administration of student financial aids. He contributed to publication of the College and University Handbook of Indiana, was appointed by the Governor to assist in the development of The College Student Loan Plan of Indiana. Bob has appeared before Congressional Subcommittees to speak on behalf of student assistance and Federal legislation.

In 1967 Mr. Sinnaeve was appointed as Executive Secretary of the State of Indiana Scholarship and Loan Commission where he served

*From *The Poetry of Robert Frost*, edited by Edward Connery Latham. Copyright 1923, © 1969 by Holt, Rinehart, and Winston. Copyright 1951 by Robert Frost.

until joining the nationwide, not-for-profit organization, United Student Aid Funds, where he currently is Vice President for Program Development and Services in New York City. Mr. Sinnaeve is a member of the American Personnel and Guidance Association, the American College Personnel Association, and the American Association of Higher Education. He is active in regional and national student financial aid organizations and contributes to the professional development of the campus financial aid officer.

**Ernest E. Smith, Jr.**

# Every Person
# A Sales Person

*There are many kinds of salesmen* who sell many kinds of products and services, even ideas. Initially, I must confess that I have never considered myself to be a professional salesman in the truest sense of the word—I do not earn my livelihood through the sale of a product. For this reason, when asked to contribute to this book, I questioned the appropriateness of my participation. As a public administrator who carries out the provisions of law and regulations enacted and promulgated by the Congress and state legislature, I am not a salesman. A salesman is that glib and persuasive person who could sell ice to the Eskimos!

After reflecting over the request for some time, however, it occurred to me that in every respect, virtually everyone is a salesman. In fact, any person with an idea or responsibility and a true commitment to see it to fruition must be a salesman. These persons must see the need to "sell" the idea, or all will be for naught. Thus "salesman" covers the spectrum from the parent seeking to sell children on the need to choose those values and life styles the parent seeks to instill, to the minister seeking to sell the Gospel, to the employee seeking to sell management on his or her solution to the corporate problem, to the banker seeking to sell the services of his bank to the potential depositor, to the public administrator seeking to sell the public service program that requires a commitment and participation by the private, nongovernmental sector. It is in this last example that my story would appear to be appropriately considered in this book.

Let me begin by stating that, from my personal perspective, any salesman who wants to be considered a success must be committed to a product. To try to sell some good or service in which the seller has no personal belief or respect is not likely to result in a satisfied buyer or a successful seller. Equally important is the challenge provided to the seller. In the typical sales environment, such a challenge would be provided by the management and supervisor of the employing corporation. For the public administrator, the challenge will most likely come through the authorizing legislation of a program or through the direction of the regulatory authority. While the challenge provided to persons in the private sector may be more direct and clear, the challenge provided to the public administrator can be equally compelling. Most of the challenges will provide a goal that cannot be obtained without the belief and commitment required of the salesman, and only through a better effort on the part of the person being challenged. Some might even go the point of saying that most challenges would represent a level of success that the person making the challenge does not feel can be reached.

In this context of challenges, my task in the spring of 1977 was a challenge that most reasonable people would have considered to be virtually impossible to complete. As the Administrator of Student Financial Aid for the Florida Department of Education, the state education agency in Florida, I was given the "challenge" of developing the response Florida would make to certain provisions of the Higher Education Amendments of 1976 enacted by the 94th Congress in November 1976. The language of this act reconfirmed the Federal purpose and policy to create local student loan guaranty agencies in the fifty states and territories of the United States. Aside from the media debate concerning the welfare and food stamp programs, there are few, if any, public service programs that can generate conversation to the degree that student loans can. In the mid-1970s—and today—student borrowing was considered to be a topic about which virtually everyone but the proverbial mountain hermit would express an opinion. Unfortunately, the great majority of such conversations are negative and ill-informed. Most conversations are filled with *ugly* words: "default," "bankruptcy," "delinquency," "fraud," "ripoff," "bums," and so on. Although these terms are attributable to the student loan program with a great degree of accuracy in some cases, what is most often not recognized and very seldom discussed is the fact that these words are appropriate for discussing some persons and accounts involving the extension of any kind of financial credit! An informed conversation with the man on the street involving student loans or other types of credit would include the same ugly words, but "profitable," "thrift," "character," "investment return," "investment in the future," "foundation for future credit," "tomorrow's customer base," and similar phrases, would be added. Notwithstanding the previous comments, the student loan environment in the period of challenge facing this public administrator was a falling barometer, high winds, rough seas, all in a boat the public felt would not and should not float!

With a personal belief in the program and the challenge provided by the Congress, the staff of the Florida Department of Education proceeded to develop a plan for responding to the new law. The plan was presented to the 1977 Session of the Florida Legislature with the blessing and support of the Commissioner of Education and his management staff. Legislative support was given to the plan by Commissioner of Education Ralph Turlington, and sponsorship of the actual required legislation by then Senator, now Governor, Bob Graham. The plan received scrutiny and overwhelming support in both Houses of the Florida Legislature, not receiving a single negative vote in either body.

The plan called for the creation of a state-chartered nonprofit corporation to serve as the policy implementation body for student financial assistance in Florida. While primary emphasis and impetus came from the Guaranteed Student Loan Program, the new Florida Student Financial Assistance Commission was charged with the administration of the comprehensive program of grants, scholarships, loans, and loan guarantees authorized by Florida law. The composition of the Commission is nine members appointed by the Governor and confirmed by the Florida Senate. The constituent representation in Commission membership is three persons representing financial institutions, three persons representing educational institutions, two persons representing the public at large, and one enrolled student.

Given the needed legal and administrative framework, the Commission entered the required agreements with the U.S. Commissioner of Education to become the guarantor of student loans made in the State of Florida. The next step involved the greatest challenge facing the new Commission—convincing the private financial community that the Florida Guaranteed Student Loan is a viable form of credit, involving no loss to the prudent lender and serving an acceptable social and educational purpose. Florida bankers can be accurately and affectionately described as among the more conservative in the nation. If questioned about students loans in 1977 virtually all bankers in Florida would have wanted to put an end to student loans made in their institutions and the State of Florida. Although about $25 million in student loans was provided by the private sector in 1976, the vast majority was loaned to primary customers for the purpose of retaining good accounts. There was essentially no competitive approach to student lending except among a very few savings and loan associations. It was actually difficult to determine where the students were able to obtain the loans that were being made.

Obviously the new program was successful, or this story would not be told. The real story, however, is the approach taken by the Commission, the very fortunate events, and the response given to the program by the private financial community, once the true story on student loans was heard by the bankers.

The conservative Florida banker does not hold the "faceless bureaucrat from Tallahassee" in the highest esteem. When the bureaucrat represents the educational establishment and wants to talk about making student loans to "guitar-packing longhairs," the expected reception is not warm. The missing element was the understanding of the banker that the person making a student loan presentation was informed, had a working understanding of how financial institutions operate, and could show the financial institution that the student loan portfolio can be among the most secure and profitable investments in the portfolio of the financial institution, and perhaps most important, that the Florida Student Financial Assistance Commission can deliver the services it promises to provide.

To develop the basic elements of the Florida Guaranteed Student Loan Program, the Commission was able to obtain the knowledge and experience of bankers and persons with backgrounds in commercial finance and servicing by hiring bankers and commercial collectors from the private sector. Although these persons now became "bureaucrats," they remained representative of the philosophy of their previous professions and have been recognized by the bankers as colleagues. Since three members of the Commission came from the commercial financial community, the bankers had the comfort of knowing that there were colleagues sitting on the governing body of the Commission.

The most significant contribution to the development of Florida Guaranteed Student Loan Program was made by Bob Minnick, an active commercial banker and accountant by training, who fortuitously was available to serve as temporary professional staff member of the Commission. Bob Minnick had temporarily left active banking to organize another venture. Upon learning about the new Florida Guaranteed Student Loan Program, he offered his services to the Commission, and the offer was gladly accepted.

Under the guidance provided by the banker–members, it was possible for the Commission to develop a marketing plan that included the presentation of reasonable lending demand expectations for the financial institutions which were considering participation in the student loan program. Using a fairly complicated formula—considering the student enrollment patterns in each county and major municipality in the State of Florida, the deposit bases, and market penetration of the financial institutions placed in and serving each county and municipality—it was possible for the Commission staff to approach the prospective financial institution with a realistic proposal. The previously stated opinion of many financial institution personnel was that if an institution began to open its doors to student lending, the lobby would soon be filled with thousands of students. When the institution had questions about the basic need for student loans, the prospect of being overrun by students made a realistic consideration impossible.

Student loan demand statistics reflected the philosophy that the student should seek to borrow from the hometown lender. For example, a student attending the University of Florida in Gainesville, with parents residing in the Tampa area, should reasonably be expected to borrow from a financial institution in the Tampa area. The student is far more likely to return to the Tampa area than to remain in relatively rural Gainesville. On the other hand, the student attending Santa Fe Community College in Gainesville should approach the financial institutions in Gainesville rather than seeking loans in Tampa, 150 miles away. The deposit base of the institutions located in Tampa can support the residents of Tampa who may go to a large institution outside of Tampa, whereas the relatively smaller deposit base of a financial institution located in Gainesville will not support the demands of students who move into Gainesville for the purpose of attending the University of Florida. The proposal of meeting the demands of hometown students is supplemented by the lending of a limited number of large regional lending institutions resulting in a system of referrals that can supplement the lending of the hometown institution.

In approaching prospective lending institutions, the Commission staff tried to establish a nucleus of financial institutions located around the state to ensure that at least one institution could be established to serve each major metropolitan area of Florida. After the nucleus was established, additional lenders to supplement the nucleus could be added. The philosophy followed was that once participation was developed successfully in an area, the spirit of competition would bring other institutions into the program. This has proven to be the case, with only a few exceptions. The holding company system in Florida banks has assisted in this effort. Where an affiliated institution has begun to benefit from the services of the Florida Guaranteed Loan Program, other affiliates within the same holding company have sought to participate.

Perhaps the most amazing and gratifying part of the new program has been the timing of the acceptance of the program by the private financial community. In the first full year of operation, lenders made student loans totaling over $60 million, well over twice the level of previous lending. We are now in the second year of participation in the Florida Guaranteed Loan Program and will exceed $100 million in loans.

Our goal had been to ensure that at least the same level of loans would be available as before the establishment of the local program. It is even more amazing to note that the healthy level of acceptance by the financial community has occurred during poor economic conditions in the country. The credit restraints that were imposed on the public and financial institutions did not have a negative impact on the new loan program. We know that this was due in part to a great deal of good fortune. At the same time, we can take pride in the fact that good planning and effective marketing can result in the presentation of a public program that is acceptable to the private sector.

The salesmen making this presentation were certainly faced with a challenge; they had to personally believe in their product with an intensity that led to a commitment, and the private sector has responded with a level of participation far exceeding the expectations of the Commission. It is very clear that the quality product, our service, when properly delivered by an informed and committed seller, will receive a fine response from the private sector. The student will benefit, the educational institution will benefit, the financial institution will benefit and make a taxable profit, the public will benefit from an educated citizenry, state government will have fulfilled a portion of its Constitutional responsibility of education for the citizen, and the Congressional purpose confirmed in the 1976 Higher Education Amendments will have been fulfilled.

☐ ☐ ☐

**Ernest E. Smith, Jr., Executive Director of the Florida Student Financial Assistance Commission, is a native of Mobile, Alabama, and a graduate of Marion Military Institute, Howard College (Samford University), and the University of Alabama at Tuscaloosa. He has**

served in his career as a student financial aid administrator since joining the University of West Florida, Pensacola, as Director of Student Financial Aid in 1968. In 1971, Mr. Smith joined the staff of the Student Financial Aid Section of the Florida Department of Education as Associate Administrator, with specific responsibilities for the guaranteed student loan program, research, and in-service training for campus student aid personnel.

Mr. Smith assumed responsibility as Administrator in 1974, upon the retirement of the previous administrator. During the period immediately following the appointment, the administrative placement of the Student Financial Aid Section was changed to place the function directly under the Deputy Commissioner for Special Programs of the Florida Department of Education. At the same time, the Florida Student Assistance Grants Program and the Florida Insured Student Loan Program came into maturity as a major financial resource for Florida students.

In 1977, the Florida Legislature created the Florida Student Financial Assistance Commission, a state-chartered nonprofit corporation with the primary purpose of administering the student financial assistance programs of the State of Florida. In 1978, Mr. Smith was appointed to serve as Executive Director for the Commission.

Mr. Smith has served in a variety of leadership functions in his brief career. He has served as President of the National Council of Higher Education Loan Programs, President of the Association of State Direct Lenders, President of the State Department of Education Credit Union, and President of the National Association of State Scholarship and Grant Programs. He now serves as a member of the Executive Committee of the College Scholarship Service Council. In the past he has served as a member of the American College Testing Service Advisory Council. Mr. Smith has been asked to consult with several other state agencies concerning student financial assistance in several areas of specialization.

**Milton R. Stohl**

# The Most Significant Sale in My Career

*When I was hired* by Mystik Tape Company as Vice-President and Director of Sales and Marketing, I quickly realized that we needed more effective distribution in the eleven western states. We had some very good independent distributors scattered throughout the West, doing an effective job locally in their limited geographic areas. However, there were two giant distributors of paper products and pressure-sensitive tapes who dominated the western market.

One of these was Blake, Moffitt & Towne, at that time a division of Kimberly-Clark, with over 240 salesmen in twenty-seven divisions covering all of the eleven western states. BM&T distributed 3M tapes exclusively and over the years were not receptive to changing this source of supply or taking on an additional supplier. The management team at Mystik came to the inevitable conclusion that without BM&T as a distributor we would not achieve the desired increases in sales and market share we had put in our five-year forecast.

Having established that as a prime objective, we studied competitor weaknesses versus our strengths and weaknesses with a view to showing BM&T why such a move was as advantageous for them as it was for us. We had our Western Regional Manager set up an appointment with Lloyd O'Connell, who was then General Merchandising Manager and who would have to approve our product line for distribution. Since this meeting was of critical importance, both Bob Leander, who was then President of Mystik, and I decided to pull out all stops and see him together.

O'Connell was very warm, and personable—and a shrewd businessman. He had been with BM&T for over thirty years and was getting ready to retire the following year. He had a very close relationship with our competitor, having done business with them for such a long time. So we knew we had our work cut out for us. I was lucky to have Bob with me because he is the epitome of what we would like to see in a good salesman or a good executive. He is a handsome, friendly, bright yet unassuming man. These qualities are disarmingly effective in a salesman but in the Chief Executive Officer of a company, they are powerful sales tools.

O'Connell, who possessed many of the same qualities, was no less affected by this type of charm in another person. He greeted us very cordially and then got right down to business with, "Why should we change a source of supply which has helped us make lots of money with their products for the past thirty years?" Our preparation proved its value at that point. I said, "Mr. O'Connell, 3M is a fine company with good products and they are considered number one in the field of pressure-sensitive tapes. You'd be ill-advised to change, but that's not what we're asking you to do. For all these years you've been selling 3M tapes exclusively while *they* have been selling their tapes to all your competitors as well. So it's a one-way exclusive arrangement. That doesn't make good business sense. Since you have been successful with their products, it *does* make sense to continue selling their line—but not to the exclusion of all other pressure-sensitive tapes."

He smiled and said, "What can you give us that we do not already have? 3M manufactures more types of tape than you do. They are better known and more widely accepted, so our salesmen don't have to spend as much time making a sale and *they* have more salesmen than you do. They consistently go out and get tape business which they turn over to us."

I said, "They *do* manufacture more types of tape, but we have a number of tapes they don't produce, and they don't permit you to sell their electrical tapes. We do!! This would be additional business for you. Not all of your customers love 3M and this would give them an alternative without having to buy from another distributor. The fact that they are well-known and widely accepted has turned your salesmen into order-takers. They don't know what the tapes are used for in different types of industries, so they don't contact similar industries and show them how pressure-sensitive tapes can save them time and money and help them do the job better. They depend on the manufacturer's salesman to turn over orders, and he does. But he also has to divide those orders he gets among all of your competitors, whom he also sells. That doesn't leave much for you when you look at the size of your organization. With over 240 salesmen of your own you could be getting a much greater share of the tape market if your men had the technical training to sell the product effectively. We can educate them in the techniques of selling these products. Since you are obviously much more important to us than you are to our competitor, you are assured of getting the lion's share of our salesmen's time. I can also assure you that if you took on the Mystik line of tapes, you would get three times more attention from our competitor's salesmen than you've had in the past."

O'Connell was no novice at this, and with a delighted twinkle in his blue eyes, he asked, "And who would be involved in training our people? How many trainers do you have available?" I made a quick mental count of our western salesmen, two regional managers, Bill Miller, our Director of Sales Training, our National Sales Manager, and myself and said, "About ten or eleven men." He smiled again and said, "As you know we have over 240 salesmen. All the people you assign to the training program have other duties to perform as well. How are you going to effectively train 240 salesmen before we're all too old to enjoy the fruits of this ambitious program?"

At this point necessity again became the mother of invention and I said, "We'll produce a 16mm color, sound movie film showing the uses of our various tapes in different industries and how they should be sold. We'll produce a printed manual for each salesman covering the various segments of the film, with space for notes. We'll schedule a full-day training program for the salesmen in each of your twenty-seven divisions. These will be held on consecutive Saturdays so that your salesmen don't lose any time in the field. They will be held at the various division headquarters if they have the room, or at a local hotel. Mystik will pay for the hotel meeting room and lunch, as well as for the audiovisual equipment and material. Where it is practical geographically, and the number of salesmen does not exceed sixty, we can cover two or even three divisions at one training session."

O'Connell, still smiling, asked how long it would take to produce the film and the manuals. Sensing the "kill" I rashly blurted out, "Eight weeks"!!! He quickly walked across the room to a wall calendar and circled the date eight weeks away. Then he said very deliberately, "Young fellow" (this should give you some idea of how long ago this happened), "you bring in a good training film and manual on that date—and we'll distribute your products." We had made the sale! But we still didn't have the order. There was still an *almost* impossible task to accomplish and O'Connell knew it. He told us afterward that he didn't feel he was taking any risk. He said if we didn't come back on schedule with a good film, manual, and training program, he would still have lost nothing. On the other hand, if we accomplished what we said we would do in eight weeks, he knew we could and would do anything else we promised. He knew he would then have a valuable additional supplier with an extraordinarily high level of interest in promoting new business for them and for ourselves.

For the next eight weeks we got very little sleep. Dick Kane, our Advertising Manager, Bill Miller, Ted Levine, our Manager of

Customer Service, some of our key salesmen and managers all did their parts in assembling material for the script, acting, revising, and so on. Bill Miller and I wrote the script. He did the technical product descriptions and acted as a teacher to show how the products were sold and used. I wrote the rest of the script, location scenes, selling scenes, comedy sequences—anything that would add human interest. We hired a good cinematographer and sound man, and used the production facilities of Colburn Laboratories in Chicago.

The finished film was called *The Magic of Mystik*. It was four hours long after cutting. It was divided into twenty-minute segments, each covering a specific topic. A manual covering each topic was prepared from the script. It was designed to be used as a review reference by the training seminar participants, and to amplify all film sequences.

We enlisted the aid of Bob DeWilde, BM&T's general Sales Manager, when we were about halfway through the film. He gave a brief commentary on the objectives of the film and how they paralleled the marketing objectives of BM&T. This sequence helped ensure and increase the receptivity of their salesmen and made it easier for them to relate to our product line and common objectives.

After eight weeks of sleepless nights, hard work, overcoming sound filming obstacles such as heating fans, airplane noises, town maintenance crews removing tree limbs, unexpected telephone rings and even a dog fight, we kept our appointment with Floyd O'Connell in San Francisco. We showed the finished film to him and a group of BM&T's top executives.

They were delighted with *The Magic of Mystik* and the manual and assured us that both would achieve all the predetermined objectives:

1    To give the distributor salesmen a selling knowledge of the line in one day.

2.    To describe the complete product line and outline all features and advantages.

3    To open discussions on all potential tape markets as well as specialized tape needs and applications.

4    To show how Mystik Tapes are produced (Quality Control, etc.).

5    To demonstrate how to sell tapes.

6    To illustrate product superiority by showing dramatic in-office demonstration techniques.

7    To provide written material to reinforce film sequences.

8    To present opportunities to discuss local accounts with distributor salesmen and pinpoint tape uses.

We made nine prints of the film, and in the first five years of its use we trained about 5000 distributor salesmen. Eighteen publications published articles about the film, proclaiming that it established a new horizon in audiovisual training programs.

The business results were immediately apparent in terms of dramatic increases in sales and profits. It firmly established me as an innovator in our industry and increased our profits to the point where Borden, Inc., developed an interest in acquiring Mystik. It started me in the film producing business, which I still do successfully as one of the services of my management consulting company.

Most important, it reinforced my conviction that people don't just buy a *product*. You can sell anyone if you can demonstrate through pure logic that what you're trying to sell is not just a good product but offers a definite benefit to the purchaser—it will increase profits, save time, labor, or money, or make life easier or more enjoyable for the purchaser.

When I am asked which sale did the most to further my career, I have to think of that one as the most significant.

□   □   □

Milton R. Stohl is president of his own management consulting firm, Milton R. Stohl, Associates. He was formerly Senior Vice President of Borden Chemical, and General Manager of their Consumer Products Division where he inaugurated and directed their management development programs. Among the many successful, internationally advertised products he marketed were Elmer's Glue, Mystik Tapes, Krylon Spray Paints and other familiar consumer and industrial trademarks. He was President of Waring Products, manufacturers of the Waring Blender and the Dormyer mixers. He is a Director Emeritus of the Connecticut Business and Industry Association, a Trustee of Manhattan College in New York and he has served as both officer and director of the Sales Executives Club of New York and other directing boards. Mr. Stohl has written numerous articles for a wide variety of periodicals and has been quoted in *Business Week* and other national publications as a highly respected authority on marketing and management. Scores of salesmen and managers who received their tutelage under Mr. Stohl are now running large departments, divisions, and companies. His list of current clients looks like a Who's Who in American Industry. His seminars are very popular because his vast experience as a business leader enables him to provide practical, proven solutions to specific business problems, and his sincerity and quick wit have made him as popular with salesmen as he is with Chief Executive Officers.

*Joseph Sugarman*

# The Ultimate Salesman

*My reputation was built* on my ability to write effective mail order advertisements that sell products in very large quantities. Instead of selling on a one-to-one basis, I have learned to truly duplicate myself through the power of my pen and the wide distribution of the magazines and newspapers I advertise in. All that is fine, but how did I do it? What secrets can you discover from my life that can make you a better salesman? And, finally, what was my most satisfying sale?

An officer of a major Chicago corporation once confided in me, "Joe, I consider myself a great salesman. I feel confident that I can sell anybody on a one-to-one basis. But my ability doesn't compare to what you can do. You can sell millions of people through the power of your pen. You're the ultimate salesman."

Those comments were a great compliment to me. Without realizing it, I was indeed a salesman—a salesman on a totally different plane— but a salesman nevertheless.

In selling, a salesman's personality often plays an important role in a sale. So does mine, and I reflect it very clearly in my advertisements. People have commented, "I buy from JS&A because I trust the company. I feel that you're honest and that you don't insult my intelligence." Isn't that the sign of a good salesman?

Not all of our ads are successful. But few people sell all of their prospects. Every once in a while we'll misjudge our market or select the wrong product and fall flat on our face. The principles of salesmanship, however, always apply.

My sales training really started very early in life. I sold newspaper subscriptions to earn a football when I was only eight years old. I sold lemonade—the usual entrepreneurial activities that the oldest son of another entrepreneur might do.

My father was the president of a company that manufactured and sold printing equipment, Consolidated International. I was to help my father in business after college so my future was pretty well set. But every once in a while I'd want to buy something my parents would deny me and end up creating some little business to earn the money.

While still in grammar school, with the assistance of my father, I opened up a printing company in the basement of our home. I'd sell printing to the neighbors and pay off the equipment on a time payment plan.

In high school I started my own school paper and sold advertising space to support it, and in college I sold my advertising writing services to local merchants trying to sell to the university's students.

When I look back at some of the events that affected me the most, I can remember walking alone down Seventh Avenue in New York City. I was asked to help my father at his New York office, so I left the University of Miami where I was majoring in electrical engineering and moved to New York City.

It was pretty lonely in New York. I had no friends and I was new to the city, but I amused myself by reading books on salesmanship and walking down Seventh Avenue and across Forty-Second Street.

I knew some day I would have to help my father in selling his equipment, so I would read every book I could find on selling— *Dangerous Selling, The Power of Selling, How to Be a Salesman.*

I would also visit a few of the auction galleries along Seventh Avenue. You would walk in the store and an "auctioneer" standing on a platform would auction off a real bargain. The person who bought it would be so impressed with the buy that both he and the rest of the crowd would bid and clamor for the next product, which, too, would be a bargain.

With the crowd clamoring for more and in a frenzied buying mood, the auctioneer would cleverly start upgrading the products, getting more money, and thus make sizable profits.

I would stand for hours watching the auctioneers, fascinated by their skill and amused by their techniques.

Mike Todd had recently died and I read his biography. I was programming myself to be a promoter like Mike Todd, a showman like the Seventh Avenue auctioneer, and a skillful salesman like my father. After a year in New York, I returned to school.

Things were still rough. My father was having difficulty going through the 1958 recession. He had overcommitted himself just before the recession and he was sitting on thousands of dollars in inventory that wasn't moving.

He asked me if I could earn some money to help support myself through college. I had worked for him for a year at no salary and had successfully gotten his New York office in operation again. But I had no money and I wanted to finish college and get my degree.

Back in Miami, I stopped by a restaurant on Coral Way in Coral Gables, a Miami suburb. The Ole Hickory Restaurant was empty—which seemed strange since it was dinner time.

"Where is everybody?" I inquired of the portly gentleman behind the counter.

"We just opened the restaurant last week," replied the owner, Walter Volk. "It's too early to expect much of a crowd."

As I was eating my dinner, Volk walked up to me and asked me a question. "How do I attract college students? You're from the university, aren't you?"

I thought for a moment, looked him straight in the eye, and said, "Why not advertise in the school paper?"

"Fine," replied Volk, "But what do I say?"

"Whatever you say, it's got to be different," I replied.

Volk sat down at my table. A sense of frustration appeared on his face. "I can't spell my own name sometimes, how am I going to figure out something different? Would you write an ad for me? I'll give you a free meal if you do."

"OK, I'll give it a crack," I answered. "Do you care what I say?"

"Say anything," Volk replied, "just make it work. If you want, offer them our $1.29 steak special with fries and cole slaw."

I paid my bill, left the restaurant and went home where I wrote out a crazy, wild ad. It certainly was different. The university was several miles away. I doubted if any student would travel that far to visit a barbeque restaurant when there were plenty of fine restaurants near the university. I felt I had to build up a great deal of curiosity to attract a crowd, but I also had to keep the advertisement honest. I had an idea.

The ad I wrote was actually a conversation between two university students. They discussed, in excited terms, the super special at The Ole Hickory Restaurant. They discussed the low price and the delicious food. "But there's a catch," said one of the students in my ad. "You've got to bring in $1.29 and the top of a Brinks armored car to get in."

The ad ran. I was quite curious to find out if the ad worked, so I drove out Saturday at noon to see if anyone would show up at The Ole Hickory.

As I drove down Coral Way, I thought of how I wasted this poor restaurant owner's money, if the ad didn't work. I thought of the chance I took by putting in such an unusual ad. "What possessed me to do it?" I thought.

I was so worried that the ad was going to be a miserable failure I decided to simply drive by the restaurant rather quickly. If, by chance, the ad failed, Volk would be looking out his window, and I didn't want him to see me.

As I approached the restaurant, I started to accelerate to forty-five miles per hour, ten above the limit. Zoom—I rushed past the restaurant only to notice a long line at the restaurant entrance and a policeman directing traffic at the parking lot entrance.

I was so shocked, as I was looking back, that I almost smashed into the car in front of me. I quickly pulled over, turned around and headed back to the restaurant.

After a five-minute delay getting into the parking lot, I noticed droves of students piling out of their cars, carrying pieces of tin, cardboard and plywood with the words, "Brinks Armored Car."

I cut to the front of the line to meet Volk at the door.

"What did you do to me?" shouted Volk. "I've had the health inspectors here already complaining about all this junk that's been piling up in the front of the restaurant."

The ad was indeed a great success. Walter was so elated that he hired me to write more ads. Later I sold my services to ten other stores, ranging from clothing shops to ice cream parlors, and without knowing it, I had created my first advertising agency.

Indeed, if my sales efforts are the advertisements I write, that first Ole Hickory ad had to be my most exciting. It started me in my first ad agency, helped me through college, and gave me the confidence to use the same sales principles I learned in those books on salesmanship for my advertisements.

I still write my own advertisements to this day. Walter Volk eventually moved Ole Hickory to Bird Road in Miami. More than twenty years have gone by, but Walter and I still remember that first ad.

I stopped by The Ole Hickory in 1980 to say hello to Walter, after not seeing him for ten years. In those ten years I had managed to start a small mail order business in the basement of my home, building it into America's largest single source of space-age products. Our ads appear in over 100 national magazines and we are the largest advertiser in many of the magazines we advertise in. We were the first to introduce the pocket calculator in 1971, the first to introduce the liquid crystal digital watch in 1973, the first company to introduce toll-free credit card order-taking and a host of other "firsts" that have been recognized in the electronics as well as marketing and advertising industries.

Walter had gained a little weight, his hair was completely grey, but I recognized him right away despite the years.

"How are you doing, Walter?"

"Fine, Joe. How are you doing? What business are you in?"

"Electronics, Walter. I sell electronic products through the mail."

"Joe, you had me fooled. I thought for sure you'd end up in advertising."

☐ ☐ ☐

Joseph Sugarman is president and creative director of the JS&A Group, Inc. In addition to directing his large organization, he is responsible for writing the copy for all his advertisements and is involved in every step of the creative process.

He was born and raised in the Chicago area, and attended the electrical engineering college at the University of Miami in Florida. He then spent three and a half years in Germany with Army Intelligence and the CIA before returning to the United States to form a ski lift sales company and then his own advertising agency. After six years with his own ad agency, he saw the pocket calculator as an exciting direct marketing opportunity and formed a company to market it from his basement.

That company grew very rapidly to become America's largest single source of space-age products.

Mr. Sugarman recently was selected as Direct Marketing Man of the Year in New York by the Direct Mail Marketing Association.

*Don Van Der Weide, CLU*

# *Finding Problems and Solutions*

*I live in a small community*, a town with a population of about 4500 people.

Orange City is not crowded with financial institutions—in fact, it is far removed from the big business and financial districts of any large city. Yet I was determined to be in business for myself—in the life insurance business—in Orange City, Iowa. I had always been a believer in life insurance and what it could do for people. As I entered the life insurance business I felt that the only way to succeed while living in my area was to write many applications. I did not believe the opportunity for writing large applications existed. Little did I realize how wrong I was.

Early in my business career I talked, visited, and watched the giants of the insurance industry. I learned from them that writing a sizable number of applications, 200 to 400 per year, was the right direction and right goal for me to set in my early years in the insurance business. This gave me a good foundation to stand on. Then, as many of my policyholders began to grow, I was growing with them. I soon realized that I did not have to be in the large metropolitan areas in order to reach my goals. In those days, though, my goal was to write 200 applications per year.

I soon began expanding my knowledge in the area of insurance as it applied to businesses and people in business. I found that I was surrounding myself with successful people. It was somewhat like having a board of directors upon whom I could lean when I needed business advice or when I needed places to go. These men were most helpful in my career. I tried to run my business as a businessman should. I operated out of an office on Main Street, and my office held all the necessary equipment to do business, and the business functioned in a responsible manner with personal duties separated from business affairs.

**345**

I soon realized that these men with whom I had surrounded myself not only were willing to help me but recognized that they too needed help in the area of estate planning—and they looked to me for advice. This encouraged me to sharpen my mind in the area of estate planning and business planning more than I had ever intended when I started in the business.

The results were phenomenal. I once dreamed about writing larger policies, and it was now happening to me at a very early point in my life. I found myself writing million-dollar and multimillion-dollar policies in a rural community and surrounding communities. I found that I did not have to be in the large metropolitan areas to achieve this kind of business.

Many sales stand out of my mind; permit me to tell you about one of them. I often work on a referral basis. I was referred to this particular client by another satisfied client. The referral was made by telephone so it was easy for me to go to the prospect and introduce myself and tell him what I needed. He preferred that I start by talking with his in-house accountant. After obtaining as many details as I could regarding this man's business, the stock ownership, the value of the business, the earnings of the business, reviewing the financial statement and the profit and loss statement, I was able to get a good handle on this business.

One thing was missing, however: the accountant could not state the personal objectives of the business owner, nor could he give me any details of the personal finances. I therefore had to set up a second appointment with the prospect. I always feel that if I have all of the details about the business, I am equipped to do a better job for my prospect. If I have all the facts, and my prospect knows that I have all the facts, he too will be more receptive to the recommendations that I make.

The second appointment was made. This time I visited with the owner of the business. I was pleasantly received. We had a good visit and he understood why I had to talk to him this time. Obviously the accountant relayed much of our discussion to his boss. I believe this employer was favorably impressed that I had the businessman and his business' best interests in mind. After this discussion with the owner of the business I uncovered several needs. I feel it is important to learn the object of the business owner. He wanted to keep the business intact, hoping his sons would be interested enough to want to continue this business. His sons were just beginning to start work in the business and therefore it was too early to know whether they would be serious about it. I presented a smorgasbord of ideas, trying to make up for the many years over which this prospect had done very little to plan for the future. He wanted to leave his business to his sons if they were interested in operating it, and to provide equally for his daughter. He wanted his wife to live well. How did I go about satisfying these needs?

One of the first things that we talked about was estate liquidity. If all of his money was tied up in his business and inventory when he died, the business and the estate would be in a financial bind. It was therefore necessary to discuss liquidity for his estate and try to provide this liquidity with the use of corporate dollars as opposed to personal dollars. Other ideas that I discussed with him then were salary continuation, pension and profit-sharing plans, improvement of his group life insurance and medical coverages, the recapitalization of his stock, gifts, and updating his will and possibly using trusts within his will. He recognized that there were a lot of things that needed his attention and that much help was needed. I told him that it was impossible to do all things at once, but that it would be important to get started at some point. I suggested that we try to provide the estate with the cash that would be needed at the first death and the second death (the death of the husband and the death of the wife). I suggested he undergo physical examinations and with results in hand we could talk with his attorney about my ideas. He agreed and we were on our way.

He was examined, appointments were set, and insurance was issued. The attorney agreed that we were on the right track. The attorney proceeded to prepare a section 303 agreement to allow for a tax-favorable exchange of stock for cash at the death of the business owner. He also prepared a salary continuation agreement with the stockholder which was certain to take care of him financially.

Now how could he leave his business to his children? We discussed the recapitalization of his stock. It was decided that work should begin immediately in this direction. New stock was issued, both class A and class B (voting and nonvoting), and a gifting program was put into effect. He started giving shares of nonvoting stocks to his children.

One million dollars of insurance was put into effect with the company being the premium payor, the beneficiary, and the owner. Someone might argue the point that we have now increased his stock in his corporation at his death by 1 million, but this thinking is wrong since this business has obligations or liabilities at the death of the stockholder. These liabilities would come near the amount of insurance that was put into effect. An interesting sidelight here: the corporation carried a lot of cash on hand and the accountant was constantly worried about unnatural accumulations or excess accumulations. One nice thing about the insurance policy was that the cash value did not count in this excess accumulation.

We have continued the gifting program of nonvoting stock to the children up to the allowable limits each year. All went well for a couple of years. During that time the business established a pension and profit-sharing plan, and a yearly contribution was started at approximately $100,000 to this plan. I updated the group life insurance and the medical coverages. As a result of updating the group life insurance, over $1 million of group life was put into effect on the lives of the employees of this business. Another interesting sidelight: as the group life was put into effect on the lives of these employees, I persuaded the employer to make an additional contribution to purchase permanent insurance on the lives of all these employees. This would be tax deductible to him and naturally picked up as income to the employee. How could the employee decline? I obtained a guaranteed issue and as a result every employee was presented with permanent insurance contracts in addition to the group life insurance contracts and the only cost to the employee was the tax liability proposed on the amount on the premium paid. This was offset by the dividends that were payable on the policy each year.

Now the two sons who started in the business the first year that I got acquainted with the owner were becoming more entrenched in the business and were becoming larger stockholders. Their sister lived elsewhere and was not involved with the business. I suggested that we have the attorney prepare a buy/sell agreement for the minority stockholders' interests. In other words, have a market created for this minority stock. All parties thought it was a good idea and the attorney was asked to prepare this instrument. At this point in time there really was no need for the business to insure the lives of these minority stockholders, since little cash would be needed to purchase this stock should they pass away at their young age. I did, however, suggest to the business owner that the business provide split dollar insurance on the lives of his two sons with the collateral assignment back to the corporation for the amount of cash value of the policy and the balance of the death benefit to be payable to the wives of these two young sons. The business owner thought it was a good idea and $100,000 of insurance was placed on each life.

As the years went on the business continued to flourish and the stock values increased at record pace. We now had an additional problem. The sons wanted to purchase the stock at their father's death but did not have the money to do so. I suggested the use of a stock purchase agreement funded by life insurance using the split dollar concept. The business owner agreed and immediately a half million dollars of insurance was placed on the life of the business owner on a split dollar basis with each son as the owner and beneficiary for the death proceeds.

But this was not the end of the problems to be solved. Another year went by and the stock values took substantial increases again, and gifting was continued, but now it was apparent that the corporation would have to purchase insurance on the life of each child. This resulted in a sale of $500,000 of life insurance to each of three children for stock redemption purposes of the stock that the children owned on their own lives. This insurance was used to fund the stock purchase agreement that was put into effect requiring the corporation to purchase this stock from the estate of the deceased children.

In addition to this recommendation I could see that the problems were going to continue to mount in the future if this business continued to operate as it had in the past. I therefore recommended to the attorney and the corporate owner that an additional corporation, a leasing corporation for the rolling stock, be established. I suggested using the preferred stock owned by the father and the common stock owned by the sons, leaving the voting powers in the preferred stock. This then would have the tendency to freeze the value of the father's stock in the newly formed corporation and allow for the growth portion of the stock to take place in the sons' names. All parties agreed that this was the way to go and an additional corporation was set up to provide for leasing agreements and arrangements between the two corporations.

As you can see much has been done in this corporation in only seven years. I didn't tally the amount of coverage issued but it runs in the millions. This was a good-sized operation in a small community that I obtained on a referral basis, and had I not been equipped with the knowledge to assist this businessman, chances are no one would have taken care of his problems. The story will not end here for I will continue to service this account. I will continue to grow as they continue to succeed. Finding problems that have a price tag on them and solutions that can best be solved by the use of life insurance—this is the role of the life insurance agent.

□   □   □

Don Van Der Weide, CLU was born in Orange City, Iowa, and has lived there all of his life. He graduated from Morningside College, receiving a BA degree in 1955.

He signed his New York Life Insurance Co. contract August 1, 1957, and has been a member of the Million Dollar Round Table each year that he has been associated with New York Life. Indeed, he has consistently qualified for the Million Dollar Round Table for the past twenty-four years and is a life and qualifying member.

Mr. Van Der Weide serves on the Executive Committee on the National Board of the Reformed Church in America. He is a member of the Board of Directors of the Northwestern State Bank, and a member of the Development Corporation of Orange City, Iowa. He is active in the civic, church, and business life of his community.

*John M. Volkhardt*

# Focus on the
# User Benefit

*The year was 1939.* The great depression was a very vivid memory, with its effects still lingering. I was a senior at Brown and even though my scholastic record, if I say so myself, was not too bad, I was worried about finding a job.

One of the few companies visiting the Brown campus that year was the Vick Chemical Company, makers of Vick's Vapo-Rub. This company had developed a program called the Vick School of Applied Merchandising, matriculation provided to twenty-five selected young men for a twelve- to fifteen-month term, much of it field work, euphemistically described as "bridging the gap" between college and business. The few survivors of this rigorous rubdown (and most fell by the wayside) were offered a highly coveted junior executive marketing position.

Education was comprised of correspondence courses in business subjects to be completed while selling the Vick line to druggists and placing advertising point-of-sale materials in drugstores. In the winter, the Vick crew, with its panel trucks, went South to escape the snow and to sell to the general stores, where competition to Vick's products usually was born.

□

Winter was also the time the Vick trainee decorated the landscape with various and sundry outdoor advertising material. My own fingers still bear the scars of cuts those sharp-edged three-quarter tins caused as I was hog-nailing them to barbed wire fences.

A typical assignment would be to receive from the New York Office an order to proceed to Bolivar, Tennessee, to cover the general stores in

Bolivar County. Bolivar County adjoined Shelby County, in which the county seat, Memphis, was located. But for us there were to be none of the lures of the big city. We were told to stay in the county seat of our assignment, which meant Bolivar, Tennessee. The "hotel" in Bolivar was not an unusual lodging for a Vick man. Many a county seat was a small rural town where the need for a hotel expired with the advent of the automobile. The bathroom was at the end of the hall, food was served family style, and you were awakened by the crowing of the rooster.

General stores could range from respectable in size, volume, and importance to some that were just a back room in somebody's small farmhouse. Placing outdoor advertising, especially Bostitching fiberboard signs to barns, seems memorable now, but at the time, it was mostly a series of miserable experiences—especially for one with no great mechanical skills or agility.

□

I can now smile about the lamentable lodgings, rutted roads, frightful food, and above all, the tremendous competition of twenty-five eager college trainees vying for those "glamorous" positions that would be offered upon graduation from VSAM.

The company had a winner in Vick's Vapo-Rub, called Vick's Salve in the South. But the trick was to sell the relatively new product, Vick's Nose Drops, and those newfangled cough drops. For those readers who may suppose that nose drops were invented by the ancient Athenians, it should be said that in 1939 they were still a totally unknown product to our general store trade. They were the very epitome of a "hard sell."

At the beginning of the VSAM course, we had our superiors—experienced salesmen—telling us neophytes what we might expect. We learned that when the buyer had his arms folded in a Bismarckian stance, it would be very unlikely he would pay any attention to our sales pitch—and that we had to get him to open his arms and say yes a few times to pave the way for that all-important sale. Above all—and this had to be done creating the statements and situations that were important to him—we had to demonstrate to him the "owner benefit."

The lengths that one traveled to create or demonstrate the owner benefit is the subject of this story, an episode I cannot forget.

□

I had spent far too much time on a rutted country road, and in the Tennessee country hills, the wet mud could be much more slippery than ice. I finally pulled up in front of what could only be described as a nondescript country store. I quickly looked to see what was in stock, and it was obvious by the dust on his merchandise that I would have to be very lucky to sell this storekeeper a dozen Vick's Salves. No sign of nose drops or cough drops, either ours or those of the competitors—only a few packages of Penetro and Rub-my-Tism salves.

Seated around the pot-bellied stove were three or four men. The one I knew instantly was the proprietor, for he was clearly in authority, a man in his late fifties or early sixties, and he had a rough resemblance to Abe Lincoln in that he had a tall, lanky frame. But what truly distinguished his face was a very large nose. It could only be described as large, dirty, and hairy.

☐

I started my pitch, and he allowed that he could take a couple of dozen Vick's Salves. With this as encouragement, I launched into the sale of Vick's Nose Drops. He obviously was not interested in Vick's Nose Drops and was ready to go back to his chair by the stove. I persisted and suggested that he could really accomplish a tremendous lot for his friends by recommending these nose drops, which were a tremendous advancement in curing the affliction of a head cold and giving you blessed relief, and that I could give him the personal realization of the product by demonstrating the product on him. I must have been terribly eloquent because he agreed. So, I got him to sit back in his chair, had his head tilted back as far as I could without his neck breaking, and taking the Vick's stopper and filling it completely to the top, I inserted it into his hairy nostril and squirted. I quickly refilled the stopper and did the same with the other nostril. I then held his head by the back of his hair, and since he was not afflicted with a cold, the Vick's really poured through him. He coughed and choked a bit, and when I finally let him up tears were streaming down his face. He said: "Bub, that's pretty powerful stuff—send me six."

☐

I have forgotten a great deal about the last forty years (and some of it deserves to be forgotten). But I will always remember that very large proprietor of that very small general store who confirmed in practice what for me, until then, had been only marketing theory—*focus on the user benefit*. When I tell the story, I find myself laughing at the absurdity of the scene and at my own youthful presumption, not to mention physical courage. But of all the many I have made since, it was the sale that I remember.

☐  ☐  ☐

John M. Volkhardt is President of CPC North America, a division of CPC International Inc., Executive Vice President of CPC International Inc., and a member of its Board of Directors. In addition, he was elected a Group Vice President of the company in 1979.

Before assuming his present position, he was President of Best Foods, the company's U.S. consumer business.

Mr. Volkhardt began a career in marketing as a trainee with the Vick Chemical Company. In 1956, he joined Best Foods as general manager of its Rit Products Division. When Best Foods merged with the Corn Products Refining Company in 1958 to form the Corn Products Company, he served the Best Foods Division as Marketing Vice President, Vice President–National Marketing Director, Vice President-Marketing and Sales, and Executive Vice President. He was made President of Best Foods in 1971, and moved up to President of CPC North America in 1978.

He was elected a CPC Vice President in 1971 and a member of the CPC Board of Directors in 1977. In 1978, he was elected an Executive Vice President of CPC.

A native of Chester, Pennsylvania, Mr. Volkhardt is a Phi Beta Kappa graduate of Brown University.

He is Chairman of the Board of Keep America Beautiful, Inc., a trustee of the Nutrition Foundation, and a director of the Chamber of Commerce and Industry of Northern New Jersey.

*William E. Walkup*

# *Selling Yourself*

*The greatest sale you will ever make* is the selling of yourself, and you don't have to be a salesman to do it. Furthermore, you never stop making that "greatest sale"—or, at least, you had better not.

In the company with which I have spent forty-one years, I never made a sale of a product. I was never in the sales department, but I was always selling. I was selling the company because I was proud of it from the first day I started, and I'm still proud of it now that I have a part in managing it. I have "sold" the merits of the company to all who would listen.

The only other sales in which I was involved were presentations to management—selling myself, partly, in helping to sell whatever program or concept the presentation embraced. And let me state one generality before I get into specifics: an effective way to sell yourself is to know how to get along with people. You can be a genius; you can have the most advanced education; you can be an expert in some specialty—but if you can't get along with people, you have a good chance of being bypassed for higher management by a less qualified generalist who can work with and through others.

Now, I can't focus on one sale that did the most for me. I can, however, select three turning points in my career, all based on the same concept, and give one example (learned from someone else) of what *not* to do. Let's take the negative before the positive, the example of what *not* to do.

I was thirty years old and had just been transferred from a field operations office to the corporate headquarters office as administrative assistant to the president. It was a completely new experience to me, quite in contrast to the informality and daily action of the field. Several of the senior executives were very considerate in trying to expose me to people and functions in the big city.

I was invited by two vice presidents and by the manager of industrial relations to attend a luncheon at the Los Angeles Biltmore Hotel where

**357**

the speaker was to be the vice president of industrial relations for one of the largest companies in the world. The man was a leader in his field and at age sixty, twice my age, obviously had a wealth of experience. I eagerly awaited his words of wisdom to a capacity crowd in the large main ballroom.

What followed was a decided letdown. He read for half an hour a prepared text which I presumed followed the company manual verbatim.

Picture the potential. Here was a man who had the respect and probably the envy of his peers as personnel director of the leading corporation in its industry. Here was a man who had worked thirty-eight years for that same company. Here was a man who had to have a veritable treasure chest of personal incidents and first hand knowledge he could relate in illustrating concepts, rules, laws, or policies. He had a wonderful opportunity to sell himself and his company, but what did he do? He read by the book.

He did himself a disservice, he did his company a disservice, and he did his audience a disservice. He did not sell himself. If you are going to make a speech or make a presentation, give of yourself. Make it *your* contribution. You have something unique, which no one else has (just like your fingerprints), so give that special something.

Enough of negation. Let's get to the positive—these three turning points all demonstrate the same premise: the sale (of myself) that did the most for me was the result of my being thrown into a situation in which I was over my head—to perform functions or assume responsibility beyond my apparent capabilities.

*Turning Point One:*    I was twenty-three years old and had been with the company only two years. I was a secretary-clerk making $150 a month supporting a wife and a year-old baby boy. One day I answered my telephone to hear the secretary of the founder–president, whom I had never met, asking me to come up to the president's office. I was very nervous as I walked in. The president asked me to be seated in front of the largest, highest desk I had ever seen. I could have used another cushion or two to reach his eye level.

"I understand you speak Spanish," he said to me.

"I don't really speak it fluently," I answered, "but I read it and write it some."

He then handed me a sheaf of papers. "Here is a proposed mining venture in Mexico written in Spanish. Do you think you could translate it?"

I briefly glanced at the top page and responded almost immediately without benefit of analysis or appraisal.

"Yes, Sir, I think so. When do you want it?" It was then a Friday morning.

"The first of the week," he answered.

"Yes, Sir," I answered and departed without being dismissed. For all I know he may have still wanted to talk to me.

Back at my desk I carefully went through the proposal and realized I did not understand a large percentage of the contents. It was a business document and it was in technical mining terms. My knowledge of Spanish consisted of five years in high school and college, and a summer session at the University of Mexico City, the most advanced courses being in Spanish literature.

With two dictionaries, I slaved over that document Friday night, all day Saturday, Saturday night, all day Sunday and typed the translation Sunday night. I not only was exhausted but I knew much of my translation was literal—but just possibly someone who understood mining technology could interpret my literal translations. I delivered the document and my translation first thing Monday morning to the president's secretary.

Two days later another call from the secretary summoned me to the president's office. The only consolation I felt was that I probably wouldn't be fired because I hadn't been hired in the first place to translate Spanish.

The President motioned me again to the same seat I had sat in before. I still could have used two cushions.

"I've read your translation," he said.

"Yes, Sir." I answered.

"How long did it take you to do it?"

That was a question I had not anticipated, but I knew one reason why he was president—he got to the heart of the matter immediately. I couldn't admit I had spent such an inordinate amount of time on it. It wasn't that I intended to deceive him. It was just that I hated to admit my own inadequacy after I had so impulsively told him I could do it.

"Oh . . . not very long," I said hesitantly.

"Approximately how long?" he persisted.

"Well, I worked on it over the weekend."

By this time he must have sensed I was not going to give him a direct answer. He thanked me, and this time I knew I was dismissed.

Seven years later this same man, Samuel B. Mosher, would call me from field operations to promote me to the position of his administrative assistant. I have no idea whether the translation helped him or was useless because of my lack of knowledge of business and technical terms. Of course it is possible he recognized my inadequacy but recognized my willingness to take on an assignment, to accept a challenge. In later years I remember him saying to someone else that whenever a job was to be done I was always willing to accept responsibility for getting it done even if I didn't know how. I must have sold myself to him even if the Spanish wasn't too good.

*Turning Point Two:* I was twenty-seven years old and had been working in an oil field production office for three years doing clerical work for the office manager, a man by the name of Jerry Krause. He did the actual accounting and I handled the routine clerical procedures. There were only the two of us because although the volume ran into many millions of dollars it was simply crude oil and natural gas produced and sold to one customer. We also had two drilling rigs developing the field, but the accounting for all the operations was relatively simple. However, if you had never studied accounting and had no real training in it, then it was as mysterious as any other unknown quantity.

Jerry Krause, the office manager, for reasons still beyond my ability to understand, had a nervous breakdown one month before the books had to be closed for the annual audit by outside professional accountants. That left me, a clerk, alone in the office to do what had been done by two of us—and one was a professional accountant, but it was not I.

How the parent company ever trusted me to effect the year-end closing of the books of their most important multimillion dollar subsidiary I'll never know. I don't even remember telling them I thought I could do it.

I was in over my head. I had never taken a single accounting course and my clerical training was very limited. I worked every night for a month!

First, I reasoned that whatever needed to be done had been done before. In other words, in the ledgers themselves were the answers. All I had to do was check back in the ledgers to the previous year-end closing for every entry and procedure, find the corresponding items and figures for the current year, and then make the same entries. My premise was correct. It worked, but it was a laborious process. I didn't know then and I don't know now the fundamentals of double-entry bookkeeping. I merely did it by rote.

When the auditor came, I turned everything over to him, crossed my fingers, said a prayer, and went about my business.

Two or three weeks later as the auditor was finishing his report, the superintendent for all those field operations went to check with him. I was in the outer office running an adding machine. I stopped the clatter of the machine just in time to overhear the auditor tell the superintendent: "He did a remarkable job—but I don't know how he did it."

*Turning Point Three:* I had been the president's administrative assistant for seven years when the controller of the company died. I found out that the executive vice president was recommending to the board of directors that someone from the outside be recruited as the new controller. I asked the president for a chance to speak to the board about the matter. Within the next day or two I was called to join a meeting. I entered the room to find the president surrounded by several directors in an informal atmosphere.

"You wanted to talk about the controller opening, didn't you, Bill?"

I then proceeded to tell them that I thought it would be a mistake to fill the job with an outsider. I pointed out that the man they were considering was well qualified but knew nothing about our industry, which was highly specialized, and that it would take any outsider two years to really have a grasp of the problems. I explained that we already had a man thoroughly qualified to step up to the controller responsibility and that he should be given the chance at it. I mentioned the man Jerry Krause, the same man who had been my boss in the field operations and whose nervous breakdown thrust me into Turning Point Two. He had subsequently recovered and been transferred to the headquarters accounting department.

They thanked me and I returned to my office. About an hour later they called me back.

"We've thought about what you've said," the president told me, "and we've decided that you should be controller and move Jerry Krause up to assistant controller. You may not know all the technical accounting, but you're familiar with it, and you can get other people to do it."

First, I found I was actually surprised that they would listen to me and reverse their decision to go outside the company. Second, I could not believe what I was hearing when they said they wanted me to be controller.

I thought about it for only a moment.

"All right," I answered. "I'll act as liaison between the accounting department and the board until I convince you Jerry Krause can be controller."

And it happened that way. Within a year Jerry Krause was named controller and deservedly so. I was temporarily without a title—except by then I had been elected a member of the board of directors at age thirty-six when all the other directors were twenty to twenty-five years older.

And for the next twenty years I kept being thrust into situations where I was over my head—but with the help of lots of good people and a little luck, things worked out.

We have all heard instances of people performing incredible feats of strength in an emergency; for instance, a hundred-pound woman lifting one wheel of an automobile which had pinned down her son. Adrenalin did it.

Cerebrally, maybe a similar condition prevails. Under the stress of our emergency, use of our brain capacity expands, since under normal conditions we supposedly use a fraction of our potential.

So don't be afraid to jump in over your head. It may be the greatest "sale" you will ever make.

☐  ☐  ☐

Starting as a mail clerk with the original Signal Oil and Gas Company in 1939, William E. (Bill) Walkup has served forty-one years with the company, completing his last eleven years as chairman of the board of The Signal Companies, Inc.

Bill Walkup joined the company following studies at the University of California, Los Angeles (UCLA) and the National University of Mexico. He moved quickly to assignments in sales, accounting, and crude oil production.

By 1948 he was serving as Administrative Assistant to the President (Sam Mosher) and in 1955 was named controller and a Director. Bill Walkup was elected Vice President-Finance in 1958, Group Vice President-Staff in March 1962, Executive Vice President and Vice Chairman of The Signal Companies, Inc. on April 30, 1968, and Chairman of the Board April 29, 1969.

Mr. Walkup continues to serve as a member on Signal's Board of Directors and Chairman of the Executive Committee.

**Harry R. White**

# A Novel Approach
# Pays Off

*Me—a salesman?* I had none of the characteristics salesmen were supposed to have. I was a rather shy young fellow, planning to be a writer, maybe a newspaper reporter. I had never sold anything in my life. And yet, at the age of twenty-one, I made a sale that changed the course of my career and started me on a lifelong study of the power of salesmanship.

The year was 1933. It was a year of failure and despair. The worst depression in our history had brought the American economy to its knees. The banks had closed. Unemployed executives were selling apples on street corners. Experienced newspapermen were out of work and willing to take any kind of menial job. Hardly a rosy scene for a graduate fresh from the Columbia University School of Journalism! I was broke. And I was in a hurry to get married. But this was out of the question without a job. And there seemed to be no job to be found anywhere.

Then one day I received a mimeographed letter. It informed me that a new organization had been started by a group of businessmen including Thomas J. Watson, Sr., of International Business Machines, William Ingersoll of "Dollar Watch" fame, and hardware tycoon Saunders Norvell. It was called the Sales Executives Club of New York and its aim was to try to rally the nation's sales talent to help sell America out of the depression. They needed an executive secretary and, since writing bulletins and letters would be an important part of the job, had applied to the School of Journalism for some likely candidates. Would I be interested?

Needless to say, I was there bright and early for the interview. And then I learned that most of my seventy-three fellow journalism school graduates had also received the letter and were being interviewed.

What could I do against such competition? Some were straight-A students. Some were experienced journalists. Three had received journalism awards. I had nothing special to offer beyond a pretty good scholastic record and a burning desire to go to work.

I knew that the only way I could possibly win this steeplechase was to do something out of the ordinary. And to do this I had to know as much as possible about the fledgling organization and what its members expected it to accomplish. Literature on the group was practically nonexistent. But their letterhead listed the directors with their titles and companies. So I started phoning them. I told them I was being considered for club secretary and it would be most helpful to me to know what they felt might be done to make the club valuable to them.

My previous encounters with businessmen had conditioned me to expect a cool reception and impatient answers. To my surprise, I found evey one pleasant, interested, and eager to give a young beginner a helping hand—a trait I later found to be common to most top executives, especially those with a sales background. I arranged five face-to-face interviews, which provided me with a notebook full of ideas for club activities and services.

But how to bring all this to the attention of the chairman of the selection committee? I thought it wouldn't be wise to ask for another interview and dump all this in his lap. If only I could get it to him in small doses—maybe an idea every day. Why not?

So I went to the post office and bought a supply of government post cards—they were only a penny apiece in those days! At the top of them I typed: "What Harry White could do for the Sales Executives Club." On each card was an idea or problem, followed by a brief description of how I would handle it. Then every day I mailed one of these cards to the chairman.

Two weeks went by with no response. I began to despair. Maybe they thought this approach was too smart-alecky, too pushy. But I learned that they weren't yet ready to announce their decision. So I might as well keep sending the daily post card.

Toward the end of the third week came that long-awaited phone call. Could I report for work at the Sales Executives Club the following Monday morning?

Later I was told that the post card campaign was the deciding factor for me. None of the other eager applicants had made any special effort beyond calling to reaffirm their interest in the job. I also learned that the committee had agreed upon me for the job after the first week's barrage of post cards but wanted to see how many more ideas and solutions I'd come up with!

That sale taught me a lesson that I never forgot. In my forty-three years with the Sales Executives Club, I had many important sales to make—to prospective members, to hard-to-get speakers, to directors of the club. I found that nearly every one ended in a "yes" if I remembered three things—do something out of the ordinary, emphasize the benefits to the prospect, and keep asking for the order—the things that enabled me back in 1933 to make that sale that did the most for me.

□   □   □

Harry R. White's career has been something of a paradox in the marketing field. He built a struggling newborn group into one of the world's largest and most influential sales and marketing organizations. Yet he never held a job as a salesman or sales manager. And, except for a two-year stint as communications officer in the Navy in World War II, he spent his entire forty-three-year business career in one job, as Executive Director of the Sales Executives Club of New York. How an aspiring young newspaper reporter happened to get into this job has already been explained.

He was born in New York City on May 5, 1911. His father was an organist and his mother a singer, so it was assumed that he'd follow a musical career. But writing seemed to be his big interest and he wanted to work on a newspaper. So he wound up his formal education in the Columbia University School of Journalism, graduating in 1933—a very bad year for newspapers and most other businesses.

He took a "temporary" job as secretary of the Sales Executives Club of New York, which had just been started "to help sell America out of the depression." It wasn't long before he decided that selling was more rewarding and exciting than the newspaper business.

"Like most college graduates of the time," he says, "I had some half-baked ideas about business and the career of selling. But it wasn't long after I started working with some of the great sales leaders of the day that I became fascinated with selling. These were vibrant, smart fellows who were making good money right through the depression because they knew how to sell. They seemed to have a keen understanding of other peoples' problems and motivations. I soon made up my mind that I wanted to spend my career working with such men."

And so he did for over four decades, taking time out to serve two years as a communications officer in the Navy in World War II. In the course of his career, he got to work with and know many great business leaders, from Charles M. Schwab to Lee A. Iacocca, most of whom were speakers at the famous weekly luncheons of the club.

With over 3000 members, the Sales Executives Club of New York not only provides weekly luncheon programs but an extensive program of research into sales and marketing methods, with findings published for the benefit of the profession. Also offered are conferences and courses in sales and marketing, a broad selling-as-a-career program and job counseling through the Man Marketing Council and the Sales Manpower Foundation.

Now retired, he does occasional consulting work and writing about sales and sales management.

# *Index*

*Advertising Age*, 61
Agfa-Gevaert, Inc., 51
Ali, Muhammad, 2
Autry, Gene, 12

Banque de Paris et des Pays-Bas
   (Paribas), 46
Bristol-Myers Products Division, 205
Brown, Courtney C., 30
Brown & Williamson Tobacco
   Corporation, 176

California Angels, 29
Carpenter, Ralph E., Jr., 36
Christie, Donald J., 42
Christie, Manson & Woods
   International, Inc., 41
Clay, Cassius Marcellus II, 8
Colgate-Palmolive Company, 113
Columbia University, 31
Coppenrath, Robert A. M., 48
CPC North America, 355

Davis, William J., 52
DeMarco, Louis F., 60
DeTurk, Frederick W., 72
Devine, C. R., 78
Dr. Scholl Foundation, 97

Early, Roland A., 84
Economos, James P., 92
Emery Air Freight Corporation, 103
Emery, John C., Jr., 98
Espy, Willard R., 104

Flaherty, Tina Santi, 112
Florida Bankers Association, 213
Florida Student Financial Assistance
   Commission, 330
Fox, James F., 120
Fox Public Relations, Inc., 125

Griffin, J. Scottie, 126

Hamel, Park, McCabe & Saunders,
   201
Hardy, Jerome S., 132
*Harvard Magazine*, 111
Hellmuth, Obata & Kassabaum, 277
Hickerson, J. Mel, 138
Hicks, Paul B., Jr., 146
Hitchcock Presbyterian Church, 131
Hyman, Richard M., 154

Jacksonville University, 161
Jefferson Standard Life Insurance

Company, 192
John M. Olin Foundation, 315
JS&A Group, Inc., 343

Kinne, Frances Bartlett, 160
Kirk, Roger M., Jr., 168

Lawrence Hall of Science, University
    of California, 58
Lewis, Aubrey C., 178
Litton Industries, Inc., 238
Lone Star Industries, Inc., 291

Macon, Seth C., 184
McCabe, Edward A., 194
McCurdy, Walter R., 202
Mickunas, Virginia, 206
Milstead, John, 212
Milton R. Stohl, Associates, 337
Mirandon, J. Wilmer, 220
Motley, Arthur H., 226
Muriel Siebert and Company, Inc.,
    308

New York Life Insurance Company,
    349

Oldfield, Colonel Barney, 232
Othmer, David, 242
Owens Brush Company, 155

Parade, 231
Phelps Dodge Corporation, 73
Pinnacle Club, 293
Putnam, Howard D., 252

Ray, Robert D., 262
Reader's Digest Association, Inc., 83
Remington, William B., 272

Reynolds, David P., 278
Reynolds Metals Company, 284

S&H Promotional Services, Sperry
    and Hutchinson Company, 91
Sales Executive Club of New York,
    365
Scheiber, Milton R., 286
Scott, David L., 292
Scott, J. L., 296
Siebert, Muriel, 302
Signal Companies, Inc., The, 363
Simon, William E., 310
Sinnaeve, Robert C., 316
Smith, Ernest E., Jr., 324
Southwest Airlines, 253
State Institutions of Higher Learning
    (Mississippi), 301
Stohl, Milton R., 332
Sugarman, Joseph, 338
Supreme Court of the United States,
    201

Texaco Inc., 153

United States Chamber of
    Commerce, 231
United States Olympic Committee,
    315
United Student Aid Funds, Inc., 145,
    225, 322

Van Der Weide, Don, 344
Volkhardt, John M., 350

Walkup, William E., 356
White, Harry R., 364
WNET/13, 251
F. W. Woolworth Company, 182
WPIX/11, 182